ICT 7 framework solutions

Stephen Doyle

OXFORD
UNIVERSITY PRESS

Great Clarendon Street, Oxford, OX2 6DP, United Kingdom

Oxford University Press is a department of the University of Oxford. It furthers the University's objective of excellence in research, scholarship, and education by publishing worldwide. Oxford is a registered trade mark of Oxford University Press in the UK and in certain other countries

First published by Nelson Thornes Ltd in 2004
This edition published by Oxford University Press in 2014

British Library Cataloguing in Publication Data
Data available

978-0-7487-8083-9

20 19 18 17 16 15 14 13

Printed in India by Multivista Global Ltd

Acknowledgements

Page make-up: Pantek Arts Ltd, Maidstone, Kent
Illustrations: Pantek Arts Ltd and Roger Fereday, Linda Rogers Associates

Contents

Acknowledgements

The author would like to thank the following people for their valuable advice and assistance in the development of this resource: Sarah Robertson and Helen Kerindi at Nelson Thornes and Helen Bannister and Robert Harries.

The author and publishers are grateful to the following for permission to reproduce material:

Lyle Zapato for the screenshot on p. 45; Yahoo! Inc. for screenshots on pp. 59, 60; Gail Renard/The Writer's Guild and Boldface for the newspaper article on p. 87; Data Harvest Group Ltd. www.data-harvest.co.uk and Rod Bowker © Flowol: Keep I.T. Easy (K.I.T.E) pp. 245, 253; www.dcsafetycameras.org p. 259; Devon & Cornwall Police p. 260; Florida Wildlife Magazine for the global temperature chart on p. 261. Air monitoring image on p. 259 provided courtesy of AEA Technology.

Photo credits:
BasicNet S.P.A. for authorisation to produce the Kappa trademark p. 121; John Birdsall Photography p. 5; P.Bucktrout/British Antarctic Survey p. 261; J Faren/British Antarctic Survey p. 266; © BBC p. 67; Bettman/Corbis p. 66; Bubbles Photo Library p. 76; Corbis pp. 88, 256; Flip Schulke/Corbis p. 75; Data Harvest pp. 262, 263, 264, 265, 266; Sally & Richard Greenhill pp.48, 164; Jessie Hall p. 133; Homepride p. 121; Kappa p. 121; LC Plastics p. 120; Lloyds TSB Bank Plc. P. 121; Mirror Syndication p. 89; News International Newspapers Ltd. p. 119; Offside Sports Photography pp. 39, 208; Penguin Books Ltd p. 121; Pressnet/Topfoto p.7; Rex Features p. 39; Science Photo Library pp. 26, 259, 263; Shell International Petroleum Company Ltd. p. 121; Shout Picture Library p. 19; Ollie Thould p.39; Topfoto p.54; Ultra Electronics Holdings Plc. p. 119; Whirlpool p. 212.

Archive images:
The Bridge by Vincent Van Gogh/Corel 303 (NT) p. 1; Corel 62 (NT) p. 260; Corel 625 (NT) p. 216; Corel 397 (NT) p.19; Jeremy Woodhouse/Digital Vision WT (NT) p. 1; Image Club/OG2 (NT) pp. 3, 86, 212; Ingram Publishing/ILV2CD6 (NT) p. 213; Photodisc 22 (NT) p. 186; Photodisc 41 (NT) p. 97; Photodisc 44 (NT) p. 259; Stockbyte 30 (NT) p. 213.

Picture research by Sue Sharp.

Introduction

Welcome to the first book of the new course, ICT Framework Solutions. This book has been designed so that it can be used on its own, although a Teacher Support Pack with networkable CD-ROM is also available, and this builds on and enhances the materials in this book.

The book supplies you with plenty of background information, enables you to work through activities and provides you with help when a new skill is introduced. Here are the features you will notice as you work through the book:

Units and lessons
The book chapters are called Units. Each unit is divided into lessons. The first lesson of each unit is a background lesson, which is really an introduction to the remaining lessons of that unit.

Find It Out
These activities involve you researching a topic in order to find something out.

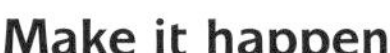

Make it happen
These activities involve using the computer to put into practice what you have been learning about.

Sometimes you will need a ready-prepared file to work on, and your teacher will provide you with this, either from the Teacher Support Pack, or from the Internet at the following website www.oxfordsecondary.co.uk

Worksheets
These are tasks, which are also included in the Teacher Support Pack as photocopiable sheets that you can write on.

Extension Activity
These are extra activities for you to do if you have finished your other work!

Questions
These are extra things to think about, which your teacher may give you as homework.

Notes and reminders
Helpful hints – read them and they could save you time!

Key Words
These are the important vocabulary that you will need to learn. They are highlighted in the margin of the book on a blue background, and also included in the glossary at the end of the book.

Index
This provides a quick way for you to find what you need in the book.

ICT is an important subject. ICT is used in all walks of life and it is becoming increasingly difficult to make your way in the adult world without understanding it well. We hope this book helps you to enjoy learning about ICT and provides you with some skills that will be very useful to you as you progress through school!

1 Using ICT

Lesson 1:
INTRODUCTION TO PRESENTING INFORMATION USING TEXT, IMAGES AND SOUND

What is a presentation?

A presentation is simply an illustrated talk on a particular topic. Usually there will be a group of people as your audience. It is important to make the information you are presenting as interesting as possible so that your audience takes notice.

ICT equipment can help you to give presentations that will keep the audience's attention. In the following lessons, you will learn how to make a good presentation using software called Microsoft PowerPoint. You will also learn the difference between a bad presentation and a good one. This unit will also teach you a lot about ICT in general.

Background theory and key information

The PowerPoint software enables you to produce multimedia presentations. Multimedia means 'many media' and can include text, sound and pictures.

Good presentations make use of more than one of the following items.

Photographs

Clip art

Pictures can be in many different forms

KEY WORDS

media – means of communication

text – letters of the alphabet, numbers and punctuation marks

sound – music, speech or sound effects

pictures – photographs, clip art, paintings, graphs, charts and drawings

Pictures can be in many different forms (continued)

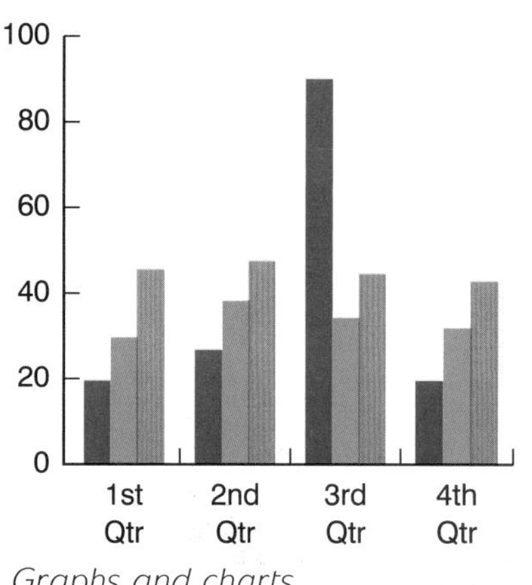

Graphs and charts

Paintings

What is a slide?

When you make a presentation it would be boring if you just stood there and spoke. You need something visual to help get your message across. This is why slides are used. Slides should contain the important points or message of the presentation and they are something your audience can look at while you are talking. A slide is a prepared document that can be projected onto a screen. If you only have a small audience you can show the slides on a computer, but in most cases you will need to project the slides onto a screen.

The material (text, pictures, etc.) is called the content. It is important that your content is clear so that your audience can understand the points you are trying to make.

Using Microsoft PowerPoint

Microsoft PowerPoint is an example of presentation software. It allows slides to be produced with text, graphics and sound. PowerPoint is also an example of a multimedia authoring package. This is the software that you will use to complete the activities in this unit.

Presentation software such as PowerPoint can be used when you have to give a talk. The purpose of the talk could be to inform people or to sell a product or service. PowerPoint takes the place of an overhead projector that uses slides (or transparencies).

If there is a large audience, the computer can be connected to a special projector, called a data projector, which projects the image onto a large white screen. If there is one in your room, you can use an electronic whiteboard to project your slides onto a large screen.

A data projector is used to project an image from a computer screen onto a large screen

What makes a good presentation?

A good presentation is one that is lively and interesting. A bad presentation is one that is dull and boring. The worst presentations are the ones where it is impossible to read the material on the slides and you cannot understand what the presenter is saying. A presentation should always relay a message to your audience, so what you say is more important than all the fancy effects.

How do I make a good presentation?

Before starting on the computer, you need to think about the purpose of the presentation and the type of audience. This will determine the language level and the tone of your presentation.

There are a number of steps you should take when producing a presentation. These are:

1 **Think about the purpose and audience of your presentation.** You need to be sure about what it is you are communicating. You need to consider your audience (what will the age group be?).

2 **Collect your content.** Content is what you put on each slide. It should include text, pictures and sound where appropriate. You need to collect the material by doing some research.

3 **Design the slides:**

- Plan what needs to be put on each slide. It is best to start off with the headings (i.e. the main points you need to make) for each slide and then split them up into a list of smaller points under each heading.
- Make sure that your audience can see your slides – do not make the text (font size) too small. See if you can read the slide from where your audience is going to sit. Also, do not use a font that is difficult to read.
- Consider the colour combination for the text and the background. Some colours work well together and others don't.

4 **Check for grammar and spelling errors.** If you are presenting your work to your classmates and teacher, it can be embarrassing to have serious spelling and grammatical errors. If English is not your strong point, get a classmate who is good at English to proof-read your slides.

5 **Add special effects.** You can add sound or animation (i.e. movement). You can alter the slide transition (i.e. the way in which one slide moves onto another).

6 **Practise your presentation.** Rehearse your presentation on your own or with a friend before you do it in front of your class. You will be able to work out the timings and what to say. You could even video your presentation and then play it back. The more you practise, the more confident you will become. Lots of people hate doing presentations, but if you are prepared it will be a lot easier and you might even enjoy it!

KEY WORDS

font – a set of letters and characters in a particular design

content – material to be put into a document

Working with networked computers

If you link computers together you have a network. When you log onto the Internet using your home computer you are making your computer part of the biggest network in the world. Throughout your Key Stage 3 ICT work you will be required to use a computer network.

Networks are used in schools because:

- resources such as printers and scanners can be shared
- it is easier for your data to be backed up (i.e. keeping copies for security purposes)
- you can all access the same files in the shared area
- your teacher/technician only needs to install software/files on one machine
- user-IDs and passwords can be used to restrict access to the network.

KEY WORDS

password – a string of characters chosen by the user. It is used to check the identity of the user. You are only allowed access to a network if you type in the correct password

User ID – a name or number that is used to identify the user of a network or system

Collecting the content for the presentation

When you are asked to do a presentation you need to collect some content. Material may be collected from lots of sources, such as the Internet, books, newspapers, etc. You need to be careful of something called plagiarism (see below).

Plagiarism

Plagiarism means stealing the thoughts or writings of someone else and then passing them off as your own. This could be copying an essay from someone else and then submitting it as your own piece of work. It could also be taking material from the Internet without altering it in any way and then saying that you have produced it on your own.

There are a number of sites on the Internet where you can get ready-made essays on almost every subject you could want. Some students may try to save themselves hours of work by copying these essays and then saying that they did them. There is software that your teacher can use to find out if you have simply copied material from the Internet.

So plagiarism can be:

- submitting work for a project or assignment done by someone else

KEY WORDS

plagiarism – copying work and passing it off as your own

shaded area – part of the network that holds files that everyone on the network can access. Clip art would be stored in the shared area

- paying someone to produce a project or assignment for you
- copying and pasting sections from someone else's work and putting them together to form a project or assignment without acknowledging the source.

In Unit 2 you will see how you can type a phrase or a sentence into an Internet search engine and find the site or sites where it occurs. If somebody suspects that you are guilty of plagiarism they could do this to find the source of the information.

Can I use other people's material?

REMEMBER!

Copying other people's work is plagiarism.

Provided you acknowledge the source of the material (i.e. mention the person who originally produced the material) then it may be OK to copy some of the material, but not usually all of it.

Some material cannot be copied at all. For example, if you had wedding photographs taken, the photographer would object to you scanning these photographs and then printing them out on your printer.

When people produce original work, such as a story or a newspaper article, it is protected by copyright as soon as the work is published. Copyright protects the producer of the work from having others illegally copy it.

Sometimes, whoever has produced the original work will be flattered that others find that what they have done is useful, and they may be happy to allow other people to use it. Such people would usually like to be mentioned if their work is used.

Good and bad slides

To make a good presentation you need good slides. In this section we will look at good and bad slides so that you can see how to make good ones.

Do not put too much text on one slide. Break down the information into several bulleted points.

Britney Spears

- Britney Spears was born on December 2nd, 1981 in Louisiana USA and has an older brother and a younger sister. Her hobbies are shopping, seeing movies and riding her go-kart. Britney's influences include Mariah Carey, Whitney Houston and Otis Redding.

Britney Spears

- Born Dec 2nd, 1981
- In Louisiana, USA
- Has older brother and younger sister
- Hobbies: shopping, seeing movies and riding go-kart
- Influences: Mariah Carey, Whitney Houston and Otis Redding

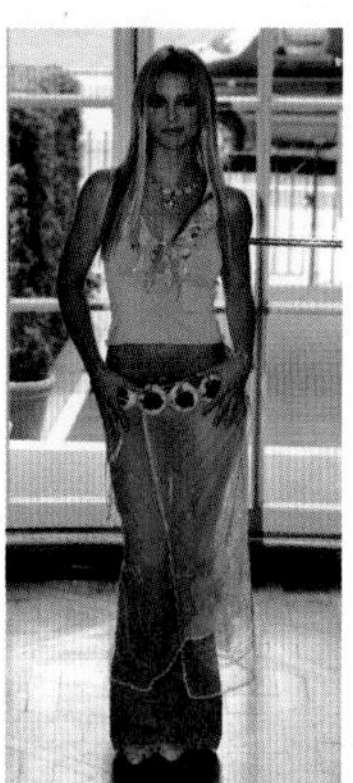

The first slide above is an example of a bad slide.
The information on this slide should be broken down.

The second slide is much better. The information about Britney has been divided into a number of bullet points. A photograph of Britney has been included and the information is much clearer.

Take a look at the good slide. There is usually something more you can do to a slide to improve its appearance. Think about the ways that the appearance of this slide could be improved.

What you should already know

You will already have used a multimedia presentation package in your Key Stage 2 work. This unit will build on the skills you already have.

What you will learn

In this unit you will:

- use a multimedia authoring package (PowerPoint) to produce a series of slides
- organise and link pages

- use text, images and sound in your presentation
- use hardware, such as scanners and digital cameras, to produce digital images.

WORKSHEETWORKSHEETWORKSHEETWORKSHEETWORKSHEET

WORKSHEET 7.1.1 How much do you already know about PowerPoint?

Below are some basic questions about PowerPoint. You may be given a worksheet on which to write your answers or you may be asked to write your answers into your books. When you have finished, your teacher will either go through the answers or give you an answer sheet so that you can check your answers yourself. You should have learnt most of this when you did your Key Stage 2 work.

1. Here are some terms used when talking about PowerPoint. Write down clearly what each term means.

   (a) Slide
   (b) Font
   (c) Clip art
   (d) Template
   (e) Bulleted list

2. Here are some buttons used in PowerPoint. Write down what they do.

   (a)
   (b)
   (c)
   (d)
   (e)
   (f)
   (g) 18
   (h)
   (i)
   (j)
   (k) Arial
   (l)
   (m)

Lesson 2: DESIGNING THE SLIDES

Background

Content means what you put on each slide. Before you make a slide show, you must collect the content and then organise it. In this unit we will not look at the research aspects of collecting material, as this will be covered in the next unit. We will be using content that is familiar to you (such as information about yourself).

WORKSHEETWORKSHEETWORKSHEETWORKSHEETWORKSHEET

WORKSHEET 7.1.2 Spot what is wrong with each slide

Your teacher may give you a worksheet on which you write your answers or you may be asked to write your answers into your books.

Your teacher will either show you a PowerPoint presentation or you can look at the slides here. The presentation (looking at the slides alone) is quite poor. You have to spot why by answering the questions overleaf.

Amy is a student in Year 7 and she has been asked to produce a presentation about herself. She has produced these slides, which will be projected onto a screen so that all her class can see them.

We will be looking at the content of Amy's slides. The content of the slides is what is written on them.

Slide 1

This is me

Amy

Slide 2

My school

- I have just started my senior school
- **Most of my mates from junior school are here**
- I like Art, PE and science best
- I hate maths
- Most of our teachers are strict so we can't mess about
- I am happy here

Slide 3

My Family

- ***My mum and dad are divorced***
- **My dad lives in London and I go to stay with him once a month**
- Being the eldest is good because I get to boss my brothers around

Slide 4

What I am like

Slide 5

What I like to do

- I love to sing and I go to singing lessons
- I love listening to music
- My mum bought me a karaoke machine so I can sing along

Slide 6

My pets

- We have a pond with lots of goldfish
- We have a dog called Roger
- He is a bulldog and all my mates are frightened of him
- He is a softy really

Slide 7

Where I live

- I live in Monmouth which is a small town in South Wales almost on the border between England and Wales. I like living here because there is plenty to do because there is the town and also the countryside. I am glad I live here rather than somewhere else.

Slide 8

The end

Look at the slides (your teacher may show these as a presentation). The presentation (looking at the slides alone) is quite poor. You have to spot why by answering the questions overleaf.

1. Imagine you are in Amy's class. Has she told you all the important things about herself? What would you like to know that she has left out?
2. Which slide contains information that should have been divided up?
3. For the slide you have identified in question 2, write a better slide by putting the information into a number of separate bullet points.
4. Was the grammar and spelling in each slide correct?
5. Were Amy's slides in a logical sequence? If you answer is no, write down the sequence you would prefer.
6. Did Amy have the correct information under each slide heading? Give reasons for your answer.
7. Did the presentation have a structure with a beginning, middle and end?
8. From the content of Amy's slides you will have developed a first impression of Amy's life and personality. Write a few sentences to describe what you think Amy might be like.

Building the structure of the presentation

Before starting on the computer, you need to think about the purpose of the presentation and the type of audience it is for. This will determine the language level and the tone. Are you presenting to adults or children? Is it a very serious subject or a fun subject?

If the presentation is extremely important, say for a job or if it is to be used over and over again, then it is worth spending a lot of time thinking about and producing it.

Here are some other things to think about:

- the number of slides
- the design template (it is best to use a design that is set up already – this called a design template)
- the colour scheme (you can choose a number of colours that work well with the chosen design template)
- a title for the presentation
- a subtitle if needed
- the animation effects
- whether other objects such as tables, clip art, drawings, etc. are to be included.

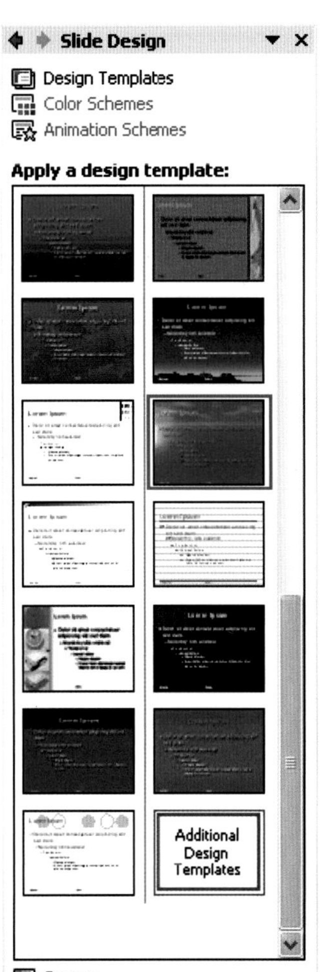

There are many templates to choose from. All you have to do is match the most suitable design to the message that you are putting across in your presentation

Using design templates

Templates determine what each slide will look like. The nice thing about templates is that specialists have chosen the background and the way items are positioned on each slide. They have even decided on some suitable colours. You are then left to think about what to put on your slides. All you have to do is add the text, graphics and sound in the places provided.

WORKSHEETWORKSHEETWORKSHEETWORKSHEETWORKSHEET

WORKSHEET 7.1.3 Selecting the best design

Your teacher may give you a worksheet on which to write your answers or you may be asked to write the answers into your exercise book.

To save time worrying about the design of your slides you can use a design template. If you use these templates, the design of your presentation will look good. You then only have to worry about what to put on each slide (i.e. the content). There is one problem in using design templates: your friends may use the same one as you and your presentation will lose its impact if they do theirs first.

Below are some design templates. Some are more appropriate than others for presenting certain information.

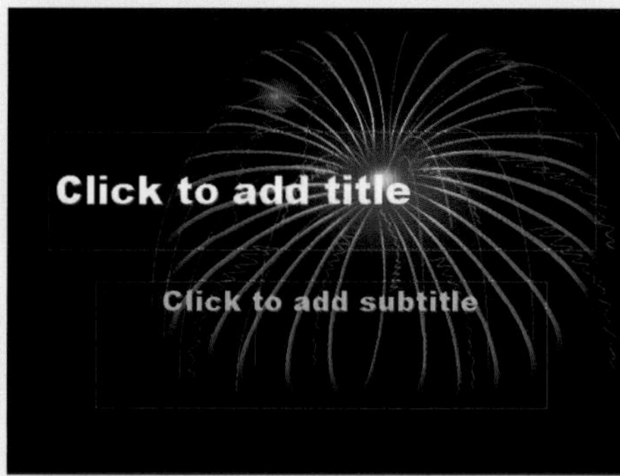

Design template 1

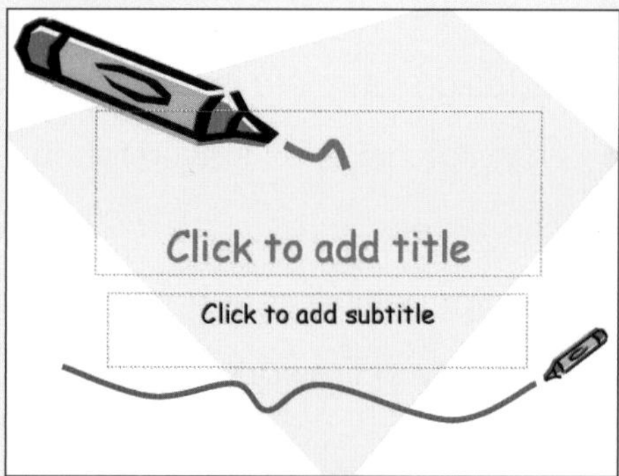

Design template 2

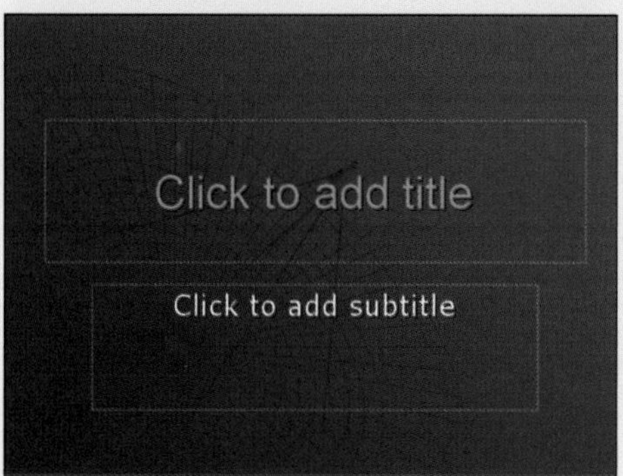

Design template 3

Design template 4

Design template 5

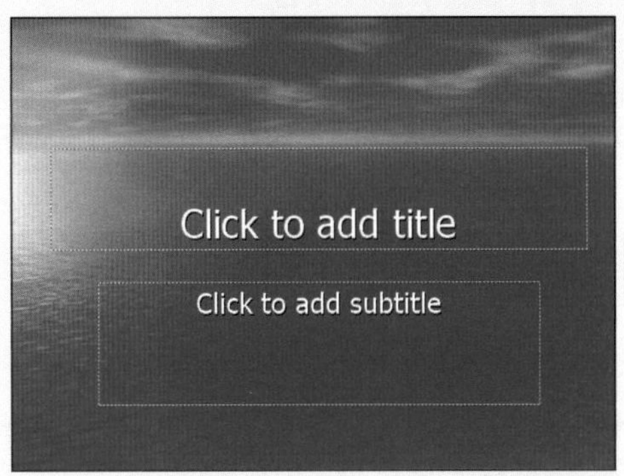

Design template 6

Design template 7

Design template 8

Which design template is best for each of the following presentations?

1. How ICT helps us stay in touch
2. The water cycle
3. Tips for getting your homework done on time
4. A history of fireworks
5. Trees
6. The Titanic
7. Weights and measures
8. Space travel

ACTIVITIESACTIVITIESACTIVITIESACTIVITIESACTIVITIESACTIVITIES

Make it happen

ACTIVITY 1: Making a presentation using a template

This activity will show you how to make two slides as part of a presentation. You will use a design template, which means you will be using a framework for your slide.

1. Load the PowerPoint software. The opening screen will appear.

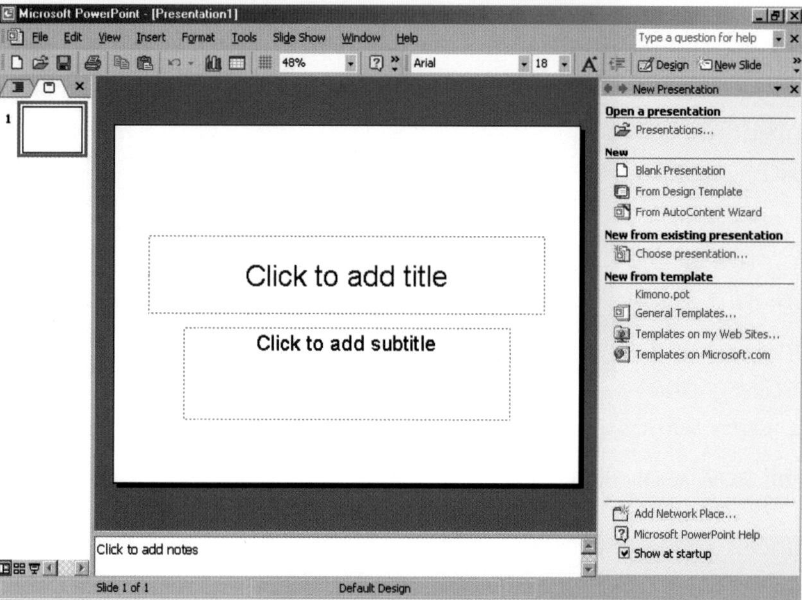

2. Click on **From Design Template** in the 'New Presentation' section of the screen. The following screen appears:

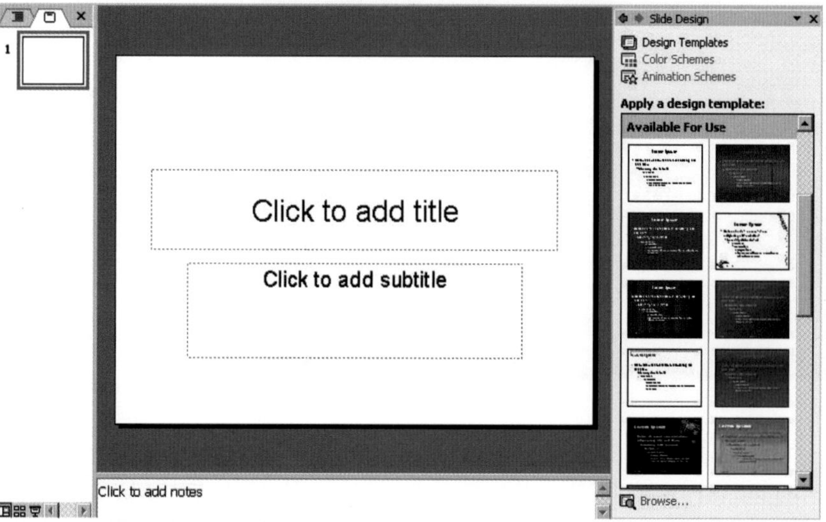

You will see a selection of templates shown as small screenshots. To choose one of them, click on the screenshot. You will now see the main screen area change.

Now that you can see a large version, you may change your mind about using it. To do this you simply click on the template you prefer.

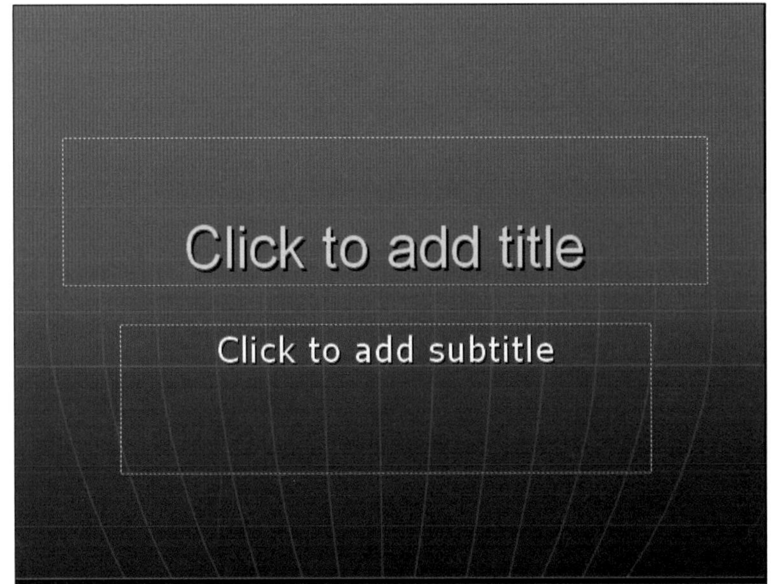

3 You will now be guided through setting up your slides. The first slide will contain a title and a subtitle. The other slides are different and allow you to add text as bullet points, as well as other content such as images and sound.

Click on the first box and type the following title: *Rules for working with ICT*

Click on the second box and type: *To work effectively and safely you need to obey some rules*

Your first slide will now look like this:

4 To make the title more eye catching, we can get the text to move about on the screen using a function called 'animation effects'.

Click on **Animation Schemes** in the 'Slide Design' section of the screen.

5 There are different levels of animation. Move to the 'Exciting' section.

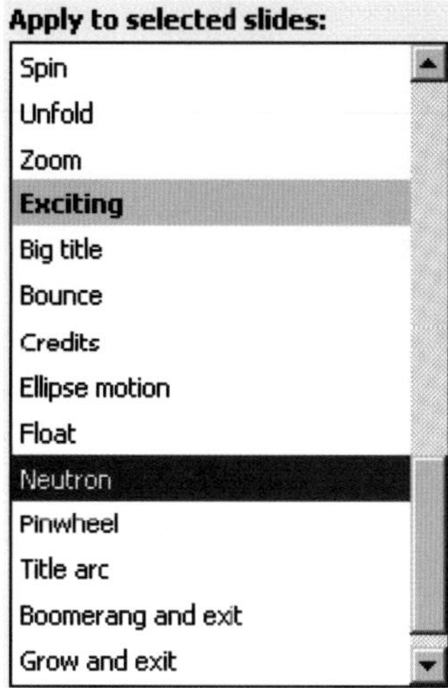

Now click on **Neutron**.

Try some of the other animation effects by clicking on them to see what happens. A word of warning: Animation effects can look good but do not use them too much as they can distract your audience.

6 You can change the background colour of the slide by clicking on **Colour Schemes** in the 'Slide Design' section. Again, if you click on each one in turn you can select a colour that you feel is right.

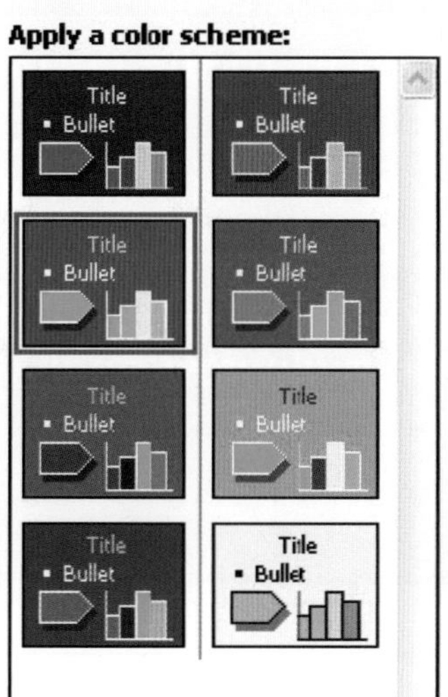

7 To create the next slide click on the following button in the toolbar:

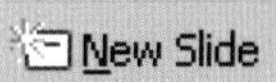

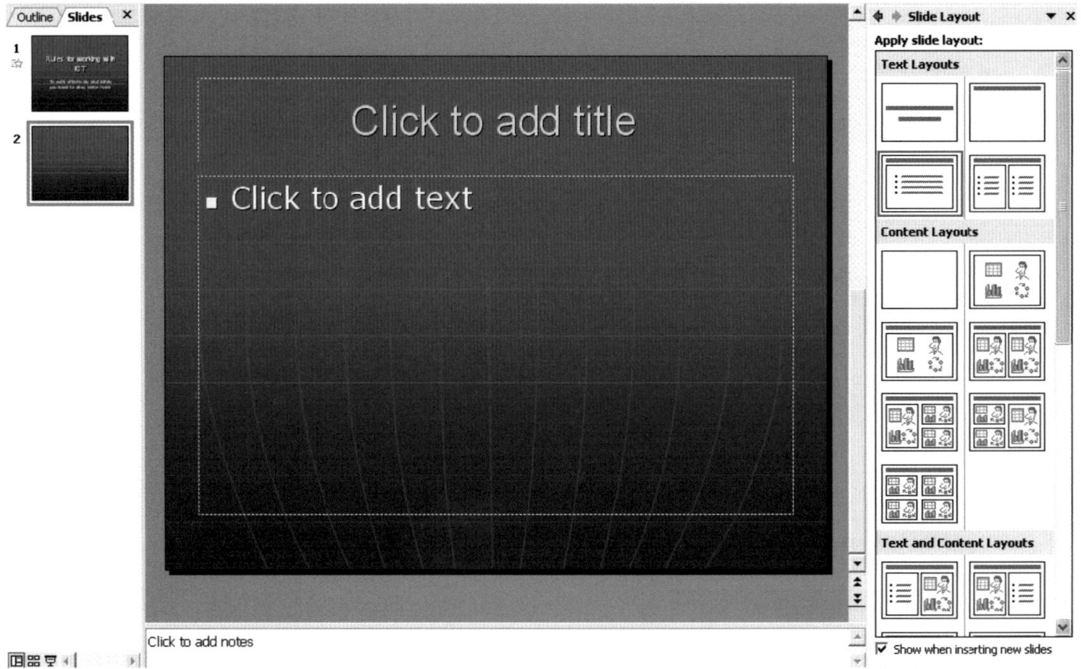

Notice that this slide is different. This is because the first slide is used to introduce the presentation. Also notice that there is a list of all the other slide layouts on the right-hand side of the screen. The one we are using is highlighted with a blue edge. When you create your own presentation you can choose any of the layouts to match your content.

8 Click on the **Click to add title** section and type in the title: *To avoid health problems you must:*

Then click on the **Click to add text** section. Key in the text as shown on the following slide:

To avoid health problems you must:

- sit upright in your chair
- adjust your chair to the correct height
- check there is no glare on your screen
- make sure your screen and keyboard are not at an awkward angle

9 Notice that as the presentation is built up, small versions of the slides are displayed to show the sequence of the slides.

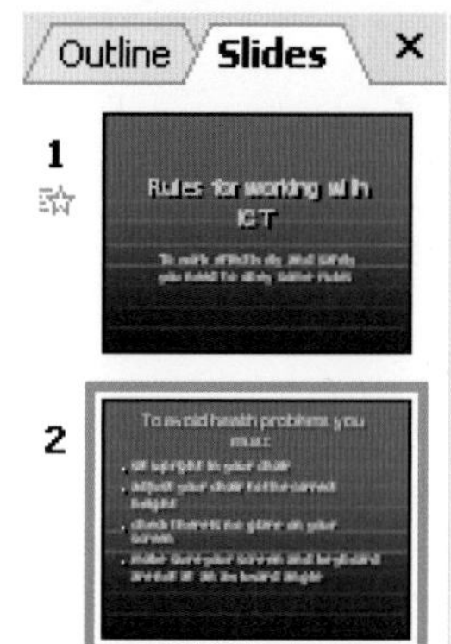

10 Click once on slide 1 in the above list. To play the presentation, click on situated at the bottom left-hand side of the screen. This starts the slide show from the current slide.

11 To save the slide click on **File** and **Save As…**.

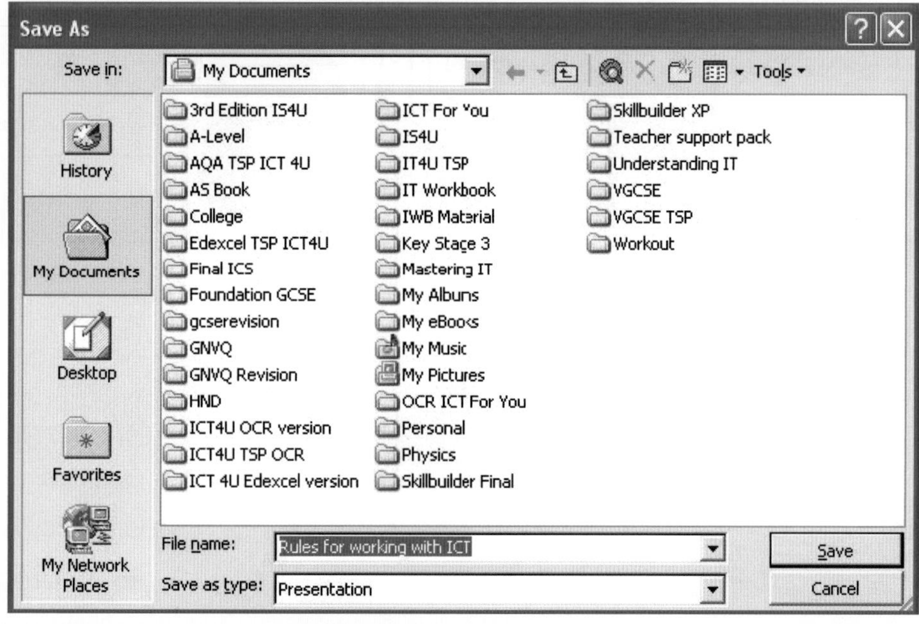

Your teacher will tell you where you will be saving your work. Check that the file name *Rules for working with ICT* is in the 'File name' box. Now click on **Save**.

Tips on slide design

Here are some tips to help you make a good slide:

- Keep a constant colour scheme and design throughout the presentation.
- Only have between five and seven words per line.
- Only have five to seven bullet points per page.
- Do not write in complete sentences (only give the main points).
- Do not overdo the animation and other special effects.
- Only put one concept on each slide.

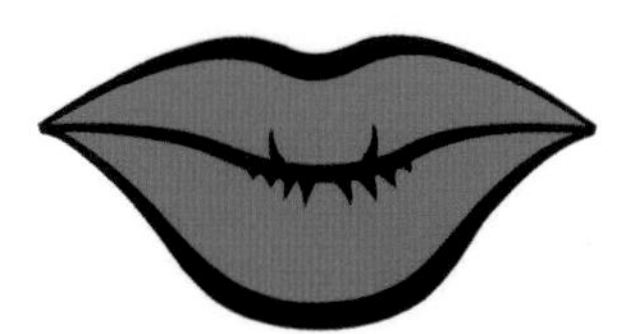

*Above all, use the **KISS** principle (**K**eep **I**t **S**imple and **S**traightforward)*

Lesson 3: ADDING GRAPHICS TO SLIDES

Background

Graphics include pictures, photographs, drawings, symbols, paintings and clip art. They are used to make slides and other documents more interesting.

In Lesson 1 a photograph was added to make the Britney Spears slide more eye catching. Including a picture also adds information because some people may not know what she looks like.

The photograph of Britney Spears is an example of a graphic.

Graphics can be:

- photographs
- clip art
- drawings
- paintings
- graphs and charts.

There is a saying that 'a picture is worth a thousand words'. Imagine trying to describe what Britney Spears looks like. It is much easier to just put a photograph on the slide.

Here are some tips about using graphics:

- Make sure that they are relevant to the message on the slides (this is called fitness for purpose).
- Don't just put them in to brighten up the page – they must be relevant.

KEY WORDS

fitness for purpose – making sure that a graphic is used in the correct context

WORKSHEETWORKSHEETWORKSHEETWORKSHEETWORKSHEET

WORKSHEET 7.1.4 Choosing appropriate images

Your teacher may give you a worksheet on which to write your answers or you may be asked to write the answers into your exercise book.

Sometimes a presentation needs to be light hearted; other times it needs to be serious. This all depends on the message you are giving.

The audience is also important. What might appeal to a group of 11 year olds may not appeal to an older audience. Knowing your audience is important.

Images (clip art, photographs, etc.) need to be chosen carefully.

Here are some presentation topics. For each one you are given two images, and you have to say which one you would choose and why.

Presentation 1: The dangers of drink driving

Image 1

Image 2

Presentation 2: Ways to encourage younger people to take cruise holidays

Image 1

Image 2

Presentation 3: British endangered species

Image 1

Image 2

Presentation 4: Things to do in a seaside resort for a senior citizens' trip

Image 1

Image 2

What are graphics and where do I get them?

Clip art

Clip art images are pre-drawn pictures that you can easily put in your own documents. When using PowerPoint you can use the clip art supplied with the Microsoft Office software. This clip art can be used with Word (the wordprocessor), Publisher (the desktop publishing package) and Excel (the spreadsheet package).

You can also get clip art from:

- clip art packages that you can buy

- free disks that come with magazines
- clip art libraries on the Internet.

Photographs

You can take photographs using a digital camera or scan in a photograph using a scanner.

Obtaining graphics using the Internet

If you see a graphic on a website and would like to include it in your presentation, you can save the picture like this:

1 Position the cursor on the graphic.

2 Right-click the mouse button.

3 Select **Save Picture As...** from the menu. Try to save your photograph as a bitmap file if you have the option. If you do save it as a bitmap file (i.e. a bitmapped graphic) you will need to add '.bmp' after the file name like this: britneyspears.bmp.

4 You can now save the graphic as a file in a suitable place.

KEY WORDS

bitmapped graphic – a file type where the image/graphic is stored as a map showing the position and colour of individual dots of light called pixels

Make it happen

ACTIVITY 2: Finding images online

This activity will help you find suitable graphics using the Internet. Suppose we are asked to produce a presentation on Paris, the capital of France. One of the landmarks of Paris is the Eiffel Tower so we would need to find a graphic showing this.

1 Go online and type in the following web address:

www.google.com

2 Click on **Images** and then type in the words: *Eiffel Tower*

Click on Google Search.

3 Some images will be displayed. Some of these are photographs and others are clip art and drawings. There are even some paintings.

Notice the huge number of images of just one thing (i.e. the Eiffel Tower) on this site.

4 Select the first picture by clicking the left mouse button. You will then see some information about the image. Most important is the copyright information and where the image comes from.

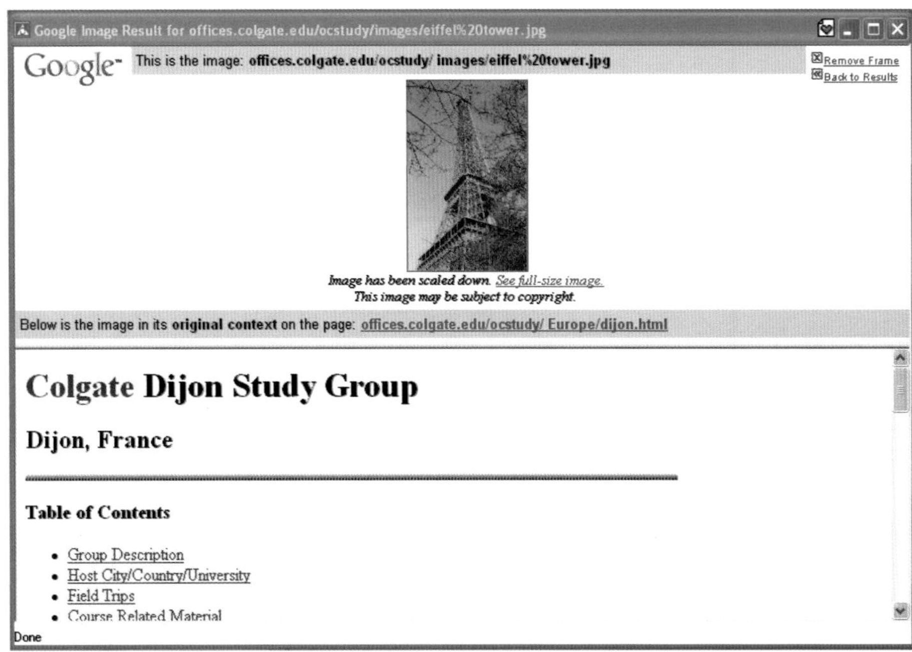

5 To save the image, position the cursor on the image and right-click. Select **Save Picture As...** from the menu.

You can now choose where you want to save the picture. You can also change the name of the file. Now click on Save.

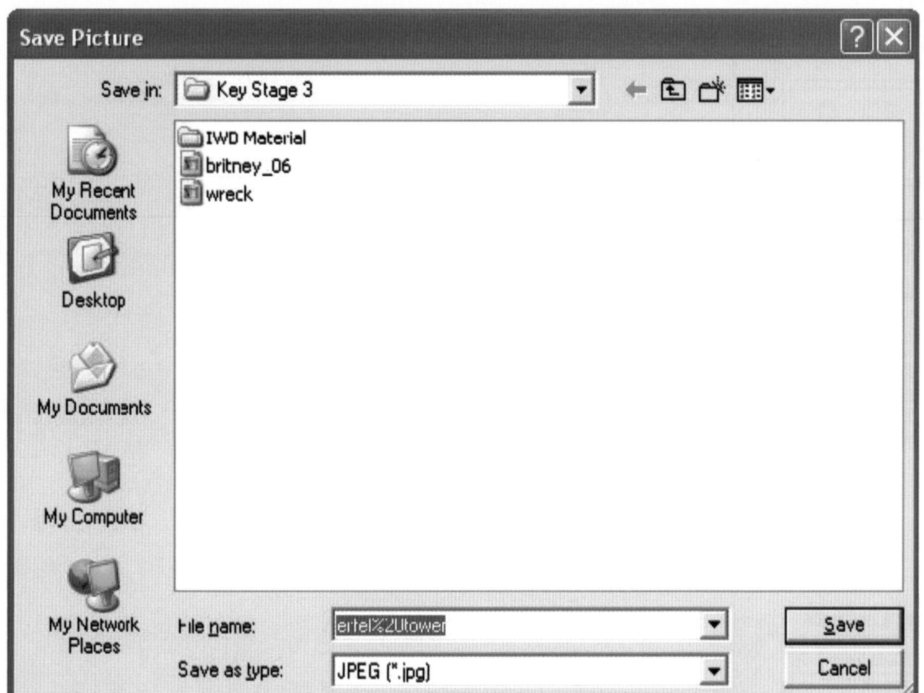

ACTIVITY 3: Adding a graphic to a slide

In this activity we will prepare a slide containing information about the Eiffel Tower. The graphic saved in the last activity will be placed on the slide.

1 Normally you would start by collecting the content (text and graphics). To save time, this has been done for you.

The Eiffel Tower
Paris's most famous landmark
Built in 1889
324 metres tall
Was world's tallest building until 1930
Sways 9 cm in high wind

2 Load PowerPoint and click on **Blank Presentation**.

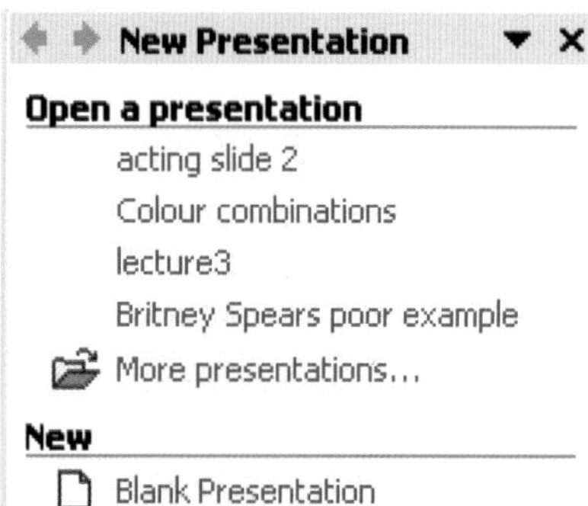

3 The following screen appears so that you can select a slide layout. Because of our content (see step 1) we need a layout that uses a title, a bulleted list and a graphic. This is called 'text and content'.

4 Choose the following Text and Content Layout by clicking on it:

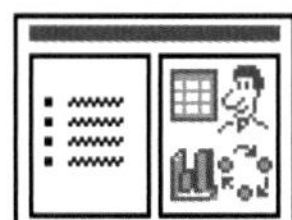

You will notice that the main area changes.

5 Type in the text so that the screen looks like this:

6 We can now insert the photograph of the Eiffel Tower that was saved in Activity 2. Click on the 'add picture' icon (it has a picture of a mountain and the sun).

The Eiffel Tower

- The most famous landmark in Paris
- Built in 1889
- 324 metres tall
- Was world's tallest building until 1930
- Sways 9cm in high wind

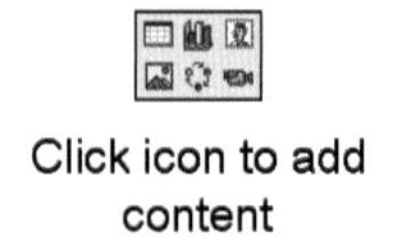

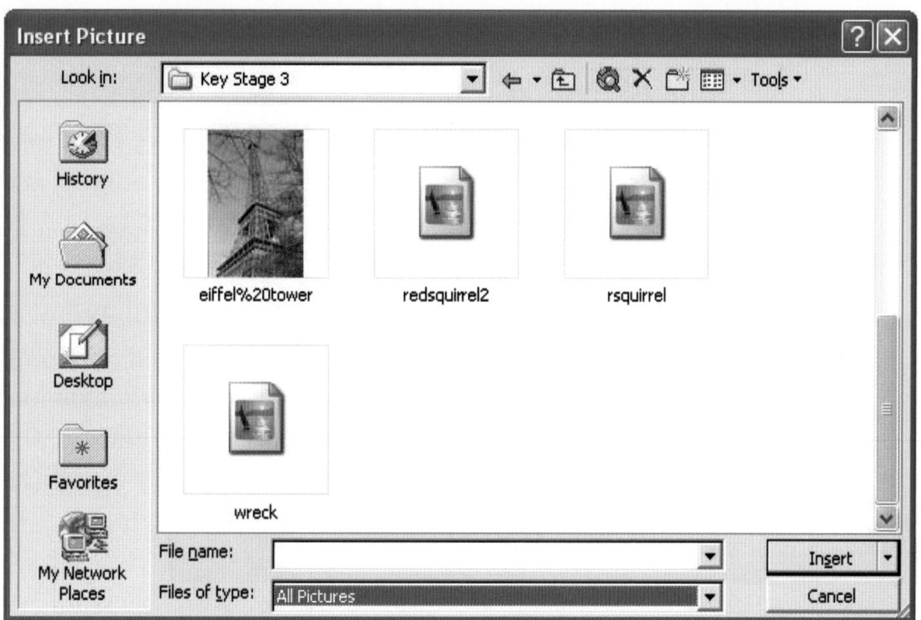

You now have to find where you stored the photograph. To insert the photo in the slide double-click on the photograph.

7 The photograph now appears on the slide.

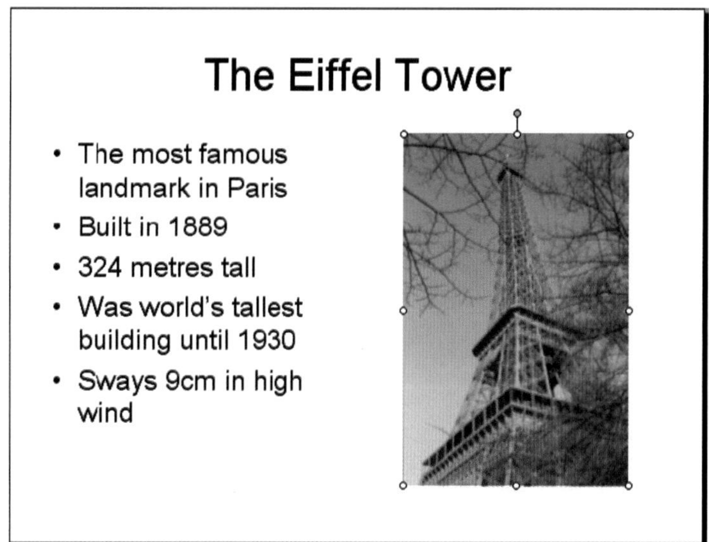

You can manipulate the image (change its position or size) by using the 'handles'. These are the small circles that appear around the image. If you want to keep the original proportions of the images you should use only the 'corner' handles.

8 Save this slide using a suitable file name.

EXTENSION ACTIVITY

1 There are other famous landmarks in Paris. Produce another two slides – one for each of these other landmarks – in the same style as this slide.

2 Experiment on the design of your slides by altering the fonts, font sizes, background colours, etc.

3 After experimenting, produce a final design and save your work using a suitable file name.

Make it happen

ACTIVITY 4: Searching for images

Finding suitable images using **www.google.com** is easy. You now have to find some and save them in a suitable place. You will be using these images later, so make sure you know where you saved them.

Later on, you will be producing a presentation about yourself. You will need some images to do with yourself. Use the website to search for suitable images on:

- the town/village where you live
- types of pets you own
- your favourite singer or group
- your favourite sport
- your favourite football team
- your favourite meal
- the TV programme you like the most
- where you like to go on holiday
- the model of car/cars your parents drive.

If you want actual photographs of your family and yourself, you will have to either take them using a digital camera or scan in a photograph using a scanner.

Searching for suitable images and sounds

Microsoft's Design Gallery Live can be found on the Internet at **http://dgl.microsoft.com/**

There are lots of new images and sounds here that can be downloaded to be used or stored with your other images and sounds.

Below is a search for the mammal 'bat'. Notice that just typing in 'bat' leads to baseball bats as well.

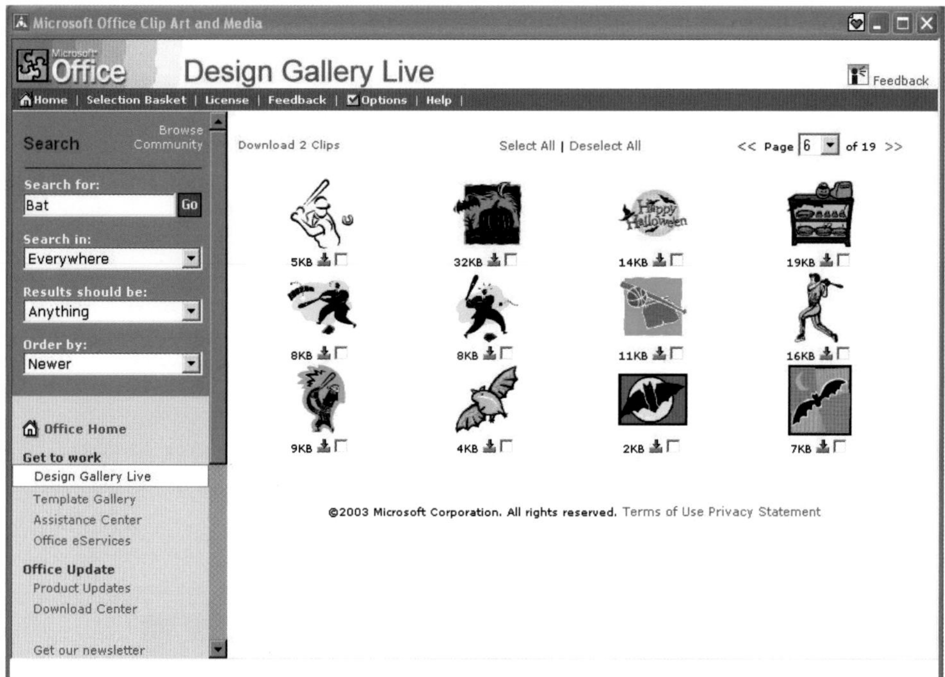

The following search is for sounds made by a cow. We have typed *Cow* in the 'Search for' box. Notice that in the 'Results should be' box we have selected **Sounds**.

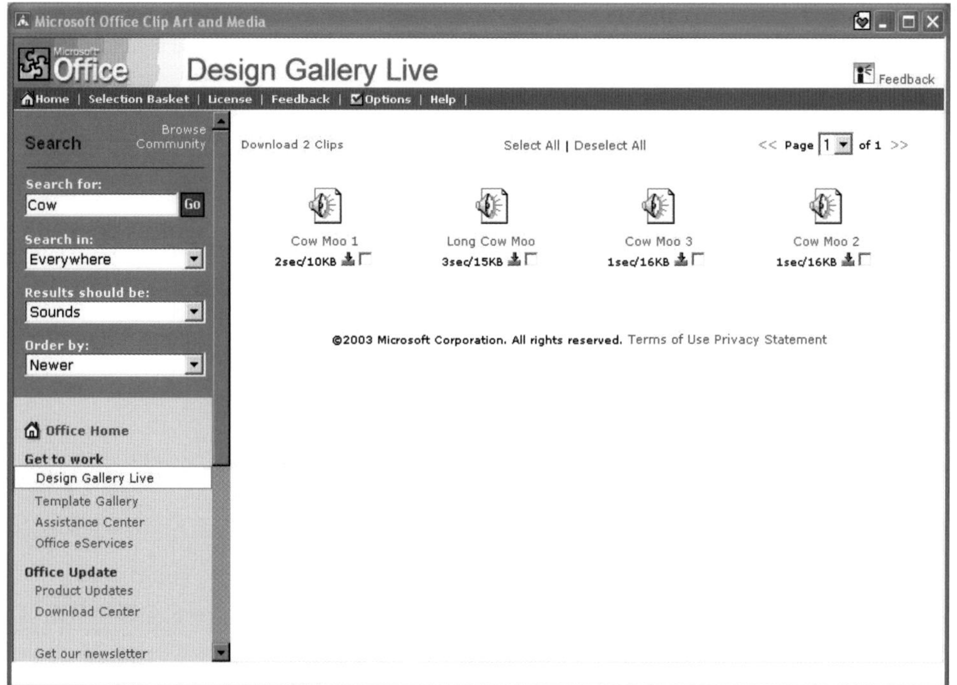

Barry's clipart server

KEY WORDS

animation – moving images

This is an extremely good on-line site to look for clip art and animations. Most of these look like clip art that moves.

Visit the site at **www.barrysclipart.com/**.

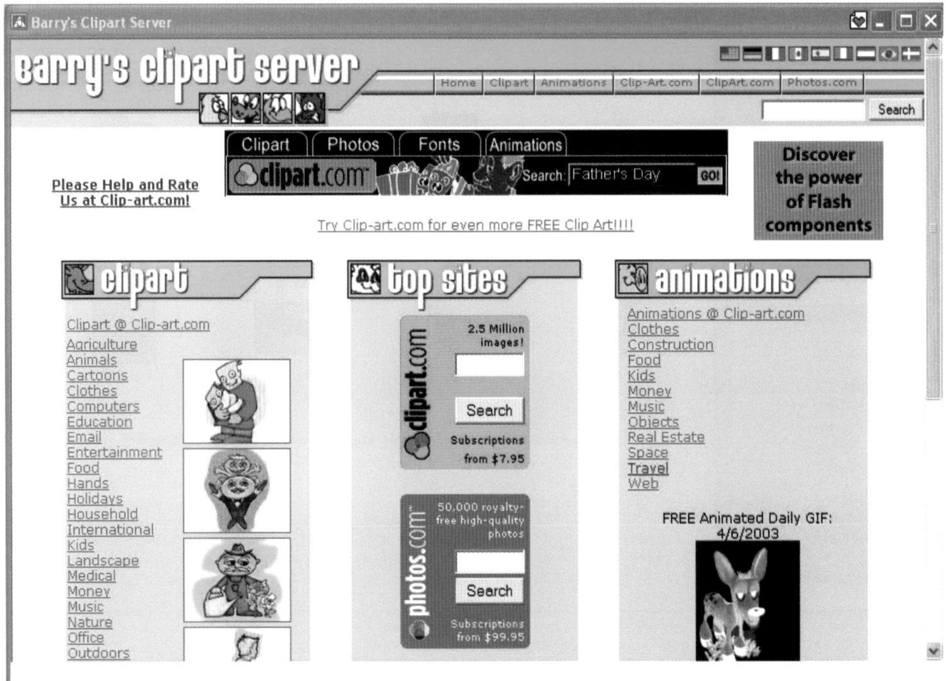

Taking photographs

Many photographs can be obtained from websites. Others you would need to take yourself. You can take photographs and store them on the computer using a digital camera. A digital camera needs no film and the image can be seen immediately on a small screen. The image can then be loaded onto the computer (usually using a wire connecting the camera and computer) and stored.

Graphics can be put into many documents and websites. Obtaining the image in the first place is called 'capturing' the image. Capturing an image can be done in the following ways:

- by using a digital camera (for a photographic image)
- by using clip art from a disk or CD/DVD, including drawings and photographs (there are also plenty of sites on the Internet where you can download free clip art)
- by obtaining an image from a website or web page on the Internet (be aware of the copyright restrictions when doing this)
- by scanning an image in (this could be a picture, diagram or photograph).

Manipulating or enhancing the image

Once the image has been captured, it may need adjusting. Graphics software is available that allows you to alter (i.e. manipulate) images. Here are some of the ways that an image can be manipulated or enhanced:

- it can be resized (i.e. made bigger or smaller)
- the contrast can be altered
- the brightness can be altered
- part of the image can be cropped (this is just like cutting the part you want out of the picture)
- individual colours in the image can be adjusted
- it can be saved in a different file format.

Modifying a graphic image

Bitmap or vector graphics

Graphic images can be either of two types: bitmap or vector.

Bitmaps

This photograph is a bitmap image. A small square of this photograph has been enlarged and you can see that the image is made up of lots of coloured squares. These are called pixels.

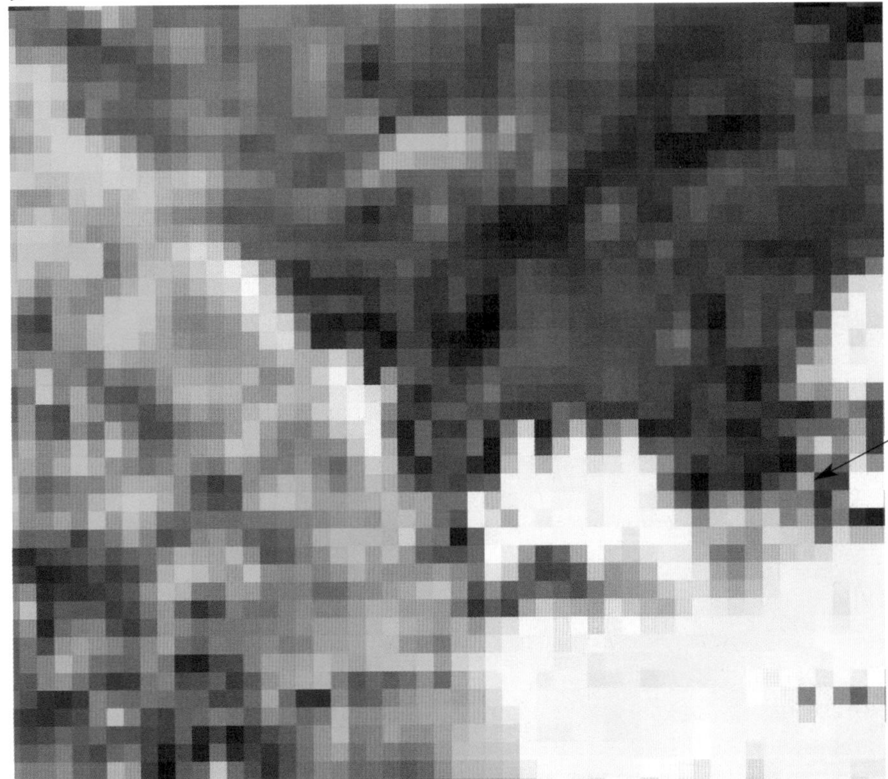

A single coloured square on the screen is called a pixel

Bitmap images are made up of millions of these pixels. Normally there are lots of these pixels and they are extremely small. This means you cannot see them in an image. If the image is enlarged, then you can start to see the pixels and the image appears blocky.

In general:

- Bitmaps are big files so they take up lots of space on a disk and take a long time to send over the Internet.
- Bitmap images can lose their sharpness when they are enlarged or reduced in size.

Vector graphics

Vector graphics are images that use maths to work out the positions and lengths of lines, curves, etc.

In general:

- Vector graphics keep their sharpness when enlarged or reduced.
- Vector images do not take up much space when stored.

KEY WORDS

Vector graphic – image/graphic represented by a mathematical formula that may be enlarged or reduced without any loss in clarity

Lesson 4: ADDING SOUND TO YOUR PRESENTATION

Background

Sound is another multimedia effect that can be added to your presentation. Sound can make a presentation more fun but it can also detract from the message being given, so it needs to be used with care. Remember that you will usually have to talk about each slide, so the sound must not last too long.

As always, you should consider your audience when adding sounds.

Make it happen

ACTIVITY 5: Adding sound to a presentation

1. Load the Powerpoint presentation software and open the file called 'Holiday presentations'.

   You will see the following screen appear:

> **Note**
> You can access this file via the 'Activity Files' link at www.oxfordsecondary.co.uk

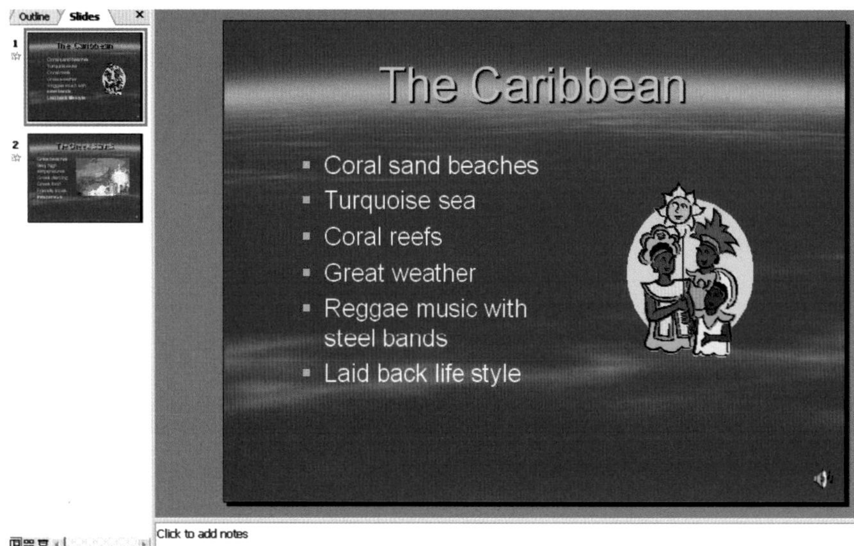

2. Start the slide show by clicking on the 'slide show' button:

   Notice the following:

   - the appropriate use of a design template
   - the use of an appropriate clip art image
   - not too much information included on each slide
   - the appropriate use of sound clips
   - the sound plays automatically.

3. Check that the slide view is normal and that the second slide has been selected. We will now create another slide. Click on the 'new slide' button New Slide on the toolbar.

4. We want to create a slide like the others. These slides have both text (bullet points) and content (image and sound). In the 'slide content' part of the screen, select the text and content shown here by clicking on it.

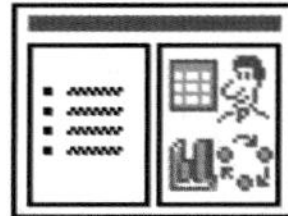

5 The screen will change to this:

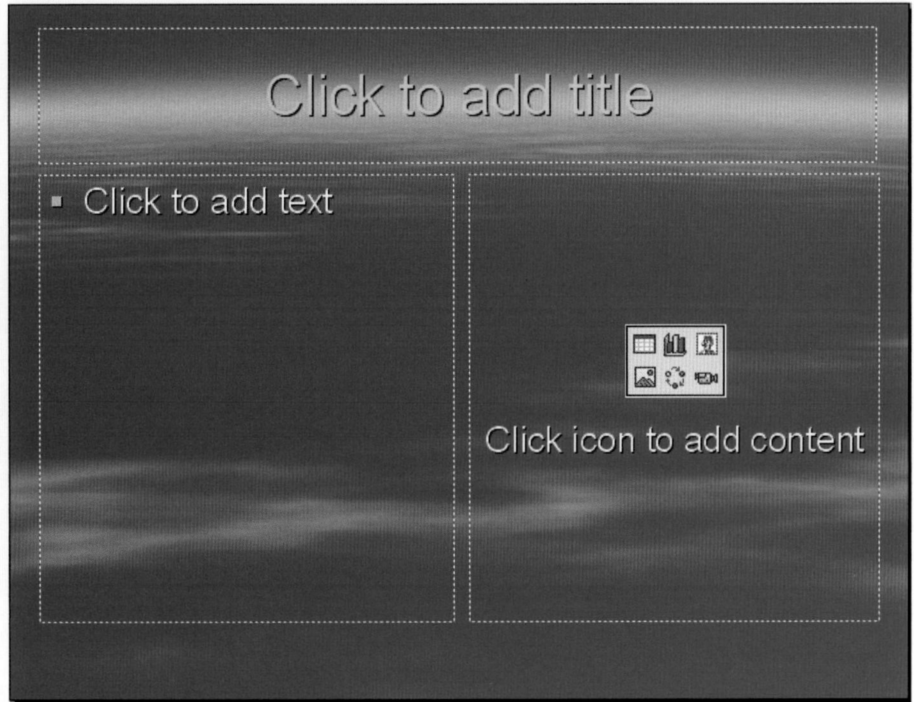

Move the cursor across each of the little icons in the 'add content' box and notice what content you can insert into the slide.

Now add text for the title and the bullet points.

Type the following as a title: *Spain*

Type in the following bullet points:

- *Easy to get to*
- *Cheap food and drink*
- *Fantastic nightlife*
- *Lovely sandy beaches*

6 Now click on the 'add clip art' icon.

The screen on the right appears. Type in *Spain* to see what clip art there is.

Click on your own choice of image and then click on **OK**.

Resize and position the image on the page by clicking on the image and dragging it or using the 'handles'.

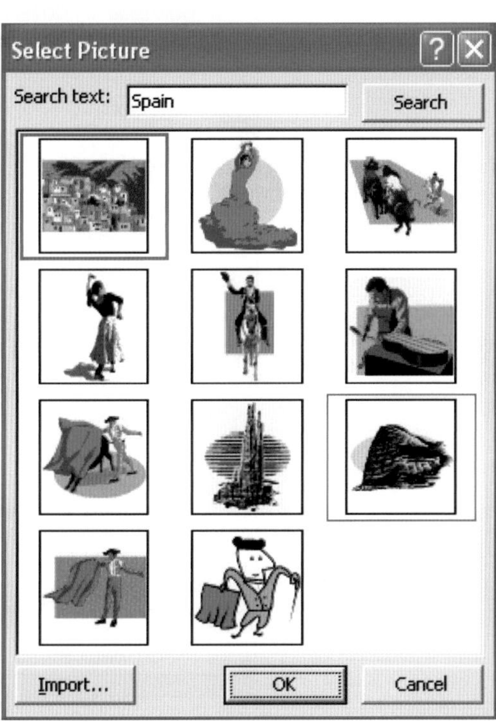

7 Your slide will look something like this, although your image may be different:

8 Now we need to add some sound. Click on **Insert** and the following menu appears, where you then click on **Movies and Sounds**.

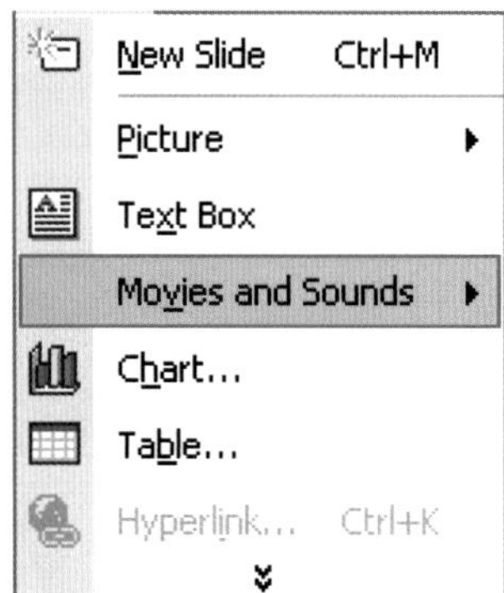

A menu now appears to allow you to find the sound file that you intend to use.

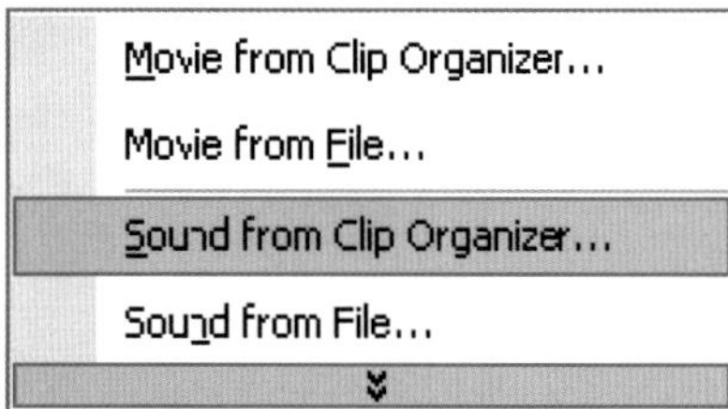

Choose **Sound from Clip Organizer…**. This is where all the sounds that come as part of Microsoft Office are kept.

9 The Clip Organizer appears with a list of sound files.

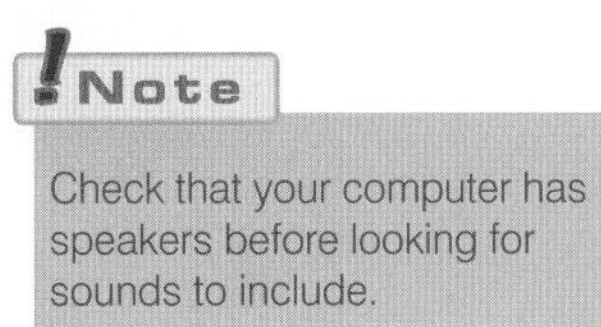

Check that your computer has speakers before looking for sounds to include.

It is hard to tell which one to choose so you will have to experiment.

Click on one of the sound files in the list and the following question appears:

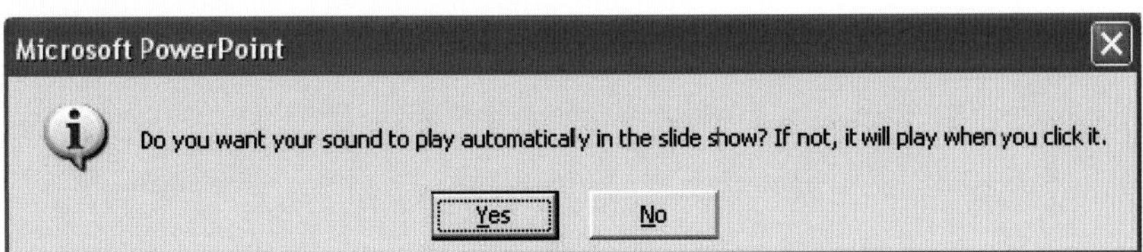

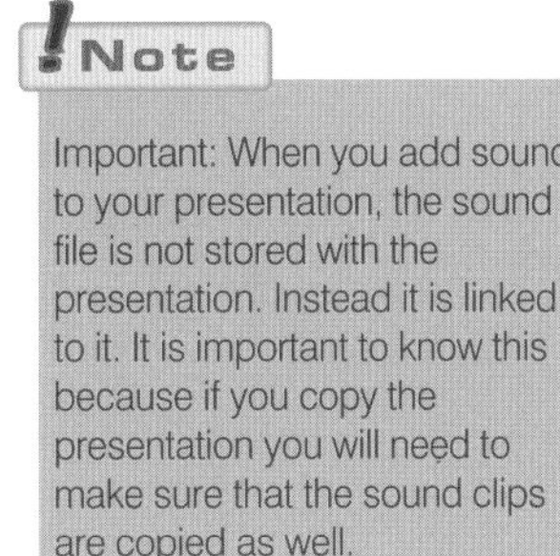

Important: When you add sound to your presentation, the sound file is not stored with the presentation. Instead it is linked to it. It is important to know this because if you copy the presentation you will need to make sure that the sound clips are copied as well.

Make your choice.

A sound file is now linked to your slide. You can attach different sounds/music to different slides in your presentation.

A small speaker icon appears like this: . If this button is in the way of material on your slides you can drag it to a better position.

Creating slides from scratch

You may wish to be original and not use a template, but instead decide on your own design for your slides. It is harder to do this and will take more time but at least your presentations will be original.

The use of colour

Before you use colour you need to think about the messages that different colours give, such as:

Red for danger, excitement

Green for go or for nature, growth

Purple for royal

Blue for cold, trustworthy, calm

Orange for vibrancy and excitement

Black for power and elegance

WORKSHEETWORKSHEETWORKSHEETWORKSHEETWORKSHEET

WORKSHEET 7.1.5 Colour codes

As we have seen, colours can convey messages. Your teacher may give you a worksheet on which to write or you may be asked to copy the table into your books and then fill it in. For each colour write down what message or messages you think it gives.

Colour	Messages
Brown	
Yellow	
Burgundy	
Light blue	
Mint green	
Pink	

In a presentation, you can use colour for:

- the background of a slide
- the font
- the colour inside a text box.

It is very important that a suitable combination of colours is used. They have to work together.

The artists' colour wheel shown on the right can be used to help select colours that work well together.

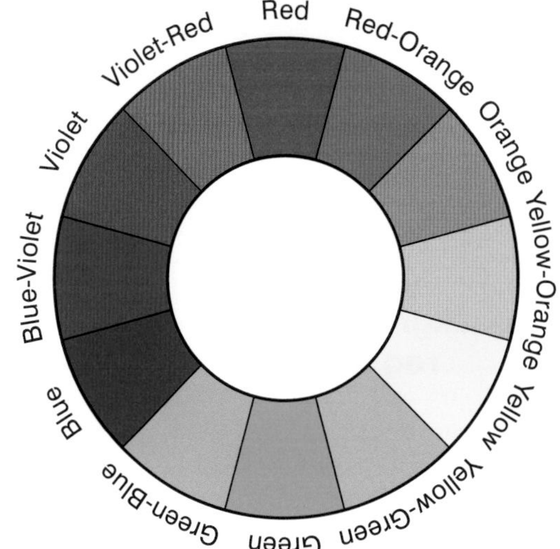

The colour wheel is divided into 'warm' and 'cool' colours. Warm colours (red, orange and yellow) tend to 'pop out' to the foreground. This makes them good for headings and other items you want to stand out. Cool colours (blue, green and violet) recede (i.e. move away). This makes them good for backgrounds.

The examples below show a combination of warm colours for the text and cool colours for the background.

Red text with a light blue background

Yellow text with a sea green background

Light yellow text with a violet background

Red text with a light pink background

You need to experiment with different fonts and background colours

Using the colour wheel to find colour schemes

Using two colours positioned on opposite sides of the colour wheel

Colours on opposite sides of the colour wheel are called complementary colours.

Blue-violet background and yellow-orange text

Yellow-orange and blue-violet (complementary colours)

Contrasting colours

These are combinations of two colours that are separated by three consecutive colours on the colour wheel. Red and yellow are two such colours.

Yellow background and red text

Red and yellow (contrasting colours)

Colour intensity

Some of these colour combinations look garish and overwhelming. You can reduce the intensity of a colour to make it look better.

Here the yellow has been made much lighter:

Yellow background and red text

You will find that pastel colours work well for backgrounds.

Thinking about colour combinations

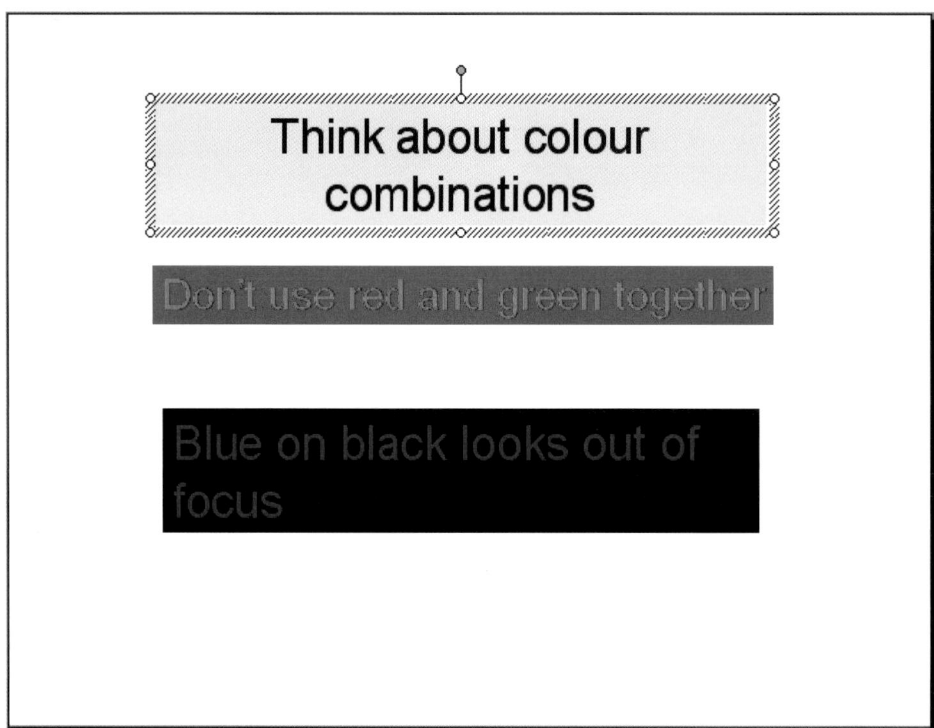

Make it happen

ACTIVITY 6: A presentation about yourself

You have to produce the slides for a presentation, although you do not need to actually give the presentation. Create four or five slides, making use of all the information and skills you have learnt in this unit.

The set of slides will be to accompany a presentation about you and your interests. You may like to refer back to the presentation produced by Amy in Worksheet 7.1.2. You will need to use some of the graphics you collected in Activity 4, such as:

- the town/village where you live
- types of pets you own

- your favourite singer or group

- your favourite sport
- your favourite football team

- your favourite meal
- the TV programme you like the most
- where you like to go on holiday

- the model of car/ cars your parents drive

Make sure you take note of everything you have learnt in this unit when producing your slides.

2 Information and presentation

Lesson 1:
INTRODUCTION TO INFORMATION AND PRESENTATION

How to search for and present information using ICT

In this unit you will learn how and where to search for information using CD-ROMs and the Internet. This information could be about anything, such as statistics, legislation, advertisements, timetables, etc.

You will also learn to be critical of the information you find so that you can determine whether to trust it or not. Information is often biased in some way, so you will also learn how to look for this.

At the end of this unit you will be asked to produce a presentation on a particular topic. This topic will be unfamiliar to you, so you will need to do some research on your own and then evaluate the material you have and use the relevant information to produce a presentation.

KEY WORDS

bias – information that has been written to favour a particular viewpoint (e.g. an article on 'should fox hunting be banned?' written by a master of the hunt would be written in favour of fox hunting)

Internet – a worldwide network of computer networks that forms the largest connected set of computers in the world

legislation – laws

statistics – facts and figures on a subject, for example the mean, mode, median, range, biggest, smallest, etc.

Background theory and key information

The word 'data' is used a lot in ICT. This is because computers use data. Data means the raw facts and figures. When data is processed, the result is called information. Processing refines the data in some way. This could be putting the data into a certain order (as in a database) or by performing calculations with it.

You can get information either by collecting data and processing it yourself or by using information already created by somebody else.

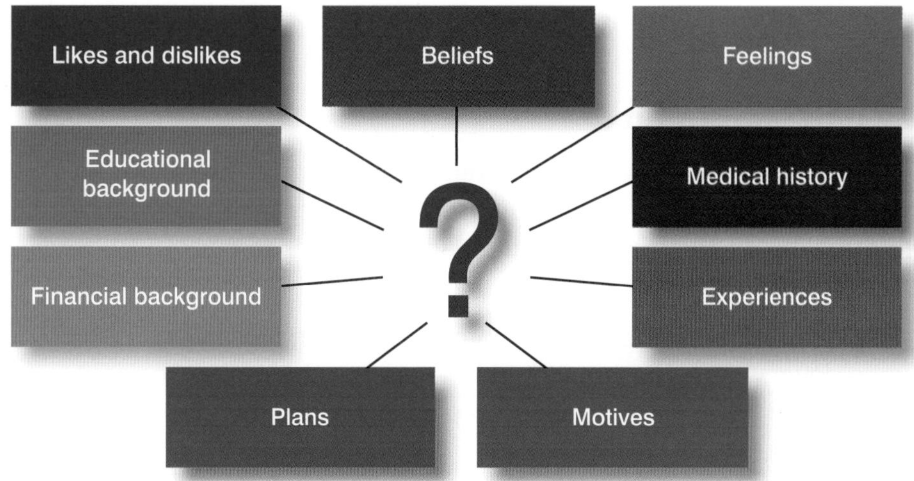

By processing data you get information

What types of information are there?

A lot of information is in the form of text, but text is not the only type of information. The main types are shown in the following diagram:

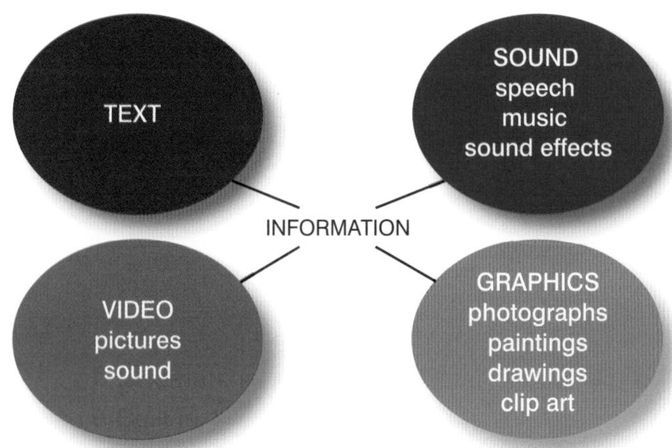

The different types of information

When you present information to others, it is best to use different types. When looking for information on a certain topic, you should be looking for graphics as well as text, and some information is best presented as sound. For example, you could be explaining the lifestyle in a certain country and have the national anthem playing or you could have people talking about their experiences during the Second World War.

Where can I find information?

There are paper-based resources such as books, magazines, newspapers, leaflets and so on. The best place to look for these is a library. Many of these resources are now available on CD-ROM or on the Internet. In this unit we will mainly look at these electronic resources.

WORKSHEETWORKSHEETWORKSHEETWORKSHEETWORKSHEET

WORKSHEET 7.2.1 Where can you find it?

You may be given a worksheet on which to write your answers or you may be asked to write your answers into your book. When you have finished, your teacher will either go through the answers or give you an answer sheet so that you can check your answers yourself.

There are many different places where you can find information. For the following pieces of information write down where you would find it. There may be more than one place. You should write down as many places as you can think of.

1. Tonight's TV programmes
2. Tomorrow's weather
3. The latest top twenty chart
4. A map of the area where you live showing your road
5. The exchange rate from pounds into euros
6. A list of the Kings and Queens of England
7. The telephone number of a local plumber
8. The opening hours of Alton Towers Theme Park
9. Where the country Albania is in the world
10. The films that are on at the cinema nearest to where you live

Using questions to obtain the relevant information

A delivery driver has just called you to ask for directions to your house. In order for you to give directions, you will need to find out where the driver is. Remember, the driver may not know the area well and you will need to be very precise in your questions to find out where he or she is.

You might ask:

- the name of the road the driver is on (you may or may not know this name)
- the nearest landmark, such as a church, pub, supermarket, railway station, etc.
- in which direction the driver is travelling.

Using precise questions to obtain information is very important in everyday life. Only if you ask the right questions will you get suitable data for processing. In the next lesson you will find out how to produce lists of questions for questionnaires.

KEY WORDS

purpose – the use to which the information is to be put

relevant – useful information that covers the topic you are looking for

reliable – trusted material

WORKSHEET

WORKSHEET 7.2.2 Collecting the information needed for particular tasks

Your teacher may give you a worksheet, in which case you will need to write your answers directly on the sheet. Alternatively, you should copy and complete the following table in your book.

Sometimes you need several pieces of information to complete a task. Here is a list of tasks and you have to say what information you need before you start. The first one has been done for you.

Task	Information needed
Plan a trip for you and your friends to the theme park Alton Towers	Date, number going, admission price, map, methods of travel, times and prices
Find out the cheapest place to order a particular CD using the Internet	
Conduct a survey to find out who the best teacher is	
Find out the weather in Spain	
Find out the cost of a family holiday on the Greek island of Corfu	
Book tickets for a local gig	
Choose a CD as a birthday present for a friend	

Can you believe the information you find?

Just because the information has come from the Internet doesn't mean it is correct. There are some sites that deliberately deceive. The main thing is to be able to spot such sites and not to use the information in them.

Anyone with a small amount of knowledge of computing can make their own website on any topic. Some websites contain completely false information and people create them as a joke. It is therefore essential to be able to spot the official sites and those produced by others that may contain inaccurate information. You must make sure that the information you use is reliable.

The rule is: when in doubt, doubt!

Watch out for bogus websites. Some are set up to misinform or part people from their money illegally.

ACTIVITIES

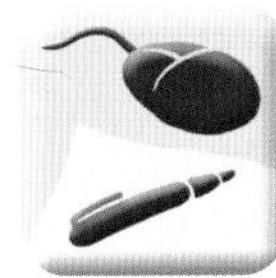

ACTIVITY 1: Is it true?

Here are some websites. For each site listed, type in the web address, read the information and then:

1. say whether you consider the information is right or wrong
2. give reasons for your decision (i.e. what was it about the site that made you suspicious).

Site 1: California's Velcro Crop under Challenge (1993), by Ken Umbach

Take a look at this site at:

www.umbachconsulting.com/miscellany/velcro.html

If you do not have access to the Internet in the room where you are working, your teacher will give you a copy of this article to read.

Site 2: A site on the dangers of the chemical Dihydrogen Monoxide

www.dhmo.org/

If you do not have access to the Internet, use the information here to make up your mind.

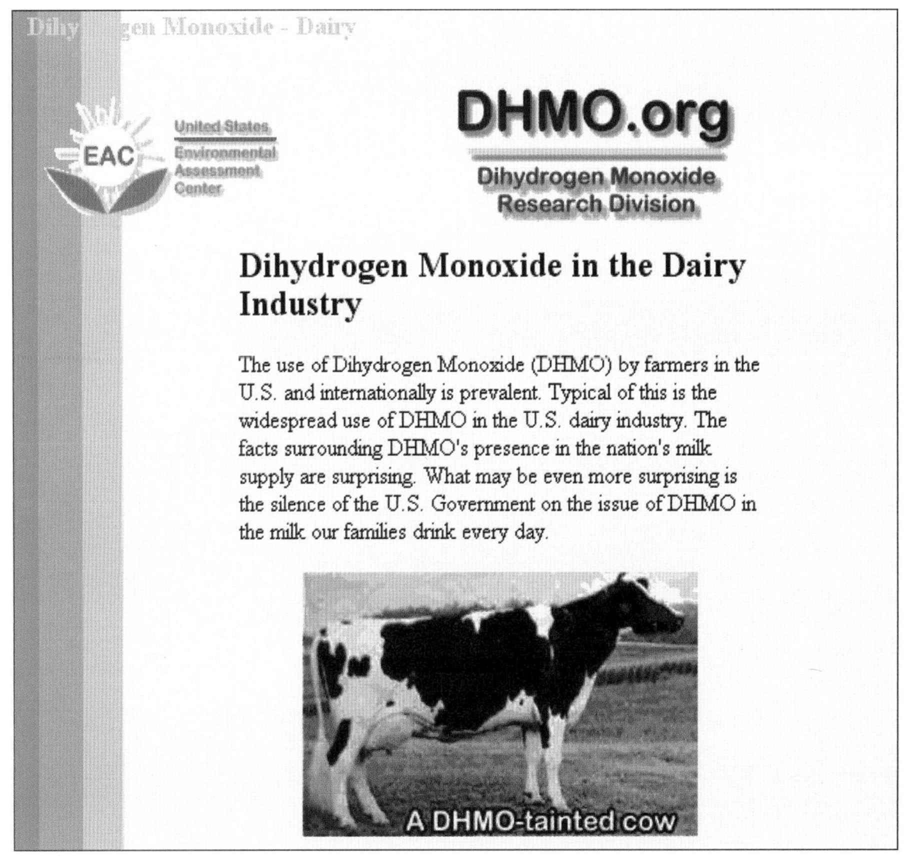

Dihydrogen Monoxide in the Dairy Industry

The use of Dihydrogen Monoxide (DHMO) by farmers in the U.S. and internationally is prevalent. Typical of this is the widespread use of DHMO in the U.S. dairy industry. The facts surrounding DHMO's presence in the nation's milk supply are surprising. What may be even more surprising is the silence of the U.S. Government on the issue of DHMO in the milk our families drink every day.

A DHMO-tainted cow

Site 3: Information about a zoo near a nuclear power station

www.brookview.karoo.net/Sellafield_Zoo/

Sellafield zoo ...where the wildlife has a half-life

Home

Home
Introduction
Bears
Elephants
Oryx
Seals
Shire horses
Gorillas
The Farm
Fishing
Souvenirs
Credits

JFH web design

The creation of the Nuclear Power Plant at Sellafield (formerly known as Windscale) was a bonus for the local zoo, as large tracts of land were made available and cheap by people moving away or dying.

In addition, our intense animal breeding program has been a tremendous success, bringing many interesting new variants of well-known species.

Follow the links on the left to explore this fascinating blend of animal life and mutation!

Site 4: A site about a creature called The Pacific Northwest Tree Octopus

www.zapatopi.net/treeoctopus.html

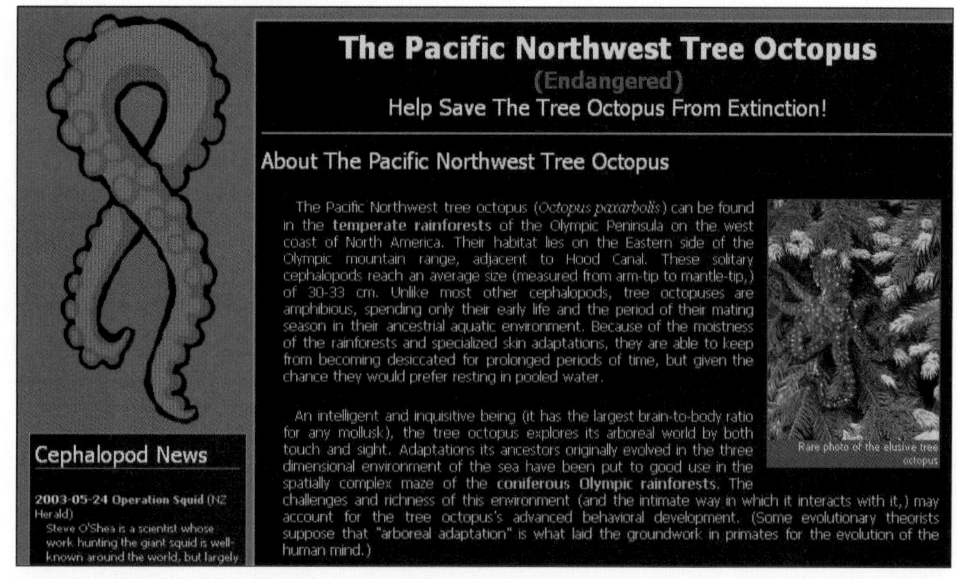

The Pacific Northwest Tree Octopus

(Endangered)

Help Save The Tree Octopus From Extinction!

About The Pacific Northwest Tree Octopus

The Pacific Northwest tree octopus (*Octopus paxarbolis*) can be found in the **temperate rainforests** of the Olympic Peninsula on the west coast of North America. Their habitat lies on the Eastern side of the Olympic mountain range, adjacent to Hood Canal. These solitary cephalopods reach an average size (measured from arm-tip to mantle-tip,) of 30-33 cm. Unlike most other cephalopods, tree octopuses are amphibious, spending only their early life and the period of their mating season in their ancestrial aquatic environment. Because of the moistness of the rainforests and specialized skin adaptations, they are able to keep from becoming desiccated for prolonged periods of time, but given the chance they would prefer resting in pooled water.

An intelligent and inquisitive being (it has the largest brain-to-body ratio for any mollusk), the tree octopus explores its arboreal world by both touch and sight. Adaptations its ancestors originally evolved in the three dimensional environment of the sea have been put to good use in the spatially complex maze of the **coniferous Olympic rainforests**. The challenges and richness of this environment (and the intimate way in which it interacts with it,) may account for the tree octopus's advanced behavioral development. (Some evolutionary theorists suppose that "arboreal adaptation" is what laid the groundwork in primates for the evolution of the human mind.)

Rare photo of the elusive tree octopus

Cephalopod News

2003-05-24 Operation Squid (NZ Herald)
Steve O'Shea is a scientist whose work hunting the giant squid is well-known around the world, but largely

Site 5: A site about ancient Greece

www.madison.k12.wi.us/whitehorse/greeceb.htm

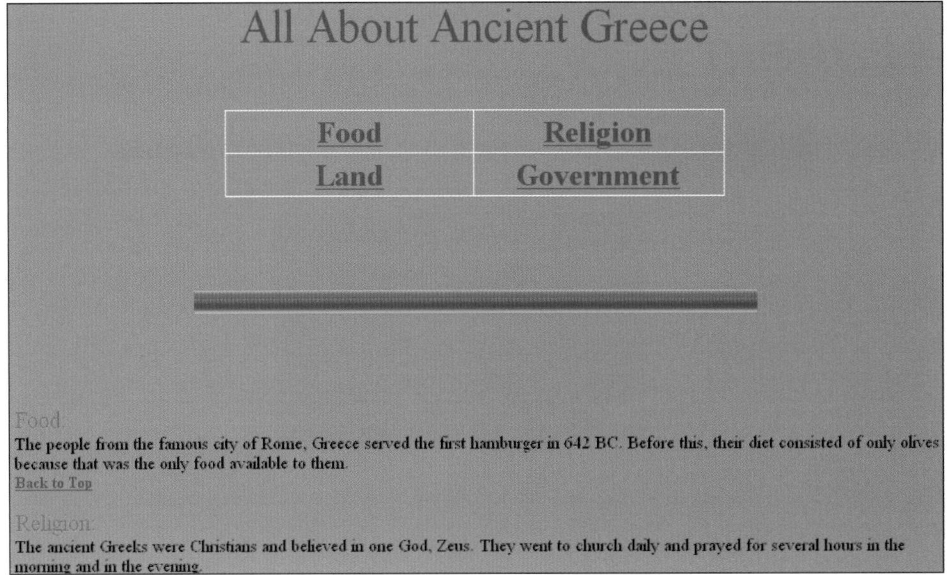

EXTENSION ACTIVITY

Bogus Internet sites can be quite entertaining – provided you realise that they are bogus. Use the Internet to see if you can find more bogus websites.

Conspiracy theories

Have you heard of conspiracy theories? These are theories which suggest that certain events, such as the accidental death of Princess Diana, can be explained in another way. Some people think the pop singer Elvis Presley is still alive or that man did not go to the moon. Some people believe these theories, and others don't. People tend to like a more interesting version than what probably happened. There is a saying: 'Never let the truth get in the way of a good story'.

There are many sites on conspiracy theories and the trouble is that people may look at them and think that they describe what definitely happened.

Bias

There are two sides to every argument and you have to ask if you are seeing both sides or just one. For example, suppose you search for information about foxhunting on the Internet. Nearly everyone has an opinion about this.

If you just want to find the facts about foxhunting in order to make up your own opinion it is quite difficult, as everyone seems to want to give you theirs.

WORKSHEETWORKSHEETWORKSHEETWORKSHEETWORKSHEET

WORKSHEET 7.2.3 **In which way are these websites biased? Or are they unbiased?**

Your teacher will either give you a worksheet on which to write your answers or you will be asked to copy your answers into your book.

Below are some websites on foxhunting. For each site, read the first page and then decide whether the website is biased in favour of foxhunting or against it. If the site is unbiased then you should say 'unbiased'.

1. **www.countryside-alliance.org/**
2. **www.animalaid.org.uk/campaign/sport/hunting.htm**
3. **www.rspca.org.uk/servlet/ContentServer?pagename=RSPCACampaigns/Banhunting/BanhuntingHomepage**
4. **http://news.bbc.co.uk/cbbcnews/hi/find_out/guides/animals/fox_hunting/newsid_1717000/1717812.stm**

How I found my information

When you are researching a topic, you should keep records on how you found the information. These records would include the following:

- How I found my information.
- Website addresses I visited.
- Ones I used, and why.
- Ones I didn't use, and why.
- How I put my point of view into the presentation.

What you should already know

You will need to be familiar with logging onto and using the Internet before starting this unit. As this unit is concerned with obtaining and using information, you will need some knowledge of how to do simple Internet searches.

Note

Being able to search for information on the Internet is an important skill. Accessing relevant information quickly will save you lots of time in your future school work.

You will be building on the following, which you covered at Key Stage 2:

- Writing for different audiences.
- Using complex searches.
- Evaluating information, checking accuracy and questioning plausibility.
- Using the Internet to search large databases and to interpret information.

What you will learn

In this unit you will:

- use different search techniques to find useful information
- learn that not all information can be relied upon
- learn how to collect your own data and use this to provide information
- learn that information is usually produced from a particular viewpoint and may be biased
- collect, evaluate and present information, bearing in mind the audience.

Lesson 2: COLLECTING DATA TO PROVIDE INFORMATION

Background

There are two ways of finding information:

- You can obtain it from sources such as websites, encyclopaedias, books, CD-ROMs, leaflets, etc.
- You can collect data (i.e. raw facts and figures) for yourself and then process it to produce information.

It is much quicker to get the information from someone else rather than find it out yourself. However, if the information comes from someone else you cannot assume that it is correct. You need to question whether it comes from a trusted source. If it doesn't then you may need to check the information by comparing it with other sources.

WORKSHEETWORKSHEETWORKSHEETWORKSHEETWORKSHEET

WORKSHEET 7.2.4 Using a large database to collect facts

Your teacher will tell you whether you are working using a worksheet.

You will be using information from a trusted source: The CIA World Facts database.

You are going to look at the many differences between the richer and poorer countries in the world.

To do this you are required to look at some information about certain countries on the Central Intelligence Agency's (CIA) website at:

www.odci.gov/cia/publications/factbook/

This is a site produced by the US government and contains information that you can rely on. It is a database (i.e. a large store of data) containing lots of organised facts and figures about each country in the world.

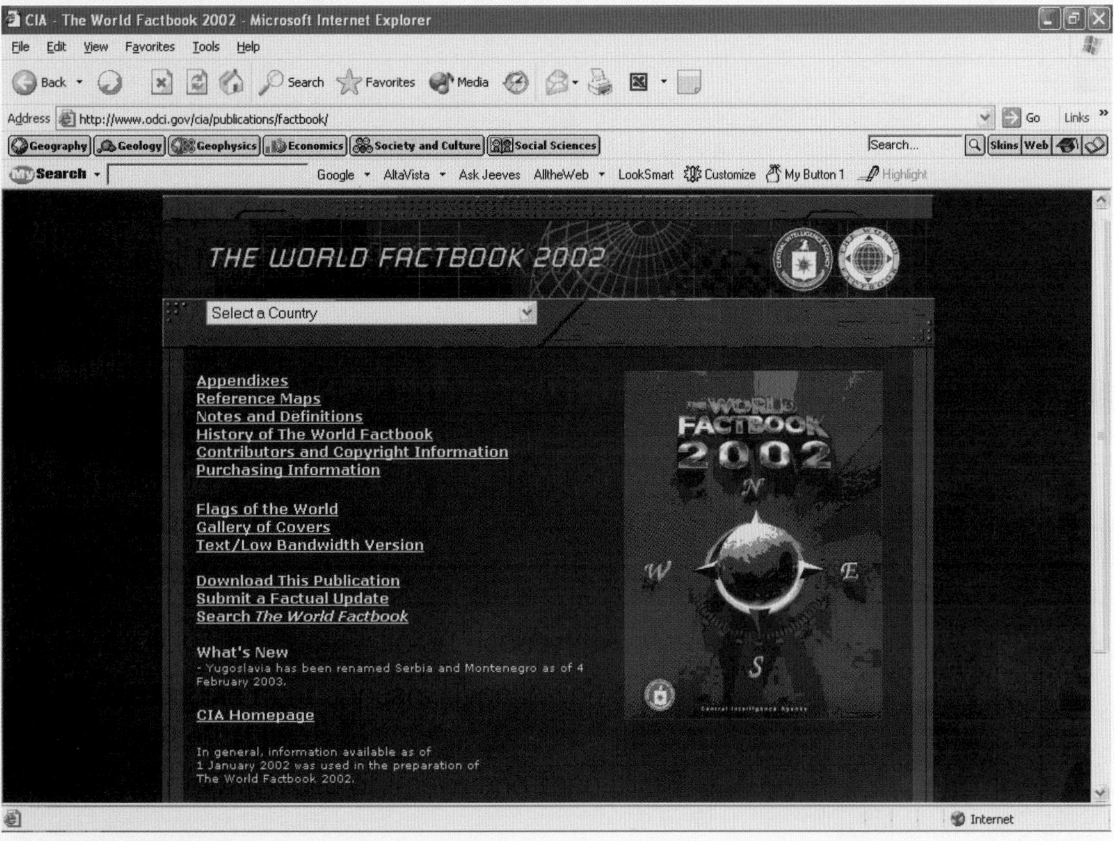

The CIA World Factbook website – good for finding out about different countries

When you get onto the website, find the United Kingdom in the list of countries and click on it. Use the information about the United Kingdom to fill in the details in the following table. Then complete the table for the other countries.

Question	UK	USA	Nigeria	Sudan	Rwanda
Population					
Life expectancy (male)					
Life expectancy (female)					
Literacy of whole population					
Gross domestic product (GDP)					
Telephone (main lines)					
Telephone (mobile)					
Internet Service Providers (ISPs)					
No of Internet users					

Explain the main differences that this table illustrates between the life of a person in a rich country (UK, USA) and that of a poor country (Nigeria, Sudan, Rwanda).

Collecting your own information: conducting a survey

KEY WORDS

opinion – a person's own interpretation of some information

opinion poll – a survey to determine people's opinions on certain topics or subjects

survey – collecting data by asking opinions or by observing

You can collect your own information by conducting a survey. A survey can be used to collect information about likes and dislikes, personal opinions, and facts about people's lives. Sometimes a survey is called an opinion poll.

What can you ask about in your survey?

The whole group about whom you want the information is called the population. The much smaller part of the population – the people you actually intend to ask – is called the sample.

It is always important to make sure that you choose a suitable sample size.

Choosing a suitable sample size

If there were 26 students in your class and you asked only three of them who their favourite singer/group was, you may not get an answer that is representative of the whole group. Why might this be?

As there are only 26 people in the group it would be possible to ask them all, although this still might not be possible as some of the group may be absent.

Suppose you collected the views of all 26 students. As this group is only one of several Key Stage 3 ICT groups in year 7, could we say that the views of the group we have sampled are typical of the views of the whole year?

Sometimes it would be impossible to ask everyone concerned with the information for their views, for the following reasons:

- it would take too long
- it would cost too much
- it is unlikely that everyone will reply to your survey.

To choose the sample size:

- if there is a large population, only a small percentage will be needed for the sample size
- if there is a small population, a large percentage will be needed for the sample size.

Once a sample size has been chosen, you then need to decide who to sample. The sample you pick should reflect the population as a whole. This means that if you stood outside a busy train station at 8.00 am on a weekday and asked people what political party they would vote for, the sample might be biased. Most people at that time in the morning would be going to work so you would only get the views of working people.

Choosing the sample composition

The sample must be representative of the whole population. For example, if you wanted to find the average wage for a professional footballer you would need to choose a mixture of footballers from all the divisions. A sample of ten footballers with five premiership players would distort the figures, since this would imply that half of all professional footballers played in the premiership, which is not the case.

KEY WORDS

questionnaire – a carefully constructed set of questions to ask a person to find out information about a topic or their opinions

representative – a sample that reflects the whole population accurately

sample – a smaller amount of data that reflects the whole set of data (or population)

sample composition – this is how the sample is made up so that it reflects the whole set of data. For example, a sample in a mixed school would usually have equal numbers of boys and girls

sample size – the number of people asked their opinion

WORKSHEETWORKSHEETWORKSHEETWORKSHEETWORKSHEET

WORKSHEET 7.2.5 Correct sampling

Your teacher may give you a worksheet on which to work or you may be asked to write your answers into your book.

Task 1: Who to sample

A national newspaper wishes to find out how people are likely to vote in a general election. It decides to use a sample of people.

1

2

3

4

5

What would be wrong with the following samples?

1. Standing outside a supermarket at 9.00 am on a weekday morning to take a survey.
2. Asking members of a local Labour club to fill in a questionnaire.
3. Asking the parents waiting outside a primary school for their opinion.
4. Getting the members of a local ladies' football team to fill in the questionnaires.
5. Asking the members of a local bowls club to supply answers to your questions.

Task 2: An unexpected result

A rail company wanted to find out how many people used the trains to travel to work in a certain city. On Monday morning, it got some of its staff to telephone 100 people and ask them 'did you travel to work by train during last week?' Only two out of the 100 they spoke to said they had travelled to work by train during the last week. They concluded that only 2% travel to work by train. This was a very surprising result.

Explain why this answer is not accurate. What was wrong with the way in which the data was collected?

Task 3: Using the wrong methods of doing a survey

Here are some results of a survey undertaken by Year 7 students:

- 90% of students in Year 7 own a computer
- 85% of students in Year 7 check their e-mail daily
- 30% of students get annoyed by surveys using e-mail.

These results are surprising. After asking how they did the research, you find out the following:

- the survey was conducted using e-mail
- replies were sent using e-mail
- only students who were not annoyed by the survey bothered to reply.

Give **two** reasons why the survey method was unsuitable.

Suggest another method to conduct this survey that would give more accurate results.

Asking questions – producing a questionnaire

To collect your own data you can ask the questions and record the answers or produce a questionnaire and get people to fill it in.

Tips for making questionnaires

- All the questions must be relevant.
- Ask the questions in simple language.

Questions may be open or closed:

- Open questions – the person you are asking supplies his or her own answers.
- Closed questions – the person you are asking picks his or her answer from a list you supply.

Here is an open question:

What type of takeaway meal is your favourite? ....

Here is a closed question:

Which of these is your favourite takeaway meal?
Pizza ☐ Fish and chips ☐ Beefburger ☐ Chinese ☐ Indian ☐

Leading questions

Avoid leading questions such as:

Do you agree that Eminem is the best rapper in the world?
Yes ☐ No ☐

Smoking is a dirty, disgusting habit. Do you smoke?
Yes ☐ No ☐

Here, you are telling them your preference in the question. You are asking for agreement so this is a leading question. You are leading them towards an answer. This type of question should be avoided in questionnaires.

WORKSHEETWORKSHEETWORKSHEETWORKSHEETWORKSHEET

WORKSHEET 7.2.6 **Spot the leading question**

Your teacher may give you a worksheet on which to work or you may be asked to write the answers into your book.

Here are some questions. You have to spot the leading ones.

1. What is your age? ....
2. Colgate is the best toothpaste. Which one do you use? ....
3. Do you agree that fox hunting should be banned?
   Yes ☐ No ☐
4. You are not going to vote Labour in the next general election are you?
   Yes ☐ No ☐
5. How many packets of crisps did you eat last week?
   0 to 2 ☐ 3 to 5 ☐ 5 to 8 ☐ More than 8 ☐
6. Most intelligent people like classical music. Do you like classical music?
   Yes ☐ No ☐
7. What is your favourite sport? ....

Now go through the questions again, this time deciding whether each question is open or closed. Give reasons for your answers.

Ranking questions

Ranking questions allow users of the questionnaire to put things in order of their preference. For example:

Put these foods in the order you prefer them (i.e. 1 for your favourite and 5 for your least favourite).

Pizza	4
Fish and chips	2
Beefburger	3
Chinese takeaway	5
Indian takeaway	1

Note

Ranking questions are often misinterpreted. People often get mixed up about numbering.

Closed questions and ranking questions may not contain every possibility

REMEMBER!

Once you have collected the results from your questionnaire, you will have to process them. You need to make sure that you ask the questions in a way that makes it easy to produce the results.

Processing the data

Data is the raw facts and figures. Performing calculations is an example of processing. Doing calculations such as working out averages produces information. Once the results of a survey are obtained they can be processed to produce information. Sometimes the processing of the data in a certain way can lead to misleading information.

Misleading information

Take the following diagram. This is used to compare the numbers of boys and girls in the same class who have their own computer. The height of the girl is 1.4 cm whilst the boy is 1cm.

A reader is more likely to look at the area of the two figures rather than just the height. The area is in the ratio of 2:1, compared to the heights, which are in the ratio of 1.4:1. The diagram is misleading.

Using different methods of calculation

You will have come across the words 'mean', 'mode' and 'median' in your maths lessons. These are examples of statistics. Statistics are useful because people can use them to describe a group of numbers.

The mean, mode and median are examples of averages. If you ask a mathematician to work out the average of a group of numbers, he or she will ask you which average you want. In ordinary conversation, if someone says the average, then he or she will understand this to be the mean.

This is a bit confusing, and sometimes people will choose the average (i.e. mean, mode and median) that suits them best. The following example shows this.

A local fast-food restaurant wanted to advertise how good its service was. Each customer who visited was given a survey form to fill in. They were asked to circle the number of the score they would give for service.

1	2	3	4	5	6	7	8	9	10
Very Poor				Average					Excellent

Here are the results of the survey for 20 customers:

1, 10, 10, 10, 2, 1, 1, 1, 10, 10, 10, 1, 5, 1, 10, 10, 10, 1, 1, 2

To calculate the mean, you would add up all these numbers and then divide by the number of customers (20 in this case).

$$\textbf{Mean} = \frac{107}{20} = \textbf{5.35}$$

To work out the mode, you look for the number that appears most frequently in the list.

Mode = 10

The median is the middle score (or the mean of the two middle scores if there is an even number of values) when the scores are arranged in order of size.

The scores arranged in order are:

1, 1, 1, 1, 1, 1, 1, 1, 2, 2, 5, 10, 10, 10, 10, 10, 10, 10, 10, 10
↑ ↑

There are two middle numbers here, so

$$\textbf{Median} = \frac{2 + 5}{2} = \textbf{3.5}$$

The three averages are:

Mean = 5.35

Mode = 10

Median = 3.5

It is easy for the manager of the restaurant to choose the average for his or her advert.

BESTBURGERS

The best service anywhere, as voted by you, the customer.

Average customer satisfaction:
10 out of 10

The manager has chosen the average that suits his or her best, which in this case is the mode. This example shows how you can use different methods of calculation for the average.

Make it happen

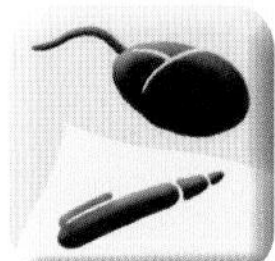

ACTIVITY 2: Averages

John is interested in finding out the weekly wage for certain occupations. He decides to perform a survey. He asks people their job and their weekly wage. The majority of the 50 people he asks refuse to answer. They tell him the question is too personal.

All the data he collected is shown in the table.

Job	Weekly pay
Decorator	£350
Teacher	£550
Security guard	£320
Caretaker	£320
Baker	£340
Accountant	£640
Professional footballer	£23,000
Cleaner	£280
Bus driver	£380

1. Work out the mean weekly wage for this sample.
2. Work out the mode for this sample.

3 Work out the median for this sample.

4 Look at the data in the table. One of the items of data is very different from the rest. Which one is it?

5 Which one of the averages – mean, mode or median – would you use if someone asked for the average weekly wage? Give a reason.

6 Explain what is wrong with the sample data that John collected.

7 John's sample composition is wrong. Explain what sample composition means and how in this case it has affected John's figures.

Lesson 3: SEARCHING FOR INFORMATION USING THE INTERNET

Background: searching for information

You have been asked to research information about endangered species in Britain. Once you have collected all the information you are required to:

- pick the bits out that are useful to you
- select some pictures that can be used
- write a page about the topic including some illustrations.

Make it happen

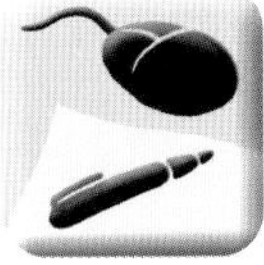

ACTIVITY 3: Creating a document

This lesson goes through the steps you might take to do a research task similar to the one described above.

1 Connect to the Internet. Your teacher will tell you how to do this.

2 Choose a search engine. There are lots of search engines to choose from. Here are some you might try:
www.yahoo.com
www.google.com
www.altavista.com

3 Type *www.yahoo.com* into the address bar like this:

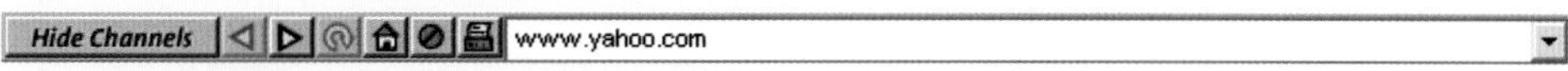

Press **enter** to go to the search engine.

4 Type in *British Endangered Species*

Press **enter** or the Search button.

Information like this will be displayed.

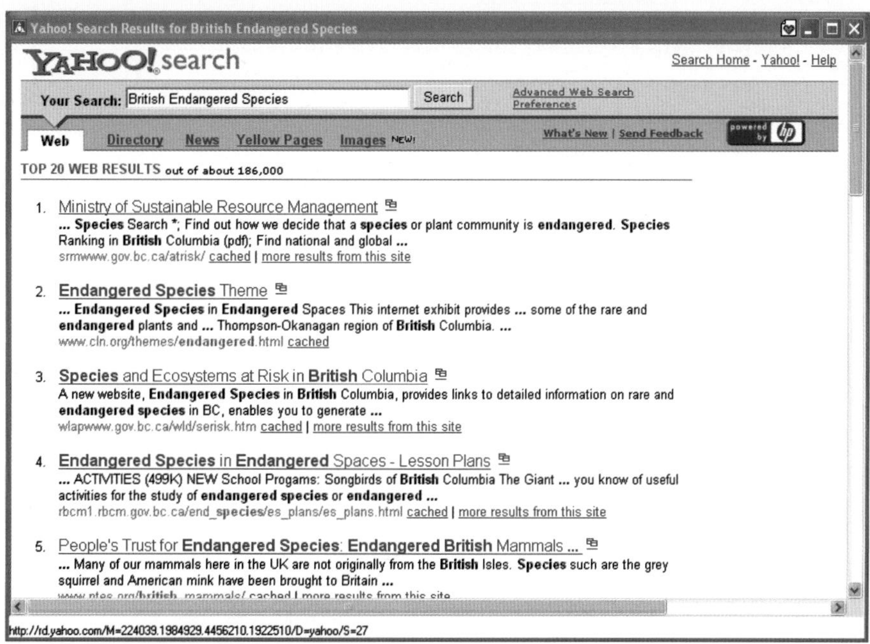

What has gone wrong? Some of these sites refer to Endangered Species in British Columbia.

This is because the search engine is looking for the words British Endangered Species in the same sentence in any order. We need these words next to each other.

If you only want sites with the words in a certain order you put the words or sentence between quotation marks like this:

"British Endangered Species"

5 Insert quotation marks and search again.

You can now see that the results are more relevant.

Take a look at some of these websites by clicking on them. Notice that some are more useful than others.

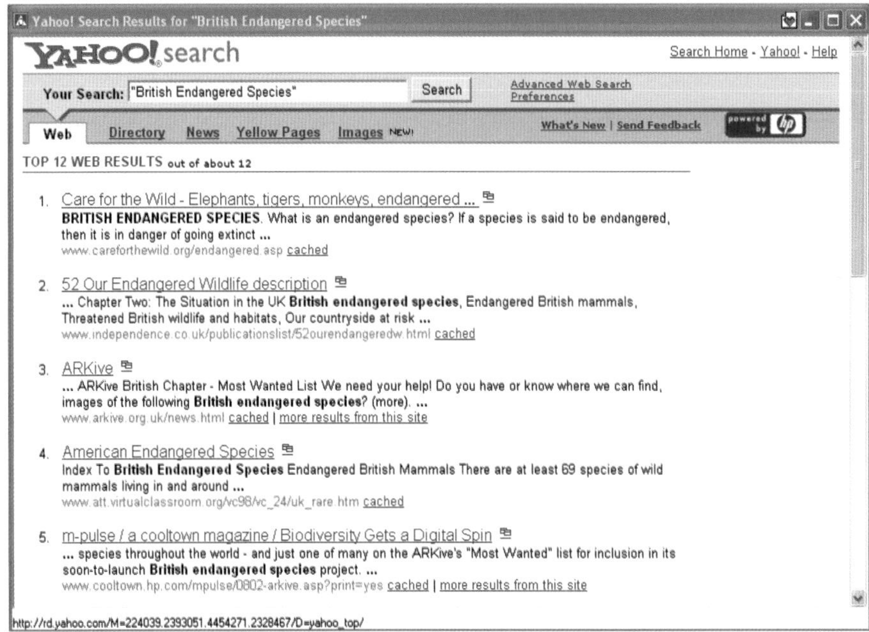

6 To find more useful websites we can type in a different phrase.

Type in "*Endangered Species in Britain*".

Again, click on the websites to see what they contain.

A web address is often called a URL.

7 Type in the following web address:

www.endangeredspecies.org.uk/

One endangered species is the Red Squirrel. Find the section on the Red Squirrel on this site. Your page should look something like this:

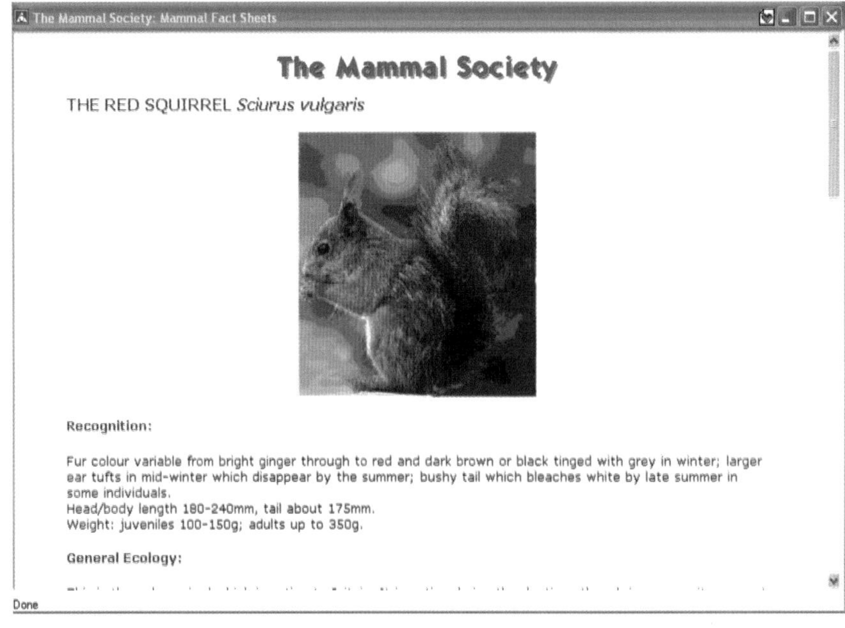

We may need to refer to this site later so we will add it to our favourites. Favourites is a list of websites and their addresses that you have found useful and will want to go back to.

To add this site to your favourites: click on the small icon of the heart at the top right of the website . You can then click on **Add to Favourites**.

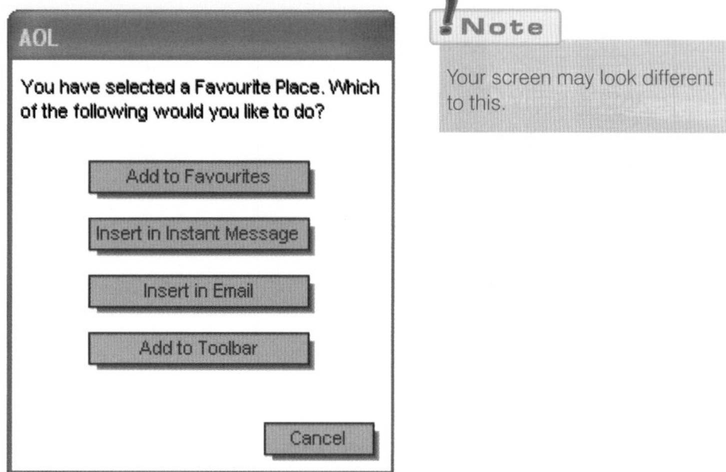

8 We are now going to learn how to save a picture from a website. We will choose the picture of the Red Squirrel.

Position the cursor on the picture.

Click the right mouse button and a menu appears like this:

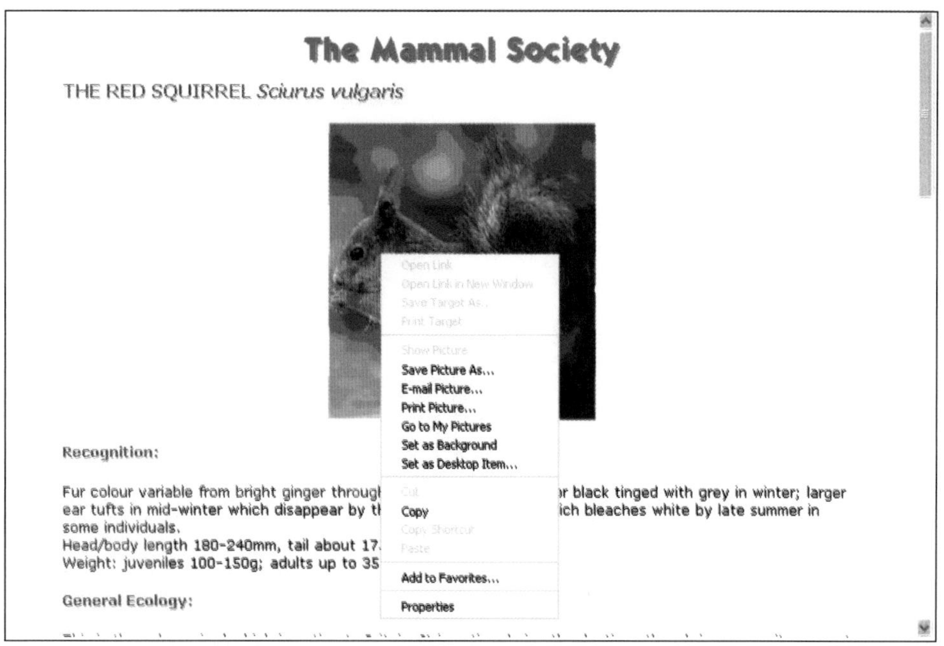

9 Select **Save Picture As ...** from the menu. The following screen appears:

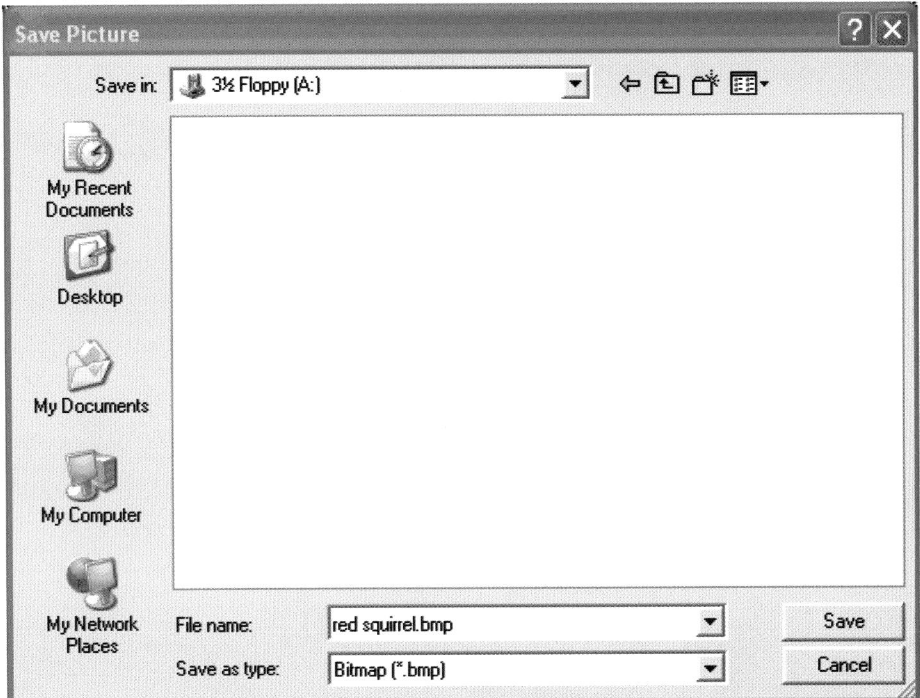

Here the picture is being saved on a floppy disk (called the A drive). Your teacher will tell you where yours is to be saved.

Change the **File name** to *red squirrel.bmp* and change the **Save as type** to Bitmap (*.bmp).

It is very important that you add *.bmp* to any filename you want to save otherwise it will save in a form that makes if difficult to put into packages such as Word. Bitmaps are big files so they take up a lot of space on the disk and also take ages to send over the Internet.

10 Now load the wordprocessing package Microsoft Word. Create a new blank document. Click on **Insert** and then select **From File ...** from the menu.

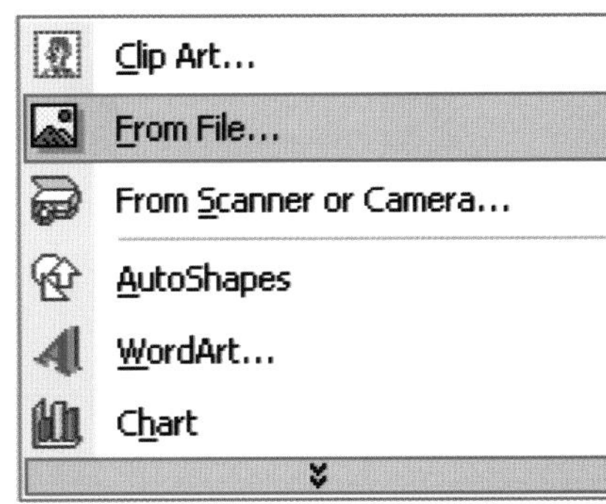

The following screen appears. Note: you need to make sure you know where your picture is saved. Here the picture was saved on the floppy disk.

Double click on the picture of the squirrel and it will be inserted into your document.

11 We now need to write some text about red squirrels. We need to do some research to find out about them. We will use the Internet for this, although you could use books from the library.

We will use the site on red squirrels that we have already found.

Because we saved this to our favourites we can easily get back to it.

Click on Favourites.

A list will appear like this:

The website is listed. Double click on the name to go to the website.

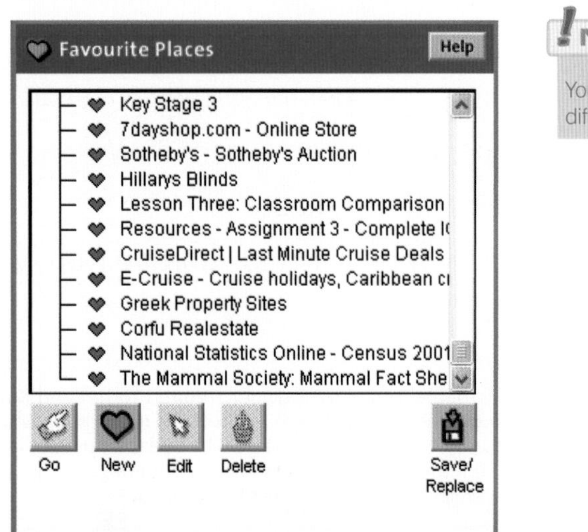

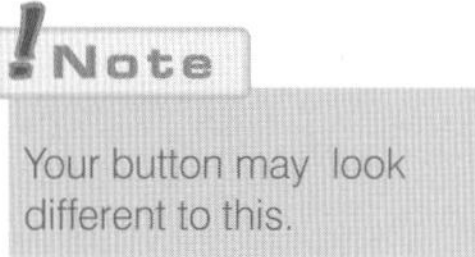

12 We need to collect some information on red squirrels so that we can write about them. One way of doing this is to print out all the information and then refer to it, but this wastes paper as we only require certain information.

A better way would be to collect, say, a page of text by copying and pasting the text from several websites. We can use this to refer to when we put it into our own words.

To copy text from a website:

- Select the text by clicking on it and, keeping the left mouse button down, drag it to highlight the required text.
- The text in blue indicates that the text has been selected.

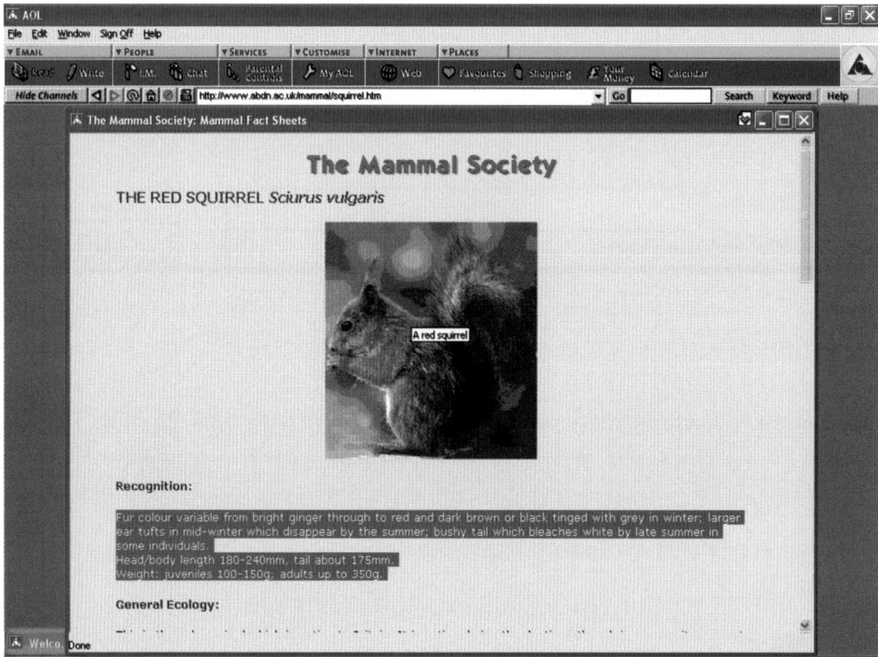

- Now click on Edit on the menu bar and then Copy. This text will be copied into a temporary storage area called the clipboard.

13 Now open a blank document in Word.

Click on **Edit** and then **Paste**.

The text will now be inserted, starting from where the cursor was positioned, like this:

Fur colour variable from bright ginger through to red and dark brown or black tinged with grey in winter; larger ear tufts in mid-winter which disappear by the summer; bushy tail which bleaches white by late summer in some individuals.
Head/body length 180-240mm, tail about 175mm.
Weight: juveniles 100-150g; adults up to 350g.

You can build up a set of notes like this on red squirrels from lots of different websites which you can save and then print.

You can then refer to this document when creating your own text.

14 Use these notes to help you write a paragraph about the red squirrel. This paragraph is to be placed near the picture of the red squirrel. Give your article a suitable title.

15 Use the spellchecker to check the spelling in your document. Also read through your text, checking for grammar and that it makes sense. This is called proof-reading. Make any necessary alterations.

16 Save your document using a suitable file name and then print out a copy.

> **! Note**
>
> There is the temptation to use some of the notes without changing them to save time. This is plagiarism (i.e. copying) and it would be easy for your teacher to spot. You must pick the essential bits and put them into your own words.

Lesson 4: HOW TO LOOK FOR AND USE INFORMATION

When searching on the Internet:

- think carefully about what you are looking for
- be specific
- use descriptive words
- say exactly what you are looking for as a sentence
- be careful with spelling; if you cannot find a match, you have probably made a spelling mistake
- do not put punctuation marks in your searches.

If you are looking for pictures, you should say that you want pictures. For example, if you need a picture of a red squirrel, type in: *photograph of a red squirrel*.

WORKSHEETWORKSHEETWORKSHEETWORKSHEETWORKSHEET

WORKSHEET 7.2.7 Where can I find it using the Internet?

Your teacher may give you a worksheet on which to work or you may be asked to write the answers into your book.

When you are asked to find out something using the Internet you need to have some idea where to look.

You often have to do some research to find out about a particular topic. Being able to find relevant and accurate material quickly is important.

Where would be the best place to look using the Internet for each of the following items of information?

1. The time of the last bus home from town
2. A list of the films that are on at your nearest cinema
3. The web address of the official Robbie Williams website
4. Information on the Great Fire of London for a history project
5. Information on how to cook a scone
6. The price of the cheapest bottle of champagne locally
7. A list of three cheap last-minute holidays
8. A list of some places to visit in St Petersburg in Russia

How reliable is information?

Just because information is on a website or even in a newspaper does not mean it is true and can be relied on. Some things you can never rely on because they depend on opinion, such as who is the best football player in England. Sometimes companies advertising products say theirs is best. But they would say that, wouldn't they?

You need to be sceptical of any information you read and be able to spot bogus information.

How can you check the accuracy of information?

Here is a statement:

The tallest man in the world was a man called Robert Wadlow, who stood 8ft 11 inches tall. He died in 1940.

How could you check this? You might:

- use the Guinness Book of Records or another trusted book
- search for websites and compare the information
- check for yourself (this would have been possible if he was still alive!).

WORKSHEET

WORKSHEET 7.2.8 I don't believe it!

Your teacher may give you a worksheet on which to work or you may be asked to write the answers into your book.

Here are some pieces of information along with their sources. Some sources are more reliable than others.

You have to decide whether to believe it or not and whether it is relevant today. You need to think carefully about where the information came from. Give reasons for your answers.

I don't believe it!

STATEMENT 1

'It will rain cats and dogs'

A pensioner at the bus stop

STATEMENT 2

'Rain will move in from the West, making the morning dry and the afternoon wet'

A report from the Internet at **www.weather.com**

STATEMENT 3

'Sunshine all day, with a light breeze from the East'

Yesterday's weather forecast from the newspaper

Differing views of the same thing

The following example illustrates how two people can have different views on the same subject.

Read the following two reports of the same football match.

Report 1

After a fairly mediocre first half the team managed to pull themselves together and score two vital goals in the second half. One goal, a penalty by Smith, was smashed into the far corner of the net. The next goal was made easy by the goalkeeper's fumbling of the ball. An excellent performance against a lacklustre team.

Report 2

There was complete domination of both halves and both goals awarded against them were against the run of play. The first goal was from a penalty. This penalty should not have been awarded and coming so near the final whistle, made it difficult to fight back. The next goal should not have been awarded, as the cameras showed clearly that the player was offside. On the whole, a good display by the team and a very bad display from the referee.

You can see that each report tells a different story of the same thing. In a football match there are two sides, and supporters of each side have a different point of view.

A slant towards a certain point of view is called bias. Although both of the reports are factual, the facts have been explained differently. Just because a report is biased, it does not mean it is wrong. Instead it means a certain point of view is attached to the facts.

People hold different viewpoints about a subject. Usually their viewpoint will reflect their interest or experience. When you are considering using information it is important to consider the viewpoint of the person who created the information.

Everyone is entitled to a viewpoint, even if you disagree with it.

Airport expansion example

There are plans to increase the size of one of the main airports in Britain.

Here are some viewpoints of people affected by this expansion:

Local resident's view

Businessman's view

Taxi driver's view

Airport's view

Environmental view

Air pollution

Destroyed countryside

Noise pollution

Congestion

Devastated wildlife

Trade unionist's view

You can see that people's views are different. They usually look from their self-interest and ask themselves 'will this expansion make *my* life better or worse?' When you look at information you need to ask whose viewpoint it is from.

WORKSHEETWORKSHEETWORKSHEETWORKSHEETWORKSHEET

WORKSHEET 7.2.9 **Biased or not?**

Your teacher may give you a worksheet on which to work or you may be asked to write the answers into your book.

Here are some opinions expressed by different people. You have to say whether they are biased or not.

1. 'Hunting is cruel' by an animal rights activist
2. 'David Beckham is the best footballer in the world' by his mother
3. 'The next train to London will be at 5.30 pm' by a member of staff at the train station
4. 'Manchester United are the best team in Britain' by the manager of Manchester United
5. 'The weather today will be dry, sunny and very warm' by the Meteorological Office
6. 'House prices will continue to rise' by the manager of a local estate agent

Look at the following articles. Are they biased or not?
How do you know?

Think about who produced the material and what they would like to promote.

You may need to access each of the websites to help you to make up your mind.

Effects of Passive Smoking – New Study in BMJ, 16 May 2003

The findings of an American study published today in the British Medical Journal (BMJ) suggest that the effects of passive smoking have been overstated, particularly in relation to coronary heart disease.

'What is quite clear from this latest study is that the body of scientific evidence certainly does not justify total bans on smoking in the workplace or other public places.'

Tobacco Manufacturers' Association

http://tma.pr24x7.com/index.php?MRMpmid=216

If you can smell it, it could be killing you! And even if you can't smell it, many of these cancer-causing chemicals can nevertheless be entering your lungs.

Moreover, many who have asthma, hay fever, allergies, emphysema, sinusitis, and many other conditions can be severely irritated by even small amounts of drifting tobacco smoke. And those with a prior history of heart problems, who are overweight, have a high cholesterol level, or are simply elderly may be at increased risk of a sudden and deadly heart attack brought on by drifting tobacco smoke.

Action on Smoking and Health, a national legal-action antismoking organisation

www.ash.org/

WORKSHEET 7.2.10 Fact detective

Your teacher may give you a worksheet on which to work or you may be asked to write the answers into your book.

A fact is a true piece of information. Some so-called 'facts' have been made up by someone to deliberately mislead. You have to decide whether these 'facts' are true or false. You will have to do some detective work using the Internet.

1. Everest is the highest mountain in the world
2. The organisation FAST stands for Finding About Software Theft
3. The Great Fire of London took place on 2 September 1666
4. The famous painting Mona Lisa can be seen at The Louvre museum in Paris
5. There is a rare toad in Britain called the Natterjack Toad
6. Pythagoras, the famous mathematician who came up with Pythagoras' theorem, was born on a Greek island called Samos

How do you decide whether a website is a good source of information for a task or project?

When looking at any information on the Internet you need to ask:

- Who made it?
- Why was it made?
- When was it made?
- Who paid to have it produced?
- What is the message being put across?
- Is it biased and how do you know?
- How good is the information?

Who made it?

Web pages can be produced by anyone. You need to be sure you are using information from a reliable source. Ask yourself the following questions:

- Does the website have the web address that you would expect?
- Is it a well-known source (e.g. BBC, newspapers, universities, companies, government departments, schools, etc.)?
- Does it say who the author is and are there contact details (e.g. name, address, tel no., etc.)?

Why was it made?

Web pages are created for some purpose, such as:

- to inform
- to sell
- to instruct
- to entertain.

It is important to ask why it was made. The trustworthiness of the information depends on the motivation of the person who made the website.

- Was it made for information, entertainment or profit?
- Does the person who made it get a laugh, a job or satisfaction from the site?
- What does the purpose tell you about the reliability of the information?

When was it made?

Information can quickly go out of date. You need to know how recent the site is by asking the following:

- Is there a date?
- When was the date last changed?
- Do the links work (sometimes links to other sites don't work if the site is old and has not been updated)?

Who paid to have it produced?

It takes time to create a good website. Creating good websites costs money. The person who pays normally has control over what is included. The person who paid for the site will use it to promote his or her own ideas or products so the site will be usually be biased.

What is the message being put across?

Ask yourself:

- What point or message is being raised?
- Is the message reasonable?
- Does it seem sensible?

Is it biased and how do you know?

Every web page you look at represents an opinion. It could be the opinion of a company trying to sell you something. It might be a pressure group trying to influence your opinion. You need to know the name of the organisation that produced the site and what the site's purpose is.

Even 'facts' can be disputed.

How good is the information?

Information may be good or bad. Ask yourself the following questions:

- Does the information look accurate (are there any spelling or grammatical mistakes)?
- Does the information fit in with what you already know about the subject?
- Does it cover what you need to know?
- Would you get better information in a book or encyclopaedia?
- A site that is good will generally have been looked at by lots of people. You can tell how many people have visited the site by the number of hits.

KEY WORDS

hits – the number of people who have accessed the website in a certain time

Make it happen

ACTIVITY 4: Conducting a survey

You have to find out about your class members' use of ICT at home. Here are some of the latest devices and services. You want to find out who uses what in your class and year.

- computer
- MP3 player
- minidisc player
- cable/satellite television
- DVD player
- mobile telephone
- digital camera
- scanner
- Internet access
- broadband

1. Design a suitable questionnaire to find out about your class's use of the latest technology at home.
2. Collect the data and process it in some way to provide information. You can calculate averages using your figures and also present some of the information using suitable graphs and charts.
3. Prepare a short report outlining what you have found out. If possible, you should try to incorporate some graphs or charts into this document.

What programs can I use for searching on the Internet?

A program called a search engine is used to make searches of the Internet easy. When you connect to the Internet you need a company called an Internet Service Provider (called an ISP for short) such as AOL, Freeserve, etc. They usually come with a search engine but there are many others you can choose from such as:

www.yahoo.com or **www.yahoo.co.uk** (depending on whether you want UK sites or worldwide sites)

www.google.com

www.lycos.com

www.ask.com (This is the same as the AskJeeves search engine.)

KEY WORDS

search – looking for specific information on a subject

search engine – a program that can be used to search for information on the Internet

URL – Uniform Resource Locator (formerly Universal Resource Locator) is the web address of the page where the information you want is located

home page – the main page; you can access all the other pages using the links from this page (these usually begin the same as the home page but have different endings)

browse – when you casually view something of interest whilst looking for something on the Internet

Finding information on the Internet

The Internet is a great place to find information on just about everything, but finding useful information can take some practice. It is important to decide what information you are looking for. Sometimes you can simply browse the Internet and suddenly find useful information. It is a good idea to keep a record of useful sites for the future.

Write a couple of sentences to describe the information you are looking for. Suppose in a history lesson you have been asked to write a short piece about the Great Fire of London. You need to type in the key words, which are: "*Great Fire of London*".

Tips for searching

- Don't bother using any capital letters. Most searches treat capitals and small letters (called upper and lower case) the same.
- Be specific. The more specific you are the better the results.
- Put your most important word first.

Boolean searches

Don't be put off by the name. Boolean searches help you save time so they are worth knowing about. When you do a simple search you may be overwhelmed by all the information. Boolean searches help you narrow down a search.

AND

If you type in the search *USA AND flag* you will get all the documents that contain both words.

If you just type in *USA Flag* you will still get all the documents that contain both words. With most search engines you do not need to type the 'AND' between the words.

AND means 'I want **only** documents that contain **both** words.'

OR

If you type in the search *USA OR flag* then you will get all the documents containing the word **USA**, all the documents containing the word **flag** and all the documents that contain both words.

OR means 'I want documents that contain **either** word. I don't care which word.'

Searching for an exact match

If you want an exact match of words (i.e. the words side by side and in the same order), put quotation marks around the words like this:

"*Recipe for a chocolate chip cookie*"

NOT

Suppose you want to search for information about different pets but you can't stand cats. You can exclude cats like this: *Pets NOT cats*.

Searching for a quotation

If you know the exact wording of the quotation, you can type it into the search engine. To get the exact match you need to put quotation marks around the words like this:

"*I have a dream*"

Martin Luther King Jr was well known for his 'I have a dream' speech. He believed that all people were created equal.

WORKSHEETWORKSHEETWORKSHEETWORKSHEETWORKSHEET

WORKSHEET 7.2.11 Who said what?

Your teacher may give you a worksheet on which to work or you may be asked to write the answers into your book.

Below are some quotations. By typing them exactly into a search engine you can find out who said them. Remember to enclose these sayings between quotation marks. Write down the name of the person.

1. I never forget a face, but in your case I'll be glad to make an exception
2. I've had a perfectly wonderful evening. But this wasn't it
3. Never put off until tomorrow what you can do the day after tomorrow
4. The best way to cheer yourself up is to try to cheer somebody else up
5. The best way to have a good idea is to have lots of ideas

Different ways of searching

There are lots of different ways you can search for information on a CD-ROM or on the Internet. Here are some of them:

Using the contents

The contents section of a book gives a list of the chapters in the book. On a CD-ROM or using the Internet you can also have a contents list. The contents list is often broken down into sections and sub-sections – just like in a book – and when you click on an item you are taken to the exact place in the website where the item is. It makes finding the information you need much easier.

This is called a hierarchical structure for the contents.

Key word searches

Key word searches are searches that you perform by entering important words into a search engine to find specific information.

Suppose you wanted to find out about the origins of bonfire night. You might try to find this information by searching using the following key words:

- Gunpowder plot
- Guy Fawkes
- Bonfire night
- Guy Fawkes night
- Fireworks.

Free-text searches

With free-text searches, you simply put a sentence into the search engine without identifying any key words. You have already used a free-text search when finding out who said a particular quote.

Indexes

These are just like an index in a book except they are electronic. You simply pick a key word from a list by clicking on it and you are taken to the sections where it appears.

Site or 'content' maps

Site or content maps are pictures that show the structure of the website. Their purpose is to show users how to find their way around the site.

You can clearly see that to get to see pictures of the person's friends you will have to go from the home page to 'pictures' and then to 'friends'.

KEY WORDS

contents list – a list of items on a website or a CD-ROM that enables you to jump straight to the section by clicking on the item in the contents list

index – a list of words that you can click on, from which you are taken to the page where the word appears

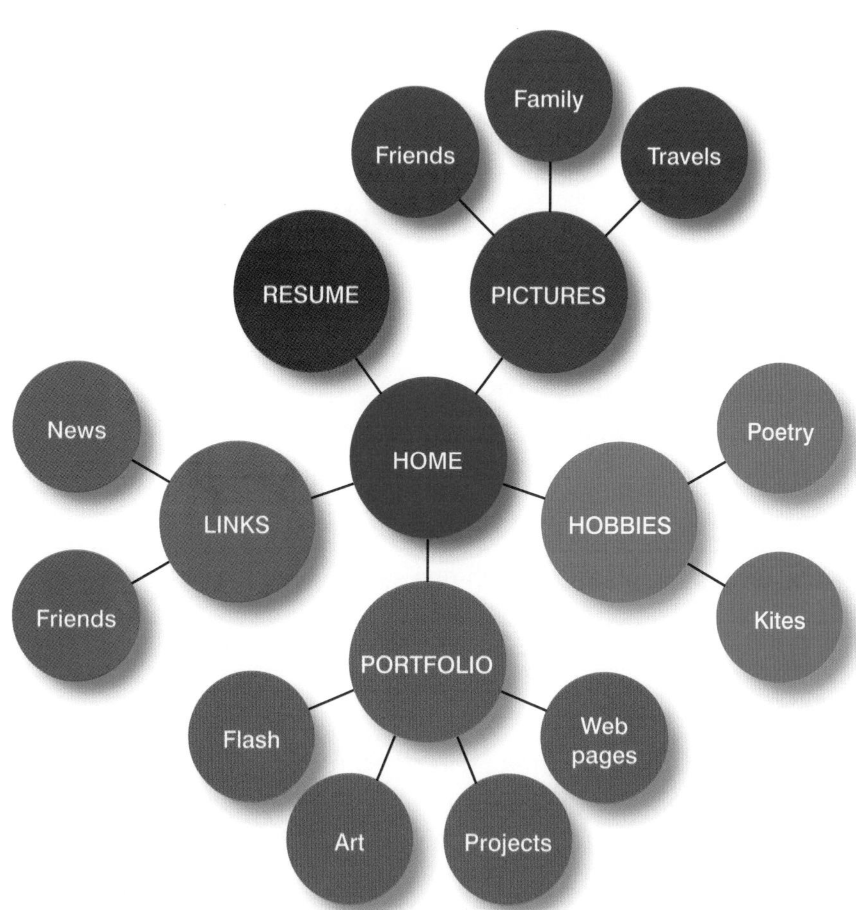

A site map for a personal website

What sorts of information are there?

KEY WORDS

home page – the first page you reach on a website, which will usually contain links to other pages

There is information on the Internet about every subject imaginable. Here are a few of the types of information.

Advertising campaigns

Advertising campaigns make people aware of a new or improved service or product. When car manufacturers release a new model they need to let people know that it exists.

Take a look at the dealer site for Nissan cars at:

www.nissan.co.uk

There are often free-to-enter competitions on car manufacturers' sites. What do you have to do to enter? What does the car manufacturer get out of it?

Have a look at the site and think of the things you can do on it.

Legislation

Legislation is the laws that affect everyone. We often need to find out about them. For example, there are certain laws affecting how we use ICT equipment. These laws cover such things as personal data, viruses, copyright and so on.

FIND IT OUT

Here are some of the laws that apply to using ICT:

- The Data Protection Act 1998
- The Computer Misuse Act 1990
- The Copyright, Designs and Patents Act 1989.

Type each of the above into a search engine to find out briefly what they apply to.

Write a short paragraph about each one saying what the Act covers.

Statistics

Statistics are facts and figures. You need to make sure that statistics come from a reliable source before you use them. As we saw earlier, great care needs to be taken when collecting statistics to make sure they are not biased in any way.

WORKSHEETWORKSHEETWORKSHEETWORKSHEETWORKSHEET

WORKSHEET 7.2.12 Website evaluation form

Your teacher may give you a worksheet on which to work or you may be asked to write the answers into your book.

When you are using a website for research you need to be sure it is useful. There are many websites that contain information that is inaccurate, biased, out of date, or not thorough enough. You can use the following form to evaluate websites or you could design your own.

Website evaluation form		
Website:	**Yes**	**No**
Source (is it clear who produced the information?)		
Is it clear why the site was produced?		
Is the information up to date?		
Is the information accurate and can it be confirmed?		
Is the information biased?		
Does it go into enough depth?		
Is the site well designed?		
Is the content free from spelling and grammatical errors?		
Do the links work?		
Did you find the site easy to use?		

Here are some websites to evaluate. Your teacher will give you one website evaluation form for each website.

Website 1

The National UFO (Unidentified Flying Objects) Reporting Centre

www.nuforc.org/

Website 2

Tintern Abbey

www.castlewales.com/tintern.html

Website 3

A conspiracy theory website on the attack on the Pentagon in America

www.asile.org/citoyens/numero13/pentagone/erreurs_en.htm

Lesson 5: SEARCHING FOR INFORMATION ON UFOs

Background

In this lesson you will research and then do a group presentation on UFOs (Unidentified Flying Objects). The research will be done using the Internet, where you will search for text, pictures, sounds, etc. that you can use to build your presentation.

Your audience for the presentation will be Year 7 students, although your teacher will be present to assess you.

You will work in a group to produce a presentation about UFOs. The presentation must last between 5 and 7 minutes.

Some people believe in UFOs and some don't. You could:

- take the view that you believe that UFOs exist
- take the view that you do not believe that UFOs exist
- take an open view and let the audience make up their own minds.

Before you start you will need to discuss with your group members:

- which one of the above approaches you will use
- how to break down the overall task into smaller tasks
- how to choose who should do each of the smaller tasks.

REMEMBER!

Remember that this is a group effort and that each member of the group must contribute their fair share to the presentation.

Make it happen

ACTIVITY 5: Researching UFOs

Use the Internet and a suitable search engine to find websites on UFOs.

When searching the Internet you would probably start by typing in UFO as your search condition. Think about as many aspects of the subject (i.e. UFOs) as you can.

Use the following diagram (or one you have produced yourselves) to help with your searches.

1. Write down the names of four of the best websites you found on UFOs.
2. Write down the URLs of these four websites.
3. Fill in a website evaluation form for each of these websites.

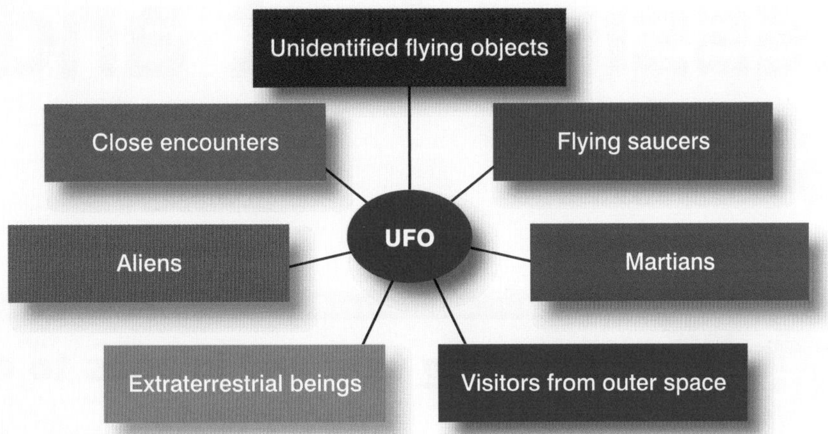

Try to think of all the aspects of the subject by drawing a diagram like this

ACTIVITY 6: Preparing your presentation

You will need to:

1. research websites containing information about UFOs
2. collect and organise your research
3. decide which parts of your research you will use
4. produce five slides to show to your audience.

ACTIVITY 7: The presentation itself

Your group will present the information on UFOs to your teacher and the rest of the group using the slides you have created.

Here are some tips:

- Practise your presentation thoroughly.
- Time your presentation to make sure that it lasts between 5 and 7 minutes.
- Try not to read from notes.
- Maintain eye contact with your audience.
- As you are working in a group, choose the most confident person/persons to do the talking.

EXTENSION ACTIVITY

In this activity you need to evaluate working in groups, which can have many advantages and also some disadvantages. You need to write about these from your own experience of producing and giving this presentation.

3 Processing text and images

Lesson 1:
INTRODUCTION TO PROCESSING TEXT AND IMAGES

Processing text and images to create documents

Modern software allows everyone with a little skill and knowledge to produce very professional looking leaflets, flyers, brochures, newsletters, etc. This unit will enable you to be confident enough to produce your own documents.

Most of this unit will refer to the desktop publishing package called Microsoft Publisher, although many similar features can be found in the wordprocessing package Word.

Background theory and key information

Desktop publishing refers to the process of using the computer to produce documents such as newsletters, brochures, books, etc. Desktop publishing combines three applications: page layout, wordprocessing and graphics. Wordprocessing is used to create text, and graphics are obtained in a variety of different ways. Sizing and positioning text and graphics on the page is called page layout.

Wordprocessing or desktop publishing?

KEY WORDS

DTP – this is short for desktop publishing

Professional publishers use specialist desktop publishing software. However, many wordprocessing packages offer similar features to DTP packages and can be used to produce professional-looking documents at home or in school.

In the past, using DTP software was quite difficult, but now there are templates and wizards to help you. The specialist DTP software supplied with Office is called Microsoft Publisher.

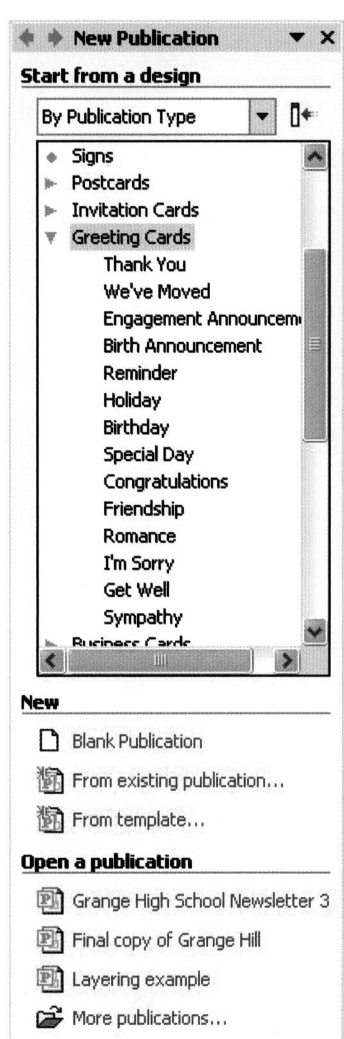

This is the New Publication wizard. The cursor is on Greeting Cards, so the wizard will guide you through all the steps you need to make a card that looks like the ones you buy

What is a template?

A template is a document with all the formatting done for you. You only have to add your own text and graphics. This can save a lot of time.

What is a wizard?

A wizard guides you through the whole process of producing a document. It asks you to make choices about the design and also to put in the text and the graphics. It produces a tailor-made document. Using a wizard is the easiest way of getting started and producing your document.

Bringing text and images together

DTP software packages make it easy to combine data obtained from lots of different sources. The two components of any document are the text and the graphics.

Where can I get the text from?

There are a number of ways you can include text in a DTP document.

You can type the text straight into your DTP newsletter.

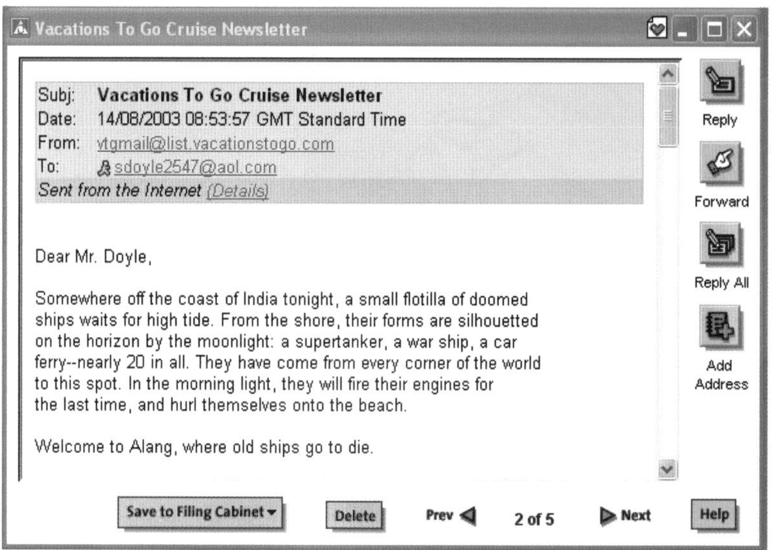

You can copy text from e-mails you have received and then paste them into your newsletter.

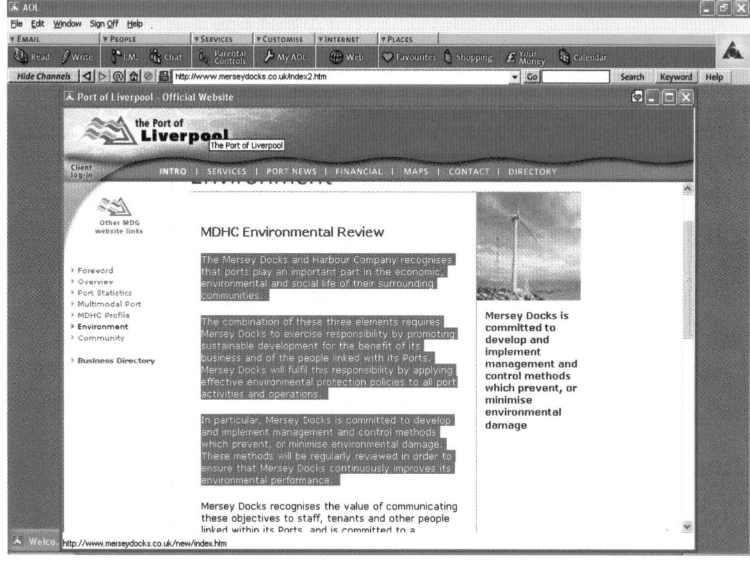

You can copy information from a website (subject to copyright restrictions).

You can even dictate straight into Publisher using speech recognition.

KEY WORDS

digital images – images that have been converted into a form that can be stored and manipulated on the computer

You can also import text from Word files on your wordprocessor. Or you can simply copy and paste the text.

Where can I get graphics from?

Images need to be in digital form so that they can be stored and then processed by the computer.

There are lots of ways to get digital images (graphics):

Take a photograph using a digital camera and put this in.

Use the clip art provided with Microsoft Office.

Search for pictures using the Internet (e.g. **www.google.com**).

You can scan photographs, pictures, etc. using a scanner.

You can use frame capture from a video camera.

Copy pictures from websites (subject to copyright).

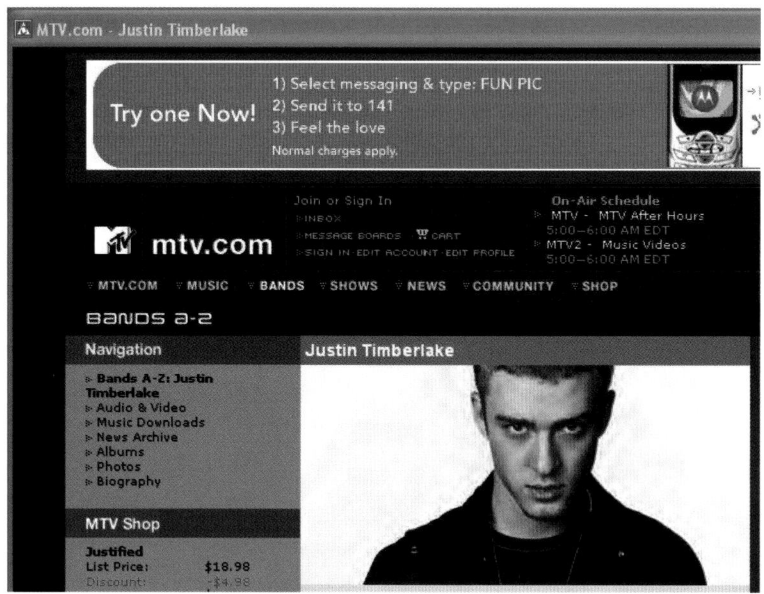

KEY WORDS

frame capture – a moving image produced by a digital video camera is made up of lots of individual pictures (or 'frames'). It is possible to take one of these images and use it as a photograph

You can use a drawing package to draw your own picture.

WORKSHEET

WORKSHEET 7.3.1 How much do you already know?

Your teacher will tell you whether you are using a worksheet. If not, you will need to write the answers in your exercise book.

If you have used Microsoft Publisher before, you should know what each of these icons means. Feel free to make an educated guess – you will probably get them right.

6

7

8

WORKSHEET 7.3.2

Desktop publishing terms

Your teacher will tell you whether you are using a worksheet. If not you will need to write your answers in your exercise book.

Below are some specialist terms used when talking about the processing of text and images. To talk like an expert, you will have to know the meaning of these terms. If you do not know the answers, try to find them using the Internet.

Explain briefly what each of the following terms means. Make sure you explain in a way that a complete beginner could understand.

1. Column
2. Text box
3. Importing text
4. Clip art
5. Template
6. Wizard
7. Cut and paste

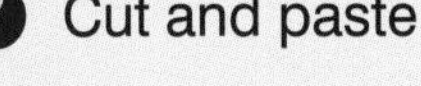

WORKSHEET 7.3.3

Design of a newspaper

Here is a section of a newspaper.

1. How many columns are there?
2. How many different fonts have been used?
3. How many different font sizes have been used?
4. How many graphic images are there?

The British Comedy Awards: fact and fiction

by Gail Renard

It was my privilege to represent the Guild at the 2002 British Comedy Awards. These are not to be confused with the Writers' Guild Awards which (a) presently don't exist and (b) wouldn't interfere with the Brit Com Awards even if they did!

The Brit Com Awards are an annual ITV event, and the brainchild of producer Michael Hurll. In his mammoth career, Michael's produced Top Of The Pops and The Two Ronnies. He was also instrumental in introducing Morecambe and Wise to legendary comedy writer Eddie Braben... and for that alone he should be sainted!

I was one of the two Guild writers on the jury, along with Jonathan Harvey. The rest of the jury consisted of the heads of comedy from various companies, as well as Bob Monkhouse. In the course of two voting days, everyone has their say. Comedy is a business which everyone takes very seriously, though people stop just short of pulling knives.

These awards are of tremendous benefit to the Guild. The Guild's name is announced loudly and proudly often throughout this peak time ITV show, and we get publicity we simply couldn't pay for. Our Assistant General Secretary, Anne Hogben, also attends on the night, and the Guild attracts many new valued members... mainly due to Anne's superb arm-twisting but officially we call it recruiting. The Guild is also given a fee for participating which, as we all know, we can well use.

There have been some slight changes in the voting procedure of the Awards. In past years, Guild members were balloted by post for some of the categories. I'm ashamed to say that the ballots actually returned were something like 17 out of 1000 members. "Poor," as Vic Reeves might say. "Very poor." Less wasteful methods have since been introduced and seem to be successful.

For those who still would like to see the Writers' Guild own awards reinstated, please reinstate away! After all, you can't honour writers enough, can you?

In the picture: Peter Kay receives the Writer of the Year Award while performing live on stage

Winners at the 2002 British Comedy Awards

- Best Comedy Actor: Ricky Gervais (The Office, written by Ricky Gervais and Stephen Marchant)
- Best Comedy Actress: Kathy Burke (Gimme, Gimme, Gimme, written by Jonathan Harvey)
- Best Comedy Drama: Auf Wiedersen Pet (written by Dick Clement and Ian La Frenais)
- Best Comedy Entertainment Personality: Graham Norton (V Graham Norton)
- Best Comedy Newcomer: Kris Marshall (My Family)
- Best New TV Comedy: The Office (written by Ricky Gervais and Stephen Marchant)
- Best Comedy Entertainment Programme: V Graham Norton
- Best International Comedy Programme: Six Feet Under (created by Alan Ball)
- Best Comedy Film: Bend it Like Beckham (written by Gurinder Chadha)
- People's Choice Award: Phoenix Nights (written by Peter Kay and Dave Spikey)
- Lifetime Achievement Award: Michael Palin
- Writer of the Year: Peter Kay

Ken slashes theatre prices

Ken Livingstone, Mayor of London, has launched a major London theatre promotion with the aim of broadening the range of theatre audiences.

The Mayor launched the promotion at the Criterion Theatre at Piccadilly Circus, alongside stars including Sir Ian McKellen (Dance of Death), Alan Davies (Auntie and Me), Michael Greco (Chicago) and Caprice (Rent).

The Mayor's London Development Agency (LDA) is contributing £350,000 to the 'Get Into London Theatre' promotion. The London theatre industry is expected to match this funding via the discounting of tickets.

Created in partnership with the Society of London Theatre, the 'Get Into London Theatre' promotion, funded via the LDA, will encourage thousands of Londoners who never or very rarely attend the theatre to give it a go, at specially reduced prices.

The promotion offers thousands of tickets to plays, musicals, dance and opera at the specially reduced prices of £10, £15 and £20. There will also be £5 tickets at specific performances for under-25s and over-60s. Many of the top West End shows are taking part, as well as venues outside the West End such as the Hackney Empire and the Tricycle in Kilburn.

"People travel thousands of miles to enjoy our theatre productions," Livingstone said. "But not all Londoners are making the most of what is on their doorstep, in particular young people. I hope that through this discounted ticket promotion they will discover what an enjoyable and rewarding experience going to the theatre can be."

8 The Writers' Bulletin **February/March 2003**

What you should already know

This unit builds on the following work, which you should have done at Key Stage 2:

- writing for different audiences
- developing images using repeating patterns
- collecting and presenting information
- evaluating information.

What you will learn

In this unit you will learn:

- how to get text and graphics for inclusion into a newspaper
- how to use a template to design a newsletter/newspaper
- how to input text and graphics into a template
- how to layer text and graphics
- how to create a page from scratch
- how to create a logo
- how to work as a team to produce a newspaper.

Lesson 2: LOOKING AT NEWSPAPERS AND NEWSLETTERS

Background

In this lesson you will be looking at newspapers/newsletters in general and those factors you would need to consider if you were making one of your own.

Intended readership

All newspapers and other documents have an intended readership. You need to know who that readership is and make the newspaper or document suitable for their needs.

The age of the readers is important, as well as their general level of education. Long sentences and unusual words should be avoided in documents aimed at younger readers.

Before you start your newspaper ask yourself:

- Who is the newspaper aimed at?
- What will be the average age of a reader?
- What is the main purpose of the newspaper?
- What will the newspaper contain?

REMEMBER!

Before producing any document, always ask yourself who the intended audience is. You can then create the content and design with this in mind.

Analysing reader needs

All documents have a purpose and a readership and it is important to think about this before you consider the design and content of the document. The 'purpose' of the document is what it is designed to do. A newspaper's purpose would be to inform its audience.

The size of the document is important, as you will need to supply enough content to fill it. The age of the readership is also important, as this will influence the design. A younger audience will be happier with a more modern uncluttered design. An older audience will be less concerned with the design and more concerned with the content.

Some subject matter is serious and it would be inappropriate to use cartoons or clip art.

Black and white or colour?

You need to decide before you start the design whether the document is to be printed in black and white or colour. Some printed materials only use a couple of colours, whilst some publications use full colour. It is much more expensive to print in colour.

There is no point in working in colour on the screen if the document is to be printed in black and white. It is hard to find clip art and photographs in black and white so it may be necessary to convert colour images to greyscale ones. Most graphics and image manipulation packages are able to do this.

DAILY Mirror
Friday August 15 2003
NEWSPAPER OF THE YEAR 32p
COMING TOMORROW
A stunning new Saturday paper
Iraq blast kills Brit
Blair heat on Kelly
THE BIG ZAPPLE
New York, Canada in giant power cut

The front page needs a good headline like this one when New York (often referred to as The Big Apple) was plunged into darkness through a power cut

KEY WORDS

greyscale – black and white images consist of an unlimited number of greys. The computer can only use a limited number so a black and white image has to be converted to a greyscale so that it can be used by the computer

ACTIVITIESACTIVITIESACTIVITIESACTIVITIESACTIVITIESACTIVITIES

Make it happen

ACTIVITY 1: Investigation

For this activity you are required to investigate the design of newspapers and newsletters.

1. Collect a number of front pages of newspapers and newsletters (at least four in total).
2. For each one look carefully at the design.
3. For each one write down the name of the newspaper or newsletter and also make some comments about the design of the page. Try to use the following words in your comments:
   - headline
   - columns
   - photographs
   - colours used (if any)
   - use of a logo
   - borders
   - background colours
   - text boxes.

Lesson 3: DESIGNING A PAGE

Background

Page design needs very careful thought. If you are not artistic, you are best using ready-made page designs where you simply select the design and then put your own text and graphics into it. Page design is made easy in Microsoft Publisher because it guides you through the processes of making the pages. It even tells you how many words your articles need to be before you write them, so that you can fit them in the space allocated.

Later in this unit you will learn how to produce your own page design from scratch. Most professional publications would do this because they would prefer to have a page design that was unique.

REMEMBER!

If you are not printing in colour there is no point in including colour in the design. Coloured text on coloured background cannot be seen sometimes when printed out in black and white.

Tips for desktop publishing

Here are some DTP tips. Try to stick to them when doing your own work.

1 Plan, plan and then plan some more.

2 Do not use more than three different fonts per page.

3 Include graphics. Pages of solid text look boring.

4 Any photos should be relevant. The reader should not be asking 'why is this here?' – it should be obvious.

5 Do not use a font that is too small. Use 10 point fonts for the main body of text.

6 Go easy with the special effects such as fancy borders, etc.

7 Take advantage of white space. A common mistake is to cram too much on the page. Leave plenty of space around the text and graphics.

8 Do not overdo the design. Some of the best designs are simple ones.

KEY WORDS

point – the unit of size for a letter, number or punctuation mark

Make it happen

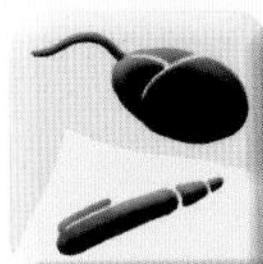

ACTIVITY 2: Using the Publisher wizard

You will be using the Publisher wizard to produce a newsletter. You will need to follow these steps carefully.

1 Load the software Microsoft Publisher.

The following screen appears:

2 Look at the list on the left-hand side of the screen. This is a list of templates. Templates are ready-made document designs. To make one of these documents you simply click on it and then enter your own text and graphics. The design works well because it has been created by someone who designs documents for a living.

3 Click on **Newsletters** in this list.

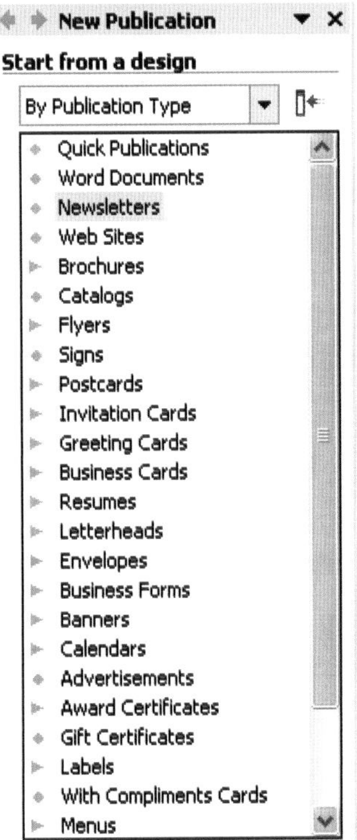

4 You get a large choice of newsletters. There are even more when you scroll down.

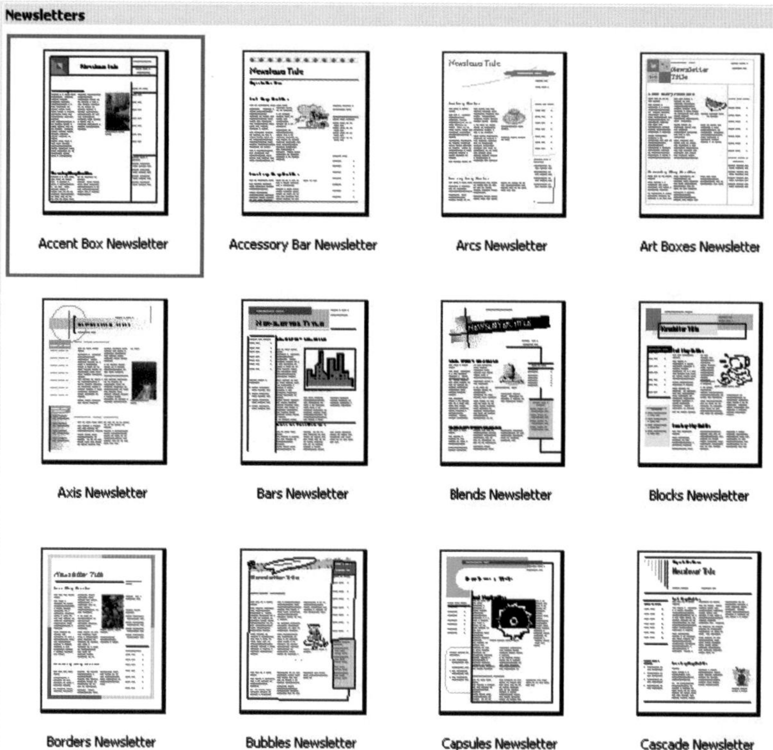

It is hard to see the designs properly because they are so small. Click on the first design **Accent Box Newsletter** to see a larger version.

5 The following screen appears:

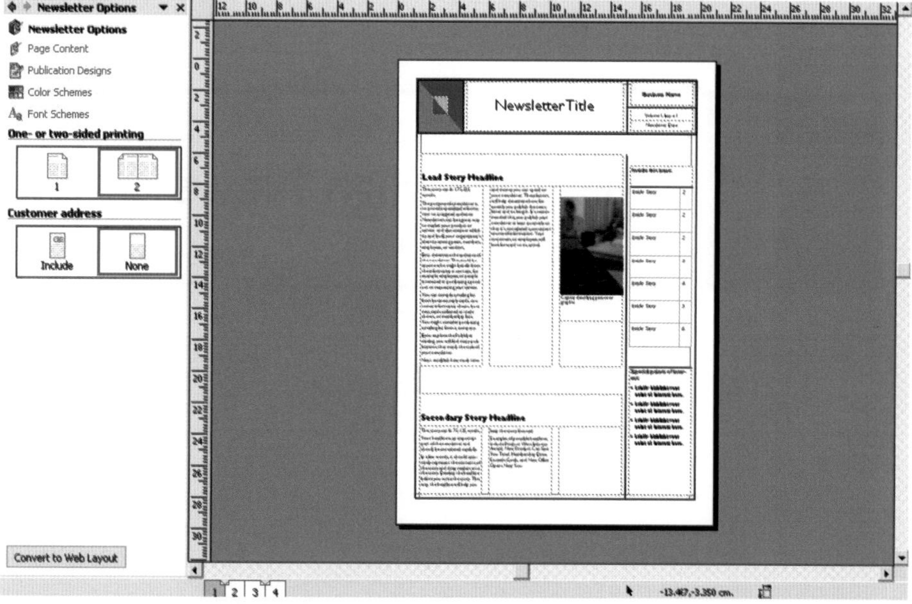

6 The text is too small to read so you can make it bigger by clicking on the 'zoom in' button . Each time you click, the page is made bigger. To make it smaller again (so that you can see the whole page) click on the 'zoom out' button .

7 Enlarge the page so that you can read the text.

Position the cursor on the text 'Newsletter Title'.

Newsletter Title

Delete this and then type in the new title: *Grange High News*.

The top of the newsletter will now contain the title.

8 Do the same to change the date to today's date and change the business name to *Grange High*. Check that yours looks similar to this:

9 Reduce the page so that you can see the two story headlines and their stories. You should now be looking at a view like this:

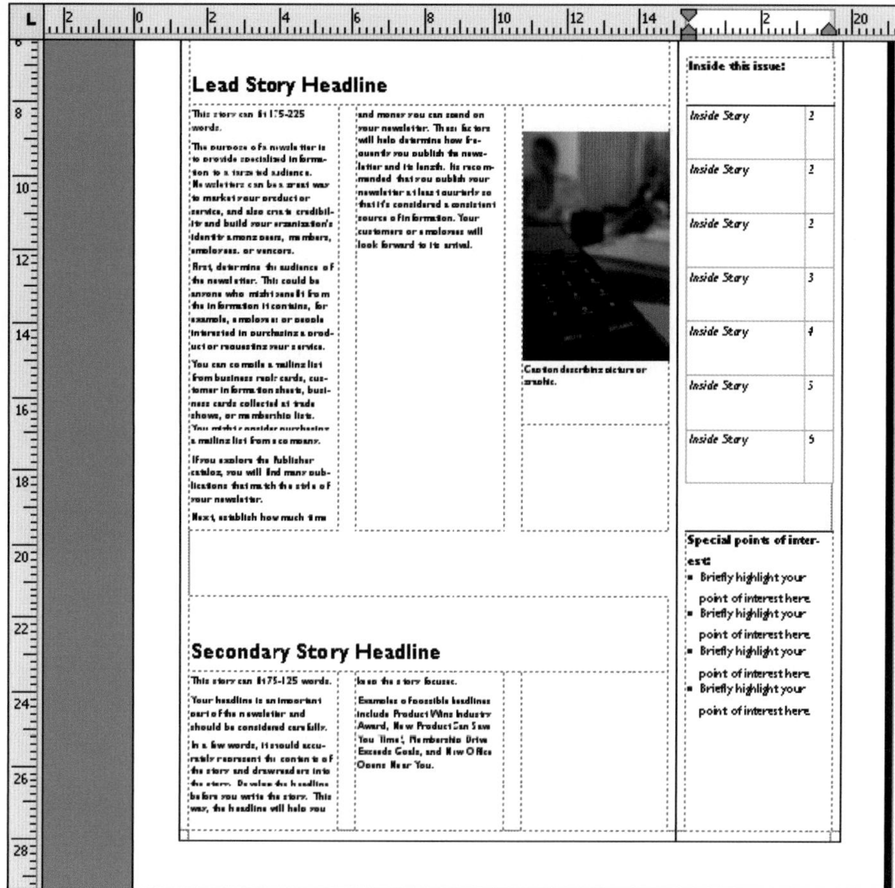

We need two headlines and their corresponding stories for the front page.

Two of your best stories need to go on this page. To fit the space, these stories have to be a certain size. The lead story has to be 175–225 words to fit the space and the secondary story needs to be 75–125 words. You also need catchy headlines for each story.

Note

You can access the files 'Lead story' and 'Secondary story' via the 'Activity Files' link at www.oxfordsecondary.co.uk

10 This is the text that needs to be added to the newsletter:

Text for the lead story

A message from your headteacher Mr Chips

It is now autumn, the season of mellow fruitfulness, and the season that marks the start of the new school year. You are sitting here reading this in your new uniform with your new pens, calculators, exercise books, etc. and wondering what the new school year holds for you.

There will be new teachers to meet, and maybe new students. The start of the school year provides an opportunity to start afresh. In some ways it is just like New Year when you make resolutions and break them a few days later.

Promises are made to yourself and to others about improving punctuality, attendance, your handwriting, your attention in class, and so on.

Ask any older person and they will tell you that your school years are the best years of your life. They may not seem so with the prospect of more lessons, homework, tests, assignments, and so on. You need to enjoy your schoolwork and the companionship of your friends, and hopefully reach the end of the year with a sense of achievement that you have actually tried as hard as you possibly could.

I wish you all the best for the following year.

Text for secondary story

A brand new ICT facility

You may have noticed lots of furniture and boxes arriving at the end of last term. These were for the new learning resource centre. This resource centre contains all the latest ICT equipment and will be open for your use every evening till 8pm, and also on a Sunday from 10am to 3pm during term time.

The suite has been made from two rooms that have been knocked into one, and contains 60 PCs that are connected to the Internet. The broadband Internet access makes it quick to access information.

As well as the computers themselves the room also has other ICT facilities. There are scanners, digital cameras, colour printers and even a plotter for doing CAD work.

You will need to put the heading into the template. You do this by deleting the existing heading and typing in the new one. You can then type the story in Word (or load it from the 'Activity Files' link at www.oxfordsecondary.co.uk) and then copy the section of text to the clipboard. Go into Publisher and make sure that the existing story has been deleted and that the cursor is in the correct position. Now paste the story into position.

You can repeat this process for the secondary story.

11. Check that the stories and their headlines have been put into the right place by comparing your page with the following screenshot:

A message from your headteacher Mr Chips

It is now autumn, the season of mellow fruitfulness, and the season that marks the start of the new school year. You are sitting here reading this in your new uniform with your new pens, calculators, exercise books, etc. and wondering what the new school year holds for you.

There will be new teachers to meet, and maybe new students. The start of the school year provides an opportunity to start afresh. In some ways it is just like New Year when you make resolutions and break them a few days later.

Promises are made to yourself and to others about improving punctuality, attendance, your handwriting, your attention in class, and so on.

Ask any older person and they will tell you that your school years are the best years of your life. They may not seem so with the prospect of more lessons, homework, tests, assignments, and so on. You need to enjoy your school work, and the companionship of your friends, and hopefully reach the end of the year with a sense of achievement that you have actually tried as hard as you possibly could.

I wish you all the best for the following year.

Caption describing picture or graphic.

A brand new ICT facility

of furniture and boxes arriving at the end of last term. These were for the new learning resource centre. This resource centre contains all the latest ICT equipment and will be open for your use every evening till 8pm, and also

3pm during term time.

The suite has been made from two rooms that have been knocked into one, and contains 60 PCs that are connected to the Internet. The broadband Internet access makes it

tion.

As well as the computers themselves the room also has other ICT facilities. There are scanners, digital cameras, colour printers and even a plotter for doing CAD work.

12 We now need to change the graphic in the template to one of our own. Ideally a photo of the new ICT facility should be taken and put in here.

You can either take a photograph of your IT room using a digital camera or look for a suitable photograph someone else has taken in Microsoft clip art.

You will need an image like this:

Whichever you choose, you will have to delete the current image. Right-click on it and select **Cut** from the menu.

You will now need to insert your image in the same position. Your teacher will tell you how to do this, as it will depend on where the image is stored. When you have done this, you will need to use the 'handles' to resize the image and you will also need to move it to its final position.

13 The page will now look like this, when you have resized the image to fit between the margins.

A message from your headteacher Mr Chips

It is now autumn, the season of mellow fruitfulness, and the season that marks the start of the new school year. You are sitting here reading this in your new uniform with your new pens, calculators, exercise books, etc, and wondering what the new school year holds for you.

There will be new teachers to meet, and maybe new students. The start of the school year provides an opportunity to start afresh. In some ways it is just like New Year when you make resolutions and break them a few days later.

Promises are made to yourself and to others about improving punctuality, attendance, your handwriting, your attention in class, and so on.

Ask any older person and they will tell you that your school years are the best years of your life. They may not seem so with the prospect of more lessons, homework, tests, assignments, and so on. You need to enjoy your school work, and the companionship of your friends, and hopefully reach the end of the year with a sense of achievement that you have actually tried as hard as you possibly could.

I wish you all the best for the following year.

Caption describing picture or graphic

14 Now replace the text under the photograph with the following: *Ben Smith working away at his Key Stage 3 ICT work*.

The caption now appears under the image like this:

Ben Smith working away at his Key Stage 3 ICT work.

15 You have now almost completed the first page of the newsletter. There are actually four pages of this newsletter. The other pages can be accessed using the following buttons at the bottom of the screen: 1 2 3 4

The page in blue is the current page.

⓰ Notice there are two other features of the page that we have not altered.

The first gives a bulleted list of special points of interest. It is best to complete this after the other pages have been completed.

The second is a contents list. We would complete this when we have completed the other pages.

Special points of interest:

- Briefly highlight your point of interest here.
- Briefly highlight your point of interest here.
- Briefly highlight your point of interest here.
- Briefly highlight your point of interest here.

Inside this issue:

Inside Story	2
Inside Story	2
Inside Story	2
Inside Story	3
Inside Story	4
Inside Story	5
Inside Story	6

EXTENSION ACTIVITY

You have seen how to use a template to complete the first page of the newspaper/newsletter. Completing the other pages is no different.

Make sure that you keep a consistent design from one page to the next. For example, do not alter the colour scheme or the fonts and font sizes from the ones selected for the first page.

For this extension activity complete the rest of the newsletter including content (i.e. text and graphics) of your choice.

Lesson 4: THE JOB OF CREATING A NEWSPAPER OR NEWSLETTER

Background

If you look at newspapers or newsletters over a period of time, you will see that although the content changes the design stays the same. This makes newspapers and newsletters easier to design because the style (fonts, font sizes, colour schemes, some graphics such as logos, etc.) can be re-used.

Creating a newspaper is quite complicated because you have to produce the content as well as the design. As there is so much to do, newspapers and newsletters are usually produced by a team of people.

Working as part of a team

Making a school newsletter/newspaper is a big job and is too much work for one person. To get the job done, it is best to work as a team, with each team member being given the responsibility of getting a small part completed.

Who does what?

The first thing you have to do when you work as a team is to decide who does what. Someone needs to be given overall responsibility for the whole task and his or her main job is to coordinate the activities of everyone else. This person is called the editor.

Before you can allocate specific jobs to people, you really need to think about what jobs there are. It is then possible to give each job to the person who can do it best.

For example, a member of the group who is excellent at English can proof-read all the articles for spelling and grammar. Another team member might be really chatty, and could be used to interview people.

WORKSHEETWORKSHEETWORKSHEETWORKSHEETWORKSHEET

WORKSHEET 7.3.4 Pick the best person for the task

A team is made up of a group of people. Each member of the group has strengths and weaknesses. When a task is allocated, you need to give it to the person with the best skills in that area.

The task of producing a newspaper has been broken down into a number of smaller tasks. You are also given the names and skills of the team members. Who do you give each task to? Draw a line between each person and the task that would suit them.

Team members

Lin Chang
- outgoing, chatty and good communicator

Jayne Horton
- wants to be a journalist when she leaves school
- has already had two articles in the local paper

Tanya Peters
- good on the computer
- has good keyboard skills

Julie Preston
- very good at English
- reads a lot of books
- excellent at spelling and knows lots of big words

Ahmed Singh
- came top last year in Art
- interested in computer art

Jim Jones
- mad on football
- produces a fan newsletter for the local team

Sam Jones
- likes surfing the Internet
- knows how to quickly find information

Tasks

1 Interviewing

2 Design a logo

3 Proof-reading

4 Article writing

5 Wordprocessing

6 Research

7 Page design

Ensuring a consistent approach

When you have lots of people each doing part of a project you need to have consistency. For example, you could agree before everyone starts work on the number of words their stories need to contain. It is a good idea to agree on fonts and font sizes and the file formats of any pictures that are used.

Doing these things makes it much quicker to put everything together.

Sharing information using a network

Note

You will need to reach agreement on all things with your team members before starting your project.

Using a network makes it easier to work as a group because work can be shared. Members of the group can easily pass work from one member to another. Sharing ideas or bouncing ideas off each other is also made easier using a network.

One of the first things you should do before you start your work is to exchange home and school e-mail addresses. Remember you can send stories, artwork, etc. to the editor or other members by attaching the file to an e-mail.

Working to a timetable

Newspapers and newsletters have to be produced on time. This means your group will have to be organised. As you will be working in a group you have a responsibility to the other members to complete your part of the work on time.

Having regular meetings

It is a good idea to have an initial meeting where deadlines for stories and artwork are agreed. Another meeting should be arranged before the deadline to check progress. If anything happens, such as the illness of a group member, action can be taken so that the deadline can still be met.

Putting it all together

All of the group members should contribute to the design of the paper as well as the content. When all the content has been collected and checked, it can then be put into the design. The whole newsletter/newspaper should then be checked again prior to printing.

Collecting the content

The content of a newsletter or newspaper is what goes into it. Content can be divided into two parts: the text and the images.

Collecting text

Collecting stories and articles for a newspaper will be done by a reporter. Some members of your group will have to act as reporters for Activity 10.

Here is a summary of the sorts of tasks a reporter would do:

- *Interviews* – chatting to staff, students, the headteacher and anyone else involved in the school.
- *Research* – finding out things about the history of the school or the area it is in, if there have been any famous ex-students, any interesting events and so on.
- *Checking accuracy of content* – proof-reading your own and other team members' articles.
- *Writing your own text* – writing your own stories from your experiences.

KEY WORDS

bitmap image – a file that represents a picture as a pattern of 1s and 0s

compression – storing data in a format that requires less space. Bitmapped graphics such as photographs are often compressed to a fraction of their normal size

dpi (dots per inch) – a measure of the resolution of an image. The greater the dpi the better quality the image

resolution – the sharpness or clarity (i.e. how clear it is) of an image

vector image – a vector image represented by a mathematical formula that can be enlarged or reduced without any loss of clarity

Collecting images

When you write an article you will need some images to go with it. Here are some of the things you would need to do:

- *Collect images* – taking photographs using digital cameras, scanning photographs or old documents, finding clip art, producing your own artwork using paint/drawing packages, etc.
- *Select the most suitable images* – normally you would get a selection of images and choose the best one (remember you can involve the other group members in the selection process). You will also need to see if the image loses its quality when its size is reduced or increased. High resolution images are best because they are much clearer. Image resolution is measured in dpi (dots per inch). The higher the dpi, the higher the resolution of the image. Bitmap images can lose their quality when they are enlarged or reduced. Vector images are easy to scale and they stay good quality. Sometimes you will need to change the file format of an image to one that you can use with the software that you are using to manipulate the image. Images are often compressed so that they take up less storage space and take less time to transfer from one computer to another.
- *Manipulating images* – cropping images (i.e. only using part of the image), sizing the image, altering the contrast of the image, converting images to a greyscale, etc.

Make it happen

ACTIVITY 3: Team work

Your teacher will put you into a team. Get together with your team members. Decide who should be the editor (i.e. the person who is to be in charge of producing the newspaper).

You will then need to find out a bit about each other so that tasks can be matched to group members. Here are some things you will need to find out about each group member:

- what computer equipment and software they have at home
- how much they know about the DTP software
- if they have easy Internet access
- their e-mail address

- other contact details such as address and phone numbers
- their interests and hobbies
- what tasks they think they are especially suited to do
- what tasks they would prefer to do
- how good or bad they are at English
- whether they have a digital camera.

This is just a basic list. Can you think of any more information you might need about each member? Ask the above questions and your own ones and record the answers for each member of the group.

Ask your teacher to photocopy your records so that every group member has a copy of the information about all the other members in their group.

Make it happen

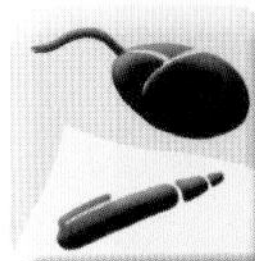

ACTIVITY 4: Listing tasks

Later on in this unit you will work together with your team to produce a newspaper.

Working as a team, write down a list of the tasks that need to be done to produce a final copy of a newspaper.

Lesson 5: SOME OF THE TECHNIQUES USED IN DTP

Background

There are many techniques used in desktop publishing that can be used to make information and graphics stand out. Here are some techniques you might like to experiment with.

Make it happen

ACTIVITY 5: Layering

Interesting effects can be achieved by layering objects. Follow these steps to find out how:

1. Open a blank document in either Word or Publisher. (We have used Publisher here.)
2. Create a text box and type in the text: *You're a winner*

   Adjust the size of the font and position the text box in the centre of the screen.
3. Insert a piece of clip art into the document. (It has to be something to do with winning but need not be the same as the one shown.)
4. Click on one of the corner handles (i.e. the little circles) to resize the image.

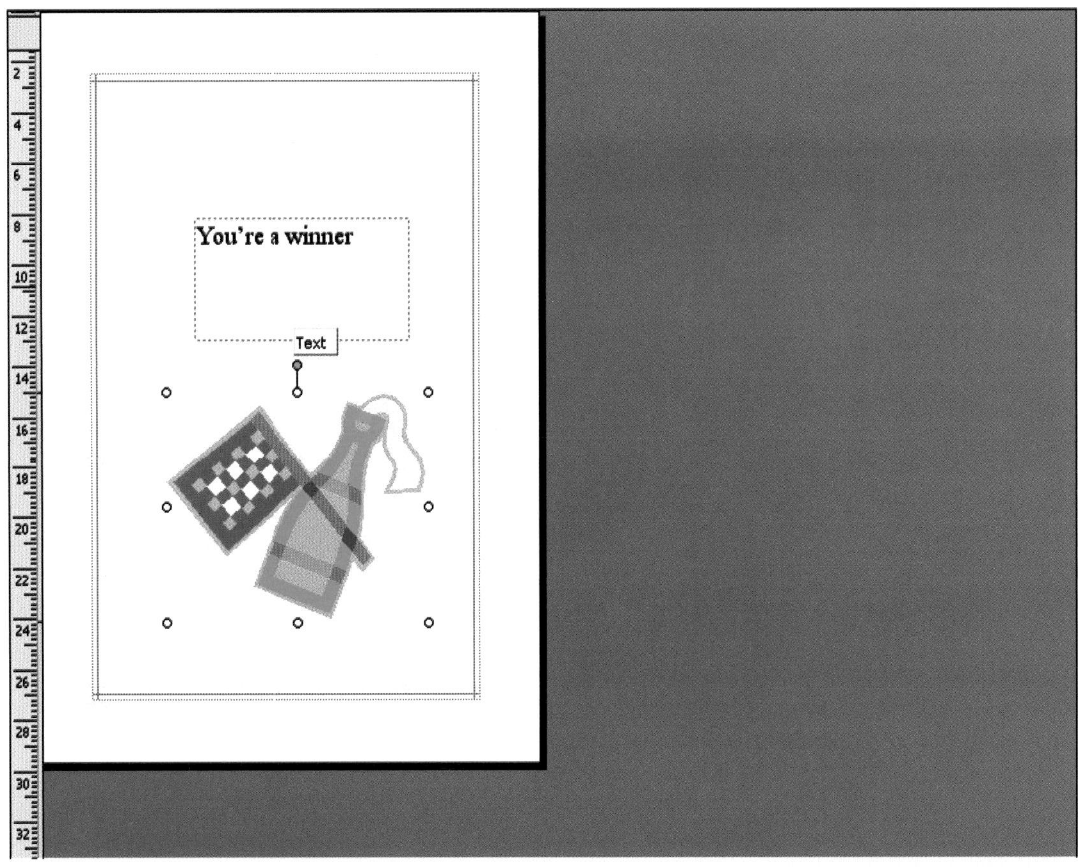

5 Click anywhere inside the graphic. You will see the cursor change to a small picture of a removals van. Click the right mouse button and keep your finger down on the button and the image will move with the cursor. Position it over the image, as shown below.

Here the graphic is brought to the front and is covering some of the text:

This is called layering. It is like having two transparencies: one with the text box and the other with the graphic image. Here the image is on top so it covers some of the text underneath.

6 If you want the text to go over the graphic image, it needs to be brought to the front. To do this click on the text box to select it. Make sure that you have only selected the text box. Now click on this button: . This brings the selected text box to the front. The text now goes over the image.

7 Now click on the graphic and then on to bring the image to the front.

Make it happen

ACTIVITY 6: Experimenting with DTP

There are so many features you can use in DTP that you could spend a whole year learning about them all. The best way to learn DTP is to experiment and see what happens. Look at the list of features below and experiment with them by creating an example of each.

Note

Don't forget: If something strange happens you have the 'Undo' button to take you back.

Some useful features explained

Formatting text

To format text, click on **Format** and then **Font**.

You can change the font, size, style, colour and character spacing.

Adding clip art

Click on **Insert** then **Picture** and finally **Clip Art**....

Enter a word or words to describe the picture (e.g. racing car).

Click **Search**.

Click on the image to insert it into your page.

Inserting WordArt

Click on **Insert** then **Picture** and then **WordArt**.

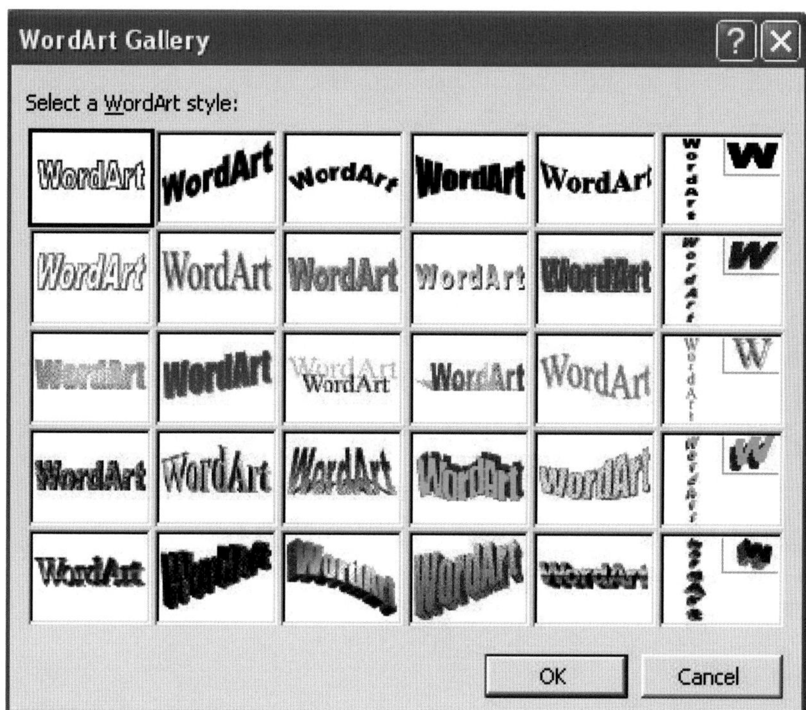

Choose the design by clicking on the choice and click on **OK**.

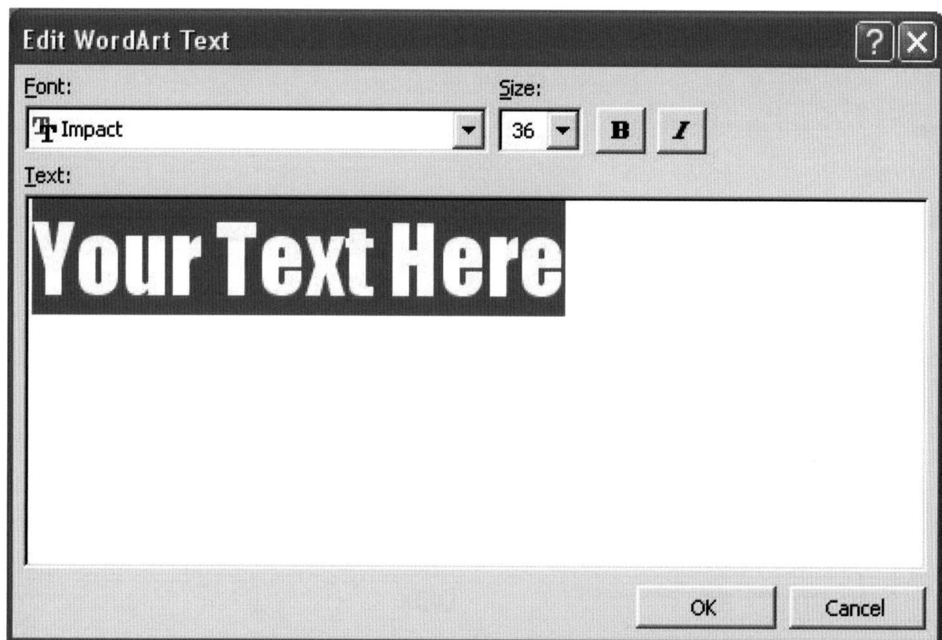

Type your text into the box and alter the font or size of font if necessary.

Click on **OK** and the WordArt will be inserted where the cursor was positioned.

Creating a text box

Text boxes are used to put text into a box. The box can be moved, resized or have its shape changed.

This is a text box. As you type, the text will fill the box.

This is a text box. As you type, the text will fill the box.

To create a text box, click on **Insert** and then **Text Box**. A cross appears on screen. Use this to draw the box by keeping the left mouse button down and dragging it.

Linking text boxes

If you link two text boxes, when one box is full with text, the other text box starts to fill up.

To link two text boxes:

- Create two empty text boxes.
- Click on the first text box by clicking on the border of the box.
- The text box toolbar will appear. Click on 'Create Text Box Link': .
- Now click in the text box into which the text will flow. The picture of the upright jug will turn to a pouring jug to show that the text can flow into the box.

Because these two text boxes are linked, as soon as one text

box is full the text continues in the next box.

You can link two text boxes to create newspaper-style columns. Linked text boxes can be on the same page or different pages. You can also link more than two text boxes.

Drop caps

The first letter of the first word drops down to add emphasis.

This is a section of text where a drop cap is used. You can use drop caps in both Word and Publisher. To drop the cap (i.e. capital letter), highlight the paragraph and then click on **Format** followed by **Drop Cap...**. The following choice appears:

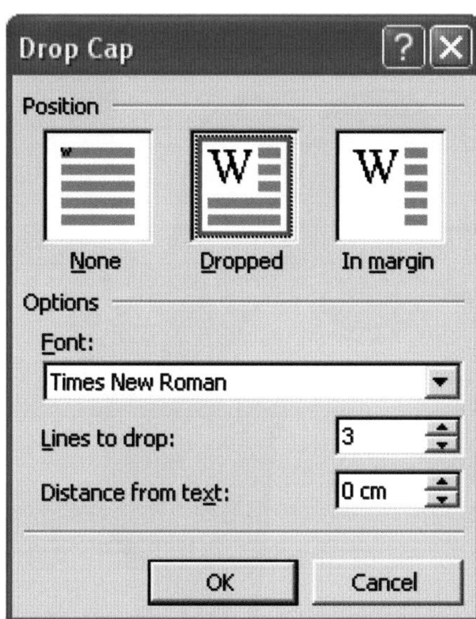

Select the middle one **Dropped** and then click on **OK**.

WORKSHEETWORKSHEETWORKSHEETWORKSHEETWORKSHEET

WORKSHEET 7.3.5 Test you DTP knowledge

Below are some questions to find out how much you know about desktop publishing. Your teacher will tell you whether you have to write the answers to the questions into your book or whether he or she is giving you a worksheet to work on.

1. What do the initials DTP stand for?
2. Give the names of three items of hardware other than the computer itself that would be useful for desktop publishing.
3. For each of the pieces of hardware you have listed in 2, say why it would be useful.
4. Templates are often used in DTP. Explain what is meant by a template.
5. Files from other software packages are often put into DTP documents. Give two types of files that you could put into a DTP document.

Lesson 6: CREATING A NEWSPAPER FROM SCRATCH

Background

Sometimes it is nice to produce something original. The disadvantage in using templates is that your newspaper can look similar to other people's work. If you do not use a template, it will take longer and you will need to have good DTP skills.

If you use templates, the newspaper can end up looking similar to others.

Make it happen

ACTIVITY 7: Creating a page from scratch

The following activity shows you how you might produce a similar newspaper to the one you created for Activity 2, but this time without using a template.

1 Load Microsoft Publisher.

2 Click on **New** and **Blank Publication**.

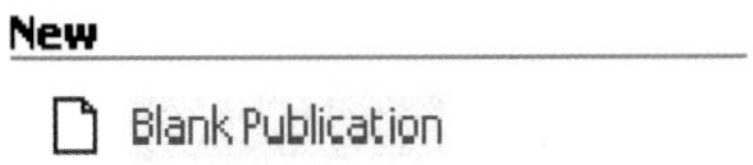

New

Blank Publication

3 Click on the 'text box' button

4 Position and size the text box to produce a long rectangular box to hold the title, like this:

5 Click inside the text box.

Change the font to Arial and the font size to 28:

Arial 28

6 Type in the title: *Grange High News*

Grange High News

7 Click on any letter in the heading and then click on the 'centre' button to centre the text in the text box like this:

Grange High News

8 Click on any letter in the heading. Then click on **Format** and then **Text Box....**

The following screen appears:

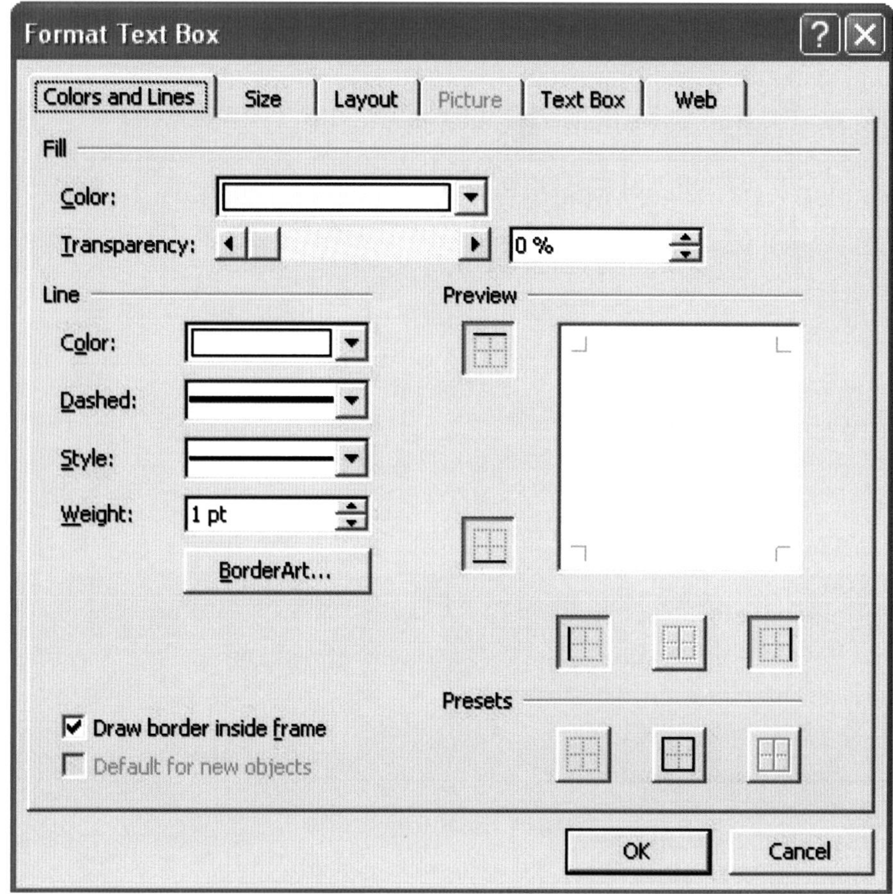

In the 'Fill' section click on a suitable light colour.

The background of the text box will now be filled with this colour.

Grange High News

9 We will now produce two columns to hold text. These two columns are simply long, thin text boxes. To make it look right we need to balance them so that they are the same width. Use the on-screen ruler to help you.

Use the 'text box' button to create two text boxes like this:

Note

Make sure that you zoom out so that you can see the whole page on the screen.

10 You now need to copy and paste the articles into the columns. The text will be the same text used when you created the newsletter using a wizard.

Load the lead story into the wordprocessor and then cut and paste it into the first column. Repeat this for the secondary story, this time putting it into the second column.

Your page will look like this:

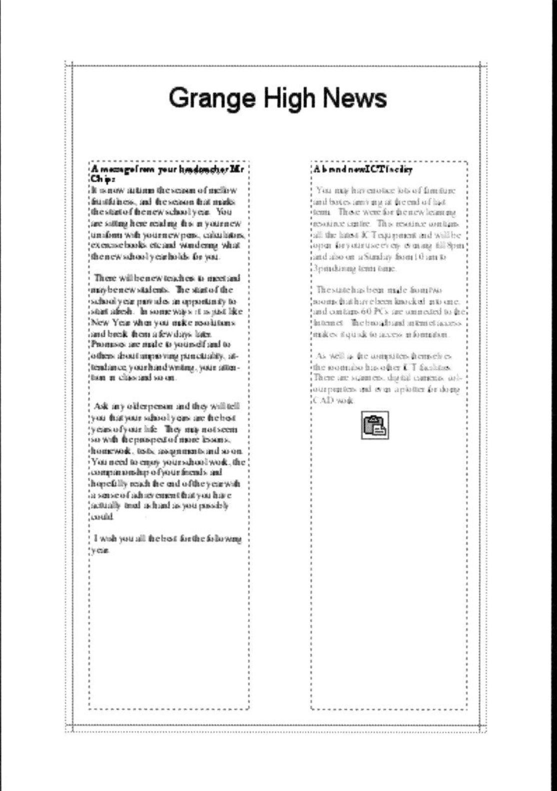
Grange High News

Note

If the lead story had taken up more space than the text box allowed, we would need to link the two boxes so that the story continued in the next column.

11 We will now add a picture to the design. We will use the same picture as before.

Make sure that the cursor is positioned between the first and the second paragraph of the story in the second column. This is where the clip art is to be inserted.

Add your clip art here →

A brand new ICT facility

You may have noticed lots of furniture and boxes arriving at the end of last term. These were for the new learning resource centre. This resource centre contains all the latest ICT equipment and will be open for you use every evening till 8pm, and also on a Sunday from 10am to 3pm during term time.

The suite has been made from two rooms that have been knocked into one, and contains 60 PCs that are connected to the Internet. The broadband Internet access makes it quick to access information.

As well as the computers themselves the room also has other ICT facilities. There are scanners, digital cameras, colour printers and even a plotter for doing CAD work.

Click on the 'insert clip art' button: .

You now need to find an image of a young person using a computer. When you have searched and found it, click on it and it will be inserted. (You could use the same image as you did in Activity 2.)

12 You may need to move and resize the picture.

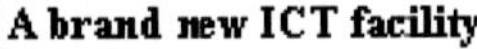
A brand new ICT facility

You may have noticed lots of furniture and boxes arriving at the end of last term. These were for the new learning resource centre. This resource centre contains all the latest ICT equipment and will be open for you use every evening till 8pm, and also on a Sunday from 10am to 3pm during term time.

The suite has been made from two rooms that have been knocked into one, and contains 60 PCs that are connected to the Internet. The broadband Internet access makes it quick to access information.

Notice the way the picture/clip art forces the text to go around it. It would be better if the text just stopped and started again after the picture.

13 You can control the way text goes around a picture.

Right-click the mouse button when the cursor is positioned on the picture.

Now click on **Format Picture…**.

14 Now select the tab called 'Layout'.

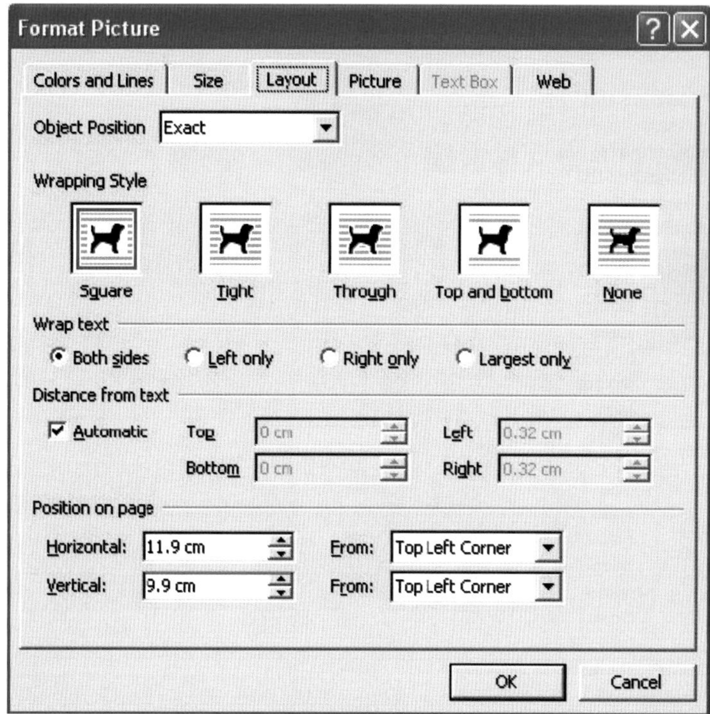

> **! Note**
>
> When you see a window appear, take a look at what is on the window before you select what you have been instructed to select. This way you learn about features that you may find useful in the future.

Select **Top and bottom** and then click on **OK**.

You may need to move the picture so that it fits between the two paragraphs.

It will now look like this:

A brand new ICT facility

You may have noticed lots of furniture and boxes arriving at the end of last term. These were for the new learning resource centre. This resource centre contains all the latest ICT equipment and will be open for you use every evening till 8pm, and also on a Sunday from 10am to 3pm during term time.

The suite has been made from two rooms that have been knocked into one, and contains 60 PCs that are connected to the Internet. The broadband Internet access makes it quick to access information.

EXTENSION ACTIVITY

You are now free to experiment to improve the appearance of the page that you have just created. Here are a number of things that you may consider doing:

- changing the background inside the text boxes
- changing fonts and font sizes
- adding borders
- drawing lines between the columns
- using WordArt.

Use your imagination and save each of your versions using a slightly different file name so that you can go back to a previous version if you need to.

Logos

A logo is a small visual tool that represents something, such as a business, place or event. Logos can be pictures or they can be pictures and text. Even text on its own can be a logo.

A logo does several things:

- it says a little about the business and what it does
- it identifies the organisation immediately
- it helps market the organisation.

Newspapers have distinctive logos. Here one is placed between the words of the newspaper title

Most newspapers/newsletters have a logo on them. Once a logo has been designed it can be put on all documents from the organisation, such as letters, forms, cards, etc.

Things to consider when designing a logo

Good logos:

- are simple in design
- are easy to see, even at a distance
- use only a few colours
- use text in a font and size that make them easy to read
- use simple graphic designs.

You will have to create your own logo later on. Make sure you consider these tips in your design.

WORKSHEETWORKSHEETWORKSHEETWORKSHEETWORKSHEET

WORKSHEET 7.3.6 **Logos**

LC Plastics is a company specialising in the buying and selling of industrial waste for recycling. The company asked a designer to come up with a logo. Rather than produce one, the designer produced four and let the customer choose.

Look at the designs carefully.

1. Put these designs into your order of preference, with your favourite design first.
2. Explain briefly why you chose the design as your favourite.

Your teacher will tell you which design the customer chose and why.

Creating a good logo is harder than you think.

Here are a few sites that will give you some ideas about creating logos.

1 See the processes by which a person created a logo at: **www.artistmike.com/test/page1.html**

2 There are lots of tutorials and advice on making logos at: **www.tutorialfind.com/tutorials/design/**

WORKSHEETWORKSHEETWORKSHEETWORKSHEETWORKSHEET

WORKSHEET 7.3.7 Name the company

If a logo is good, it should be instantly recognisable. Here are some familiar logos. Are they doing their job? For each logo, write down the name of the organisation you think it belongs to.

Your teacher may give you a worksheet on which to write your answers or you may be asked to write your answers in your exercise book.

5 

Make it happen

ACTIVITY 8: Making your own logo – a group task

For this activity your team will need to create a logo for your school. You need to create some drafts before you settle on a final design. You should do the designs on paper first because it is quicker.

Try to use the power of working as a group to come up with ideas and bounce these off each other. You could get each team member to produce one or two designs and then use the group to select the best one.

Only use the computer for the production of your final design.

You can use any drawing package for the production of the logo. There are two packages that you might consider using:

- *Word* – there are limited drawing facilities in Word. Take a look at the drawing toolbar or search for help to find out more.

- *Windows Paint* – this offers more facilities than those in Word.

The Windows Paint screen

Print a colour copy of your logo.

Make sure that you save your logo in the shared area for your group so that you can use the logo when you make up your school newsletter in the next lesson.

Lesson 7: CREATING YOUR OWN NEWSPAPER OR NEWSLETTER

This lesson brings together all the skills you have learnt in this unit and some that you have learnt in others. You will also use some of the materials you have created as part of other activities in this unit.

You will work as a team, with the same team members as before, and you will collectively produce a newspaper/newsletter for your school.

Make it happen

ACTIVITY 9: Creating your own newspaper/newsletter

You will work in the same group as before to produce a newspaper/newsletter for your school. Your group will be the reporters, editors, designers and publishers of the document.

Your teacher will tell you how much time will be allocated to this task. You may be able to work on this task in your English lesson as well as your ICT lesson. Some of the work will need to be completed at home.

Your final product will be a copy of the newspaper/newsletter.

Here is a list of what you should do and the order in which it should be done:

1. Look at a selection of other newspapers/newsletters. Decide which ideas you might be able to use. Bear in mind that you need to be realistic about what you can achieve with the DTP skills you have and in the time allocated.

2. Experiment with different designs. Each member of the group should add his or her own ideas. Remember you are working as a group so you need to help each other.

   Decide on a design and then decide what text and graphics you will need.

3. Decide who will do what. Allocate the tasks of doing research, writing articles, producing drawings, getting photos and clip art, etc. among the members of the group.

   Here are some suggestions of what you could include in the newspaper/newsletter:

- news
- school happenings
- gossip
- gripes and moans
- student spotlight – interesting material about a particular student
- letters to the headteacher
- replies from the headteacher
- jokes
- poetry and stories
- sports results

4. As this is a group task you will be relying on each other. You will need to make sure that you set deadlines so that you have all the articles and graphics when they are needed.

   Setting deadlines should be done at the start and everyone should stick to them.

5. Decide on a common approach. It will save time if you agree on the following before you each produce your own work:
   - length (number of words) for each article
   - font and font size.

6. Use e-mail or a shared area on the network to enable all the work to be commented on by all team members. Get other members of the group to proof-read your work. They might spot mistakes that you have missed.

7. Collect all the material from the members of the group and then create the design and put the various files (text and graphics) into it.

4 Modelling and presenting numeric data

Lesson 1:
INTRODUCTION TO MODELLING AND PRESENTING NUMERIC DATA USING SPREADSHEETS

What are models, how do you make one, and why are they useful?

A model represents how the real thing behaves. In ICT we use spreadsheets to make computer models. A model does not have to be made using ICT. The game of Monopoly is a model based on running a property company and the game of Cluedo models solving a murder using a number of clues. Models are easily built using spreadsheet software, although you can also buy specialist modelling software.

Background theory and key information

A model consists of a series of rules and variables. The rules are mathematical equations and the variables are the inputs to the

KEY WORDS

models – systems that mimic a real situation or thing

data – the raw facts and figures entered into a computer model (i.e. the data). The user can alter the variables to see what happens. Using a spreadsheet model makes altering these variables easy, as you will see later.

When you interact with a model you are performing a simulation. Some examples of models are:

- a flight simulator
- a computer game
- a model used to predict the weather
- a set of accounts to model the money coming into and going out of a business
- a model to predict the effect of global warming over the next 100 years.

Why bother with models?

Computer models are built by car manufacturers to simulate different types of car crash. At the press of a button the engineers can look at the inside of the car to see how it has been affected by the crash. They can alter their designs on the basis of the results to make them safer for drivers and passengers. They use computer models rather than actual cars because:

- it is much cheaper, as they do not have to make almost complete cars to crash
- the computer crash can be slowed down to see what is happening

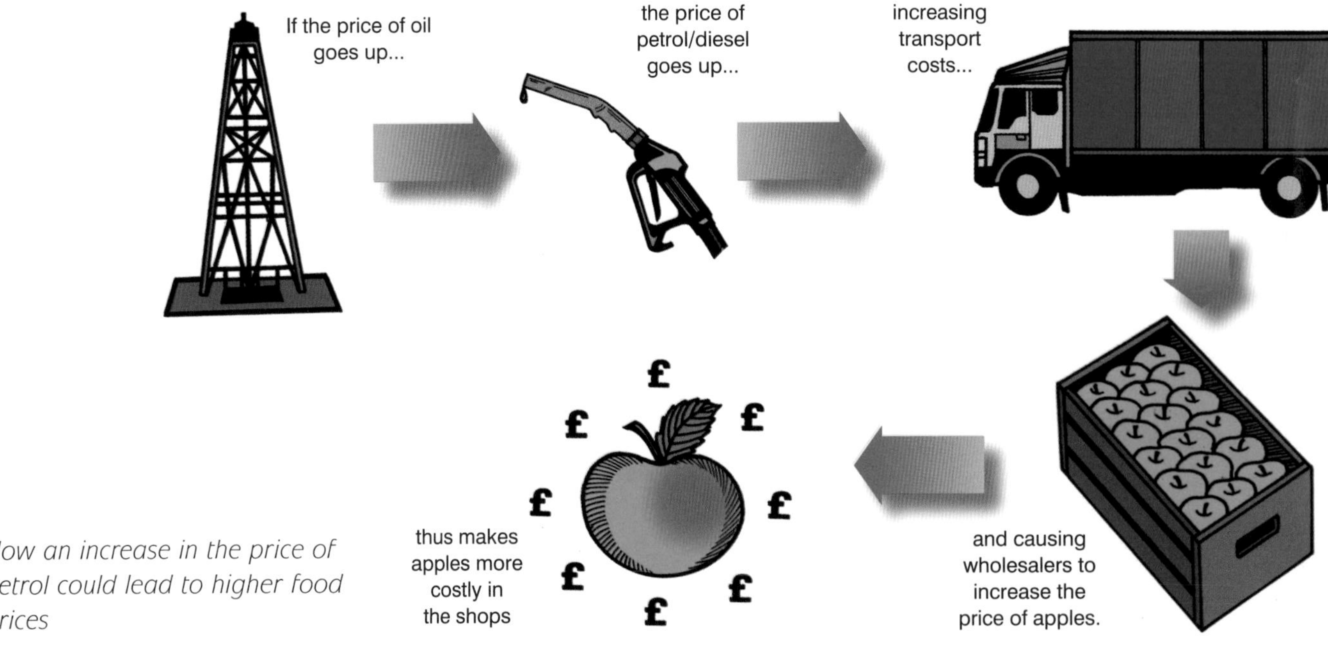

How an increase in the price of petrol could lead to higher food prices

- a lot more crashes can be analysed by the computer.

Computer models can help the people in charge of running the economy to make decisions. For example, if the price of petrol goes up, what effect might this have on employment? Different prices of petrol could be entered to see what happens to food prices. The Chancellor, who is the person who makes the decisions about the economy, could decide whether to reduce the tax on petrol to make it cheaper.

We can make models using spreadsheet software. Once a model is set up different data can be entered to see what effect it has on the outcome or output. The beauty of a model is that it is so simple to change a few numbers and the output changes automatically. Models, once created, can also be re-used with different data.

KEY WORDS

test data – data which is entered into a model to test the way it behaves

How can we check a model?

To test a model you can input the variables from a real situation and then compare the results obtained from the model with what actually happened. The more the model mimics the real situation, the better the model. Test data can also be input into the model so that you can check that the rules/formulae are working as expected.

FIND IT OUT

1 Models are used by the Met Office to predict the weather. Sensors collect the variables such as temperature, pressure and wind speed and these are entered into the model. The model is then used to produce a model of the weather and this is used to produce the forecast. Go to this website and take a look at the animation showing the weather:

www.metoffice.com/weather/charts/animation.html

Your geography or science teacher will be able to explain symbols on the map.

2 Lots of models are used in science. Here is a site you can look at to see some typical science models.

This site is called 'The Modelling Lab' and it can be found at: **www.shu.ac.uk/schools/sci/sol/invest/modelab/modelab.htm**

You can actually download, use and adapt these models. The three models you should look at are:

- How much electricity do you use?
- Stopping distances
- How much energy do you need?

You can download the 'How much electricity do you use?' model from this website. It is particularly interesting because the file is stored as a comma separated variable file (CSV for short), which means that you can use different spreadsheet software to read this file. These CSV files can be read using Excel. Here is a screenshot to show what the file looks like when loaded in Excel:

	A	B	C	D	E	F	G	H
1	Appliance	Power	Power	Time Used	Energy Un	Cost of Electrical Energy		
2		W	W	(hours)	kWh	energy (pence)		
3	Kettle	2700	EQUALSB	1.5	EQUALSC	EQUALSE3*B14		
4	Hair Dryer		EQUALSB4/1000		EQUALSC	EQUALSE4*B14		
5	TV		EQUALSB5/1000		EQUALSC	EQUALSE5*B14		
6	Electric Light		EQUALSB6/1000		EQUALSC	EQUALSE6*B14		
7	Heaters		EQUALSB7/1000		EQUALSC	EQUALSE7*B14		
8	Cooker		EQUALSB8/1000		EQUALSC	EQUALSE8*B14		
9	Electric Clock		EQUALSB9/1000		EQUALSC	EQUALSE9*B14		
10	Computer		EQUALSB10/1000		EQUALSC	EQUALSE10*B14		
11	Iron		EQUALSB11/1000		EQUALSC	EQUALSE11*B14		
12	Totals	EQUALSS	EQUALSS	EQUALSS	EQUALSS	EQUALSSUM(F3:F11)		
13								
14	One Unit o	6						

You can see that the word EQUALS appears. To use this spreadsheet you will need to delete the words 'EQUALS' and replace them with the symbol '='.

You can now think how your household uses the various appliances in the list. To use the model yourself you would need to list all the electrical devices used in your home and alter the spreadsheet to model your own household's use of electricity.

What can you do with models?

Using a model you can:

- alter the input to see what happens to the output
- ask 'what if...?' questions.

What you should already know

You will need to know the basics of spreadsheets before starting this unit.

You will have used spreadsheets in your work for Key Stage 2. In this unit most of this Key Stage 2 knowledge will be assumed. Your teacher has help sheets which he or she may supply or which you can ask for. Try to do the work on your own if you can and remember that you can always use the 'Help' function in the software.

In particular, you should already know:

- how to log on to your school network
- how and where to save your own work on the network
- how to enter and edit (i.e. alter) data in a spreadsheet
- how to make up a simple formula for a spreadsheet
- what the spreadsheet terms 'cell', 'label', 'data' and 'formula' mean
- how to use a spreadsheet to create a simple graph or chart.

What you will learn

In this unit you will:

- learn what a computer model is
- learn how models can be used
- learn how rules are used to make a model
- use rules to make up formulae
- use spreadsheet software to create a model
- use the model to ask 'what if…?' questions.

WORKSHEETWORKSHEETWORKSHEETWORKSHEETWORKSHEET

WORKSHEET 7.4.1 How much do you already know about spreadsheets?

Below are some basic questions about spreadsheets. You should have learnt most of this work when you did your Key Stage 2 work. This worksheet is to allow you to show your teacher how much you know.

You may be given a worksheet on which to write your answers or you may be asked to write your answers into your book. When you have finished, your teacher will either go through the answers or give you an answer sheet so that you can check your answers yourself.

1. Here are some mathematical symbols that are used in formulae. Write down in words what each means.
   (a) /
   (b) +
   (c) *
   (d) –

2 Here is part of a spreadsheet:

	A	B	C	D	E	F	G
1						**Costs**	
2						£32.76	
3						£12.98	
4			(shaded)			£11.00	
5						£10.45	
6						£12.65	
7						£24.12	
8						£35.50	
9							
10							
11							
12							

(a) What is the cell reference of the shaded cell?

(b) What is the column letter of the column containing data?

(c) What is the cell reference of the cell containing a heading?

(d) A vertical line of data in spreadsheet is called a …………

(e) A horizontal line of data in a spreadsheet is called a …………

3 The diagram shows a simple spreadsheet that a student uses to help budget her money.

	A	B	C
1			
2	Rent	£32.50	
3	Food	£13.00	
4	Electricity	£2.50	
5	Phone	£1.50	
6	Gas	£4.00	
7	Entertainment	£15.00	
8	Total		
9			

(a) Write down the contents of cell A4.

(b) Write down the contents of cell B7.

(c) For each of the following formulae say whether it would correctly work out the total of her expenditure when placed in cell B8. Write Yes or No.

Formula 1: =B1+B2+B3+B4+B5+B6+B7

Formula 2: =A2+A3+A4+A5+A6+A7

Formula 3: =B2+B3+B4+B5+B6+B7

(d) If the rent changed to £35.60, what other cell would change as a result? Write the cell reference of this cell.

4 Here are some statements concerning the reasons for putting formulae into spreadsheets. For each statement say whether you think it is true or false.

Reason 1: If a cell changes, then all those cells that depend on the cell will change

Reason 2: A more accurate answer is produced than with a calculator

Reason 3: It improves the appearance of the spreadsheet

Reason 4: The formulae in the spreadsheet need to be kept secret

5 Here are some buttons used in Excel. Write down what they do.

(a) B

(b)

(c)

(d) I

(e) U

(f)

(g)

(h) Σ

(i)

6 Here is part of a blank spreadsheet. Column A has been widened to enable the heading to be fitted in.

Explain how a column is widened using Excel.

	A	B	C	D
1				
2				
3				

7 Here is a spreadsheet used to work out the number and cost of the fireworks in a box.

	A	B	C	D
1	**Firework**	**Cost**	**Quantity**	**Total**
2	Bangers	£0.85	20	
3	Rockets	£4.50	5	
4	Catherine wheels	£5.20	3	
5	Roman candles	£6.00	2	
6	Jack-in-the-box	£8.90	3	
7				
8		Total number of fireworks		
9		Total cost of all the fireworks		

(a) Write down an item of data that is best described as a heading.

(b) Give the cell reference of the cell containing the data '£4.50'.

(c) Give the cell reference of any cell that contains a label.

(d) To find the total cost of the bangers a formula is needed in cell D2. Write down this formula.

(e) Explain how the formula in cell D2 can be copied down the column.

(f) Write down the formula which is put into cell C8 to add up the quantities of fireworks in column C.

(g) Write down the formula that would be placed in cell C9 to work out the total cost of all the fireworks.

(h) A mistake has been made for the price of a banger. The price should be £0.70. This is entered into cell B2. Write down a list of all the other cells which will now change as a result.

8 Printers connected to a network are shared between lots of users. Explain why you should always put your name and class on your spreadsheet (or any other work) before printing.

Lesson 2: DOING CALCULATIONS MANUALLY COMPARED TO USING A COMPUTER WITH SPREADSHEET SOFTWARE

Keeping pets

Background

Rachel keeps lots of pets. Her father is a vet and she would like to become one eventually. Rachel's pet collection seems to increase daily, so her parents have given her a budget. The budget is to cover the costs of keeping all the pets for one week.

Rachel decides to keep a list of the costs of keeping each pet. This list is kept on a piece of paper. Here is the list:

Pet	Cost to keep each pet per week	Number of pets	Total cost per week
Rabbit	£2.00	3	
Hamster	£1.00	2	
Goldfish	£0.15	10	
Dog	£5.00	2	
Budgie	£1.00	3	
Gerbil	£1.00	4	
Parrot	£3.00	2	
Cat	£4.00	1	
		Total cost of all the pets	
		Rachel's budget	
		Underspent/ Overspent	

Make it happen

ACTIVITY 1: Working with tables

Your teacher may supply you with a worksheet called Worksheet 7.4.2. Alternatively, you can write your answers into your book. If you are working in your book, you will need to copy out the above grid and make sure you do this in pencil.

Note

Important: You will need a pencil and rubber for this task. All writing should be in pencil, as you will need to make alterations.

Task 1: Completing the sheet

1. How do you work out the figure for the total cost per week for the rabbits?
2. How do you work out the figure for the total cost per week for the hamsters?
3. Work out and then fill in the last column to work out the total cost per week.
4. The total cost per week of keeping all the pets is found by adding up all the numbers in the last column. Work this out and write it in the space to the right of the caption 'Total cost of all the pets'.

5. Rachel's father has given her a budget to spend on her pets. Her budget is £40. Enter this amount on the sheet.
6. How do you work out the figure for the Underspent/Overspent?
7. Work out the figure for Underspent/Overspent and write it on the sheet.
8. Explain why the figure for Underspent/Overspent is so important to Rachel.

Task 2: Using the sheet to make decisions

Rachel can use her sheet to make decisions. Use the sheet to supply answers to the following:

1. Rachel would like to keep another dog. Can she afford to keep it?
2. Using the amount in the 'Underspent' box to guide you, give four combinations of extra pets she could buy that would still keep her within her budget.
3. Rachel's rabbits have bred, producing four bunnies and taking her total number of rabbits to seven. Can Rachel afford to keep these extra rabbits or will she have to give some to her friends?

Task 3: Altering the figures on the sheet

Make the following alterations to your sheet. You will need to rub out certain numbers and replace them with new numbers.

1. One of the hamsters has died. Reduce the number of hamsters by one on your sheet.
2. What other numbers will change as a result?
3. Rub these numbers out and replace them with new numbers.

Rachel would really like to keep a pony. Keeping a pony is expensive at £13 per week.

1. Add this to the bottom of the list of pets.
2. Now work out all the figures that need to change.
3. What is the Underspent/Overspent figure?

Task 4: Making a spreadsheet for Rachel

Instead of using pen, paper and calculator (if you need one!) you can use a spreadsheet. You will now use a spreadsheet to perform the tasks you have just completed manually. Using a spreadsheet makes things easy, as you will see.

Creating the spreadsheet

1 Load the spreadsheet software (your teacher will tell you how to do this).

2 Type in the information shown in exactly the same places as here.

	A	B	C	D
1	**Pet**	**Cost to keep each pet per week**	**Number of pets**	**Total cost per week**
2	Rabbit	£2.00	3	
3	Hamster	£1.00	2	
4	Goldfish	£0.15	10	
5	Dog	£5.00	2	
6	Budgie	£1.00	3	
7	Gerbil	£1.00	4	
8	Parrot	£3.00	2	
9	Cat	£4.00	1	
10				
11			**Total cost of all the pets**	
12			**Rachel's budget**	
13			**Underspent/ Overspent**	

To do this you will need to know:

- how to widen columns
- how to make text darker (i.e. to make text bold).

3 To work out the cost of keeping the rabbits we multiply the number in cell B2 by the number in cell C2. The formula to do this is:

*=B2*C2*

Enter the above formula into cell D2.

4 The formula needs altering slightly for each pet. The formula to work out the cost of keeping the hamsters is:

*=B3*C3*

This could be entered into cell D3 and the process repeated for all the other pets. However, there is a quick way of doing this by copying a formula.

The formula in cell D2 needs to be copied down column D. We do this by moving the cursor to the cell containing the formula (i.e. D2). You now click on the bottom right-hand corner of the cell and you should get a black cross shape. Hold the left mouse button down and then move the mouse down the column until cell D9 is reached. You will see a dotted rectangle around the area where the copying is to take place. Now take your finger off the button and all the results will be inserted. This is called 'relative copying' because the formulae are changed slightly to take account of the changed positions of the two numbers that are to be added together.

Check with this screen to make sure your totals are the same:

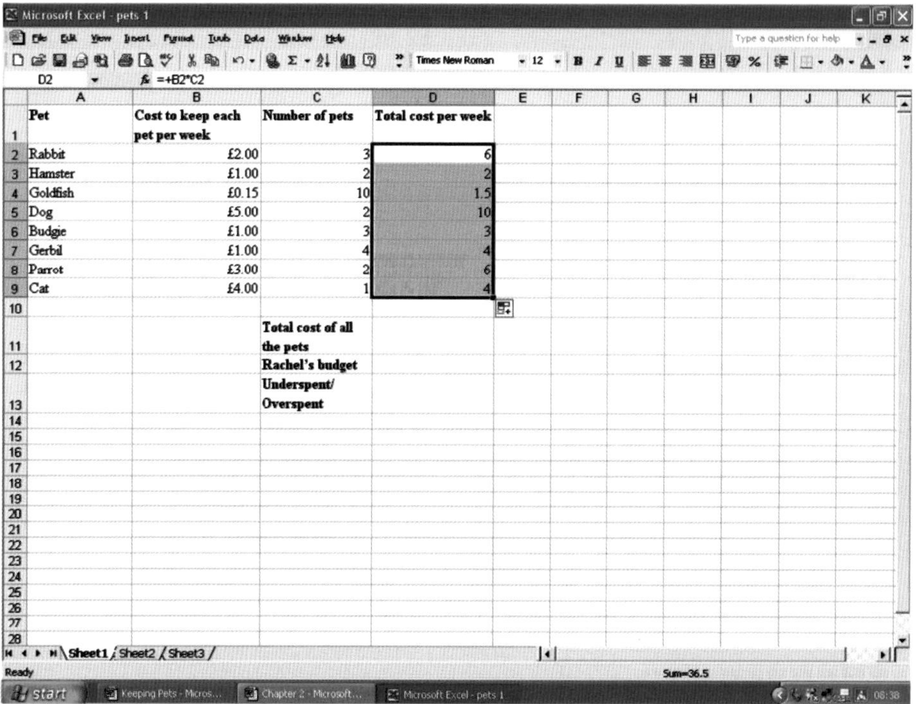

	A	B	C	D
1	Pet	Cost to keep each pet per week	Number of pets	Total cost per week
2	Rabbit	£2.00	3	6
3	Hamster	£1.00	2	2
4	Goldfish	£0.15	10	1.5
5	Dog	£5.00	2	10
6	Budgie	£1.00	3	3
7	Gerbil	£1.00	4	4
8	Parrot	£3.00	2	6
9	Cat	£4.00	1	4
10				
11			Total cost of all the pets	
12			Rachel's budget	
13			Underspent/ Overspent	

5 In cell D11 we need to put a formula which adds up all the numbers in column D from cell D2 to cell D9. A quick way to do this is as follows: click on cell **D11** and then click on the 'sum' button Σ on the toolbar. Check that it has chosen the right cells (you will see a dotted rectangle around the cells). Press the enter key and the result will appear.

The sum button saves you having to put in a formula when adding up a column or row of cells containing numbers.

6 Rachel's budget for keeping all the pets is £40 per week. Enter *40* into cell D12.

7 Put the formula *=D12-D11* into cell D13.

8 Notice that numbers like 36.5 appear. This is supposed to be money so we need to change all the numbers in column D to currency. This is called formatting the cells to currency. When formatted to currency the numbers will have a pound sign and two decimal places.

Highlight the cells in column D by clicking on the column letter (i.e. D). All the cells except the active cell are highlighted. Now click on **Format** and select **Cells**. You will now see a screen like the one shown in the diagram. In the 'Category' box, highlight **currency**. Notice that the decimal places are automatically set at two and also a pound sign is included. Click on **OK** and the final worksheet is produced.

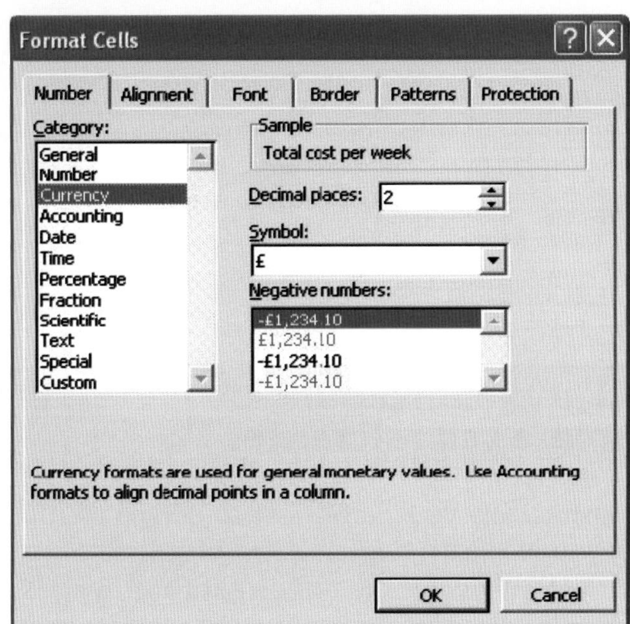

Note

Take a look at the Category box. it shows all the different categories a number can have. Look through this as you may find some of these useful when doing your own work.

Check your spreadsheet is the same as this:

	A	B	C	D
1	**Pet**	**Cost to keep each pet per week**	**Number of pets**	**Total cost per week**
2	Rabbit	£2.00	3	£6.00
3	Hamster	£1.00	2	£2.00
4	Goldfish	£0.15	10	£1.50
5	Dog	£5.00	2	£10.00
6	Budgie	£1.00	3	£3.00
7	Gerbil	£1.00	4	£4.00
8	Parrot	£3.00	2	£6.00
9	Cat	£4.00	1	£4.00
10				
11			**Total cost of all the pets**	£36.50
12			**Rachel's budget**	£40.00
13			**Underspent/ Overspent**	£3.50

You will now repeat the tasks you completed earlier except this time you will use the spreadsheet.

Use your spreadsheet to complete the following tasks:

Task 2: Using the sheet to make decisions

Task 3: Altering the figures on the sheet

See how much easier these activities were using the spreadsheet!

QUESTIONS

1 Explain two ways that the use of the spreadsheet makes it easier for Rachel to stay within her budget.

2 Give the names of three of the features used in the spreadsheet that can save Rachel time.

3 Rachel can save different versions of her spreadsheet using different names. Give one reason why she might want to do this.

4 Give two reasons why a person might still choose to work with a pencil and paper rather than a computer with spreadsheet software.

5 You had to format some cells. Explain what this means. Give the names of three different types of format a cell may have.

Background: learning about relative and absolute cell references

In the last activity you learnt how to copy a formula relatively. In this activity you will learn how to copy a formula absolutely. It is very important to know this when you need to make your own spreadsheets and models.

A company that sells computer supplies needs to show the price excluding VAT, the VAT and the price including VAT on their invoices (another name for bills). VAT stands for Value Added Tax and is added to most things you buy, except most food, children's clothes, books and newspapers.

Make it happen

ACTIVITY 2: Using absolute cell references

Note

You can access this file via the 'Activity Files' link at www.oxfordsecondary.co.uk

1 Open the spreadsheet 'Computer supplies'. Make sure you have loaded the following spreadsheet.

	A	B	C	D
1	**ABC Computer Supplies**			
2				
3	Rate of VAT	17.50%		
4				
5				
6	**Item**	**Price excluding VAT**	**VAT**	**Price including VAT**
7	A4 Photo Quality Paper	£12.00		
8	Smart media card (128MB)	£34.95		
9	Smart media card (64MB)	£18.95		
10	DVD-RW	£4.50		
11	DVD-R	£1.50		
12				

2 The VAT for each item needs to be worked out and placed in column C. To work out the VAT we multiply the percentage in cell B3 by each of the prices in column B in turn.

Put the following formula into cell C7:

*=B7*B3*

Now if this is copied down the column it will be copied relatively. This means that if we copy the formula to cell C8 the formula in C8 will change to: =B8*B4. This is not what is wanted because there is no number in cell B4. We want all the formulae in cells from C7 to C11 to refer to cell B3. To keep the reference to cell B3 when it is moved we need to have B3 as an absolute reference.

Instead of cell B3 we used B3. The dollar signs show that this is an absolute reference. If we used B3 it would be a relative reference.

Change the formula in cell C7 to:

*=B7*B3*

3 Copy this formula down the column as far as cell C11.

4 Now add a formula to cell D7 that will add the Price excluding VAT in cell B7 to the VAT in cell C7. You have to make up this formula yourself. Check that it works by adding up cells B7 and C7 manually.

KEY WORDS

absolute reference – in this type of reference, a particular cell is used in a formula, and when this formula is copied to a new address, the cell address does not change

relative reference – when a cell is used in a formula and the formula is copied to a new address, the cell address changes to take account of the formula's new position.

5 Copy the formula in D7 relatively down the column. Because there are no absolute cell references, there are no dollar signs in the formulae.

6 Check that your spreadsheet looks identical to this one:

	A	B	C	D
1	**ABC Computer Supplies**			
2				
3	Rate of VAT	17.50%		
4				
5				
6	**Item**	**Price excluding VAT**	**VAT**	**Price including VAT**
7	A4 Photo Quality Paper	£12.00	£2.10	£14.10
8	Smart media card (128MB)	£34.95	£6.12	£41.07
9	Smart media card (64MB)	£18.95	£3.32	£22.27
10	DVD-RW	£4.50	£0.79	£5.29
11	DVD-R	£1.50	£0.26	£1.76

Lesson 3: MODELLING USING A SPREADSHEET AND PRESENTING NUMERIC INFORMATION

There are two main tasks in this lesson, a modelling task called Modelling Luke's money and a task called Ways of presenting data from a spreadsheet.

Modelling Luke's money

Luke has been working away from home for several months. He is worried because he never seems to have enough money. Luke decides to use spreadsheet software to produce a simple model showing the money coming in and the money going out for a typical month.

Make it happen

You can access this file via the 'Activity Files' link at www.oxfordsecondary.co.uk

ACTIVITY 3: Creating the model

You will need to use a computer with spreadsheet software to enable Luke to juggle with his finances.

1 Load the spreadsheet software.

2 Load the file called 'Modelling Luke's money'.

3 By double-clicking on each of the numbers in turn you can find out which cells contain a formula and also view the formula itself. The formulae used in a model are called rules.

Copy and fill in the following table by writing the cell references of cells containing a formula and also write the formula that appears in the cell.

Cell reference	Formula in the cell

KEY WORDS

rule/formula – a mathematical equation that can be used to describe how the real thing behaves

formulae – the plural of formula

4 Type in your name and form in the places provided on the spreadsheet and then print the spreadsheet out.

5 The landlord increases the rent to £220 per month. Change the amount in cell B8 to £220. Notice that some of the numbers in the other cells now change. Write down the cell references that are altered as a result of this rent increase.

6 Notice that the 'Amount left at the end of month' is now a negative amount in red on the spreadsheet. This means that Luke has spent more than he has earned in wages. Write down the amount he owes at the end of the month.

7 Luke gets the offer of a part-time job working behind a bar. He will take home £220 for this job. Put a suitable explanation for this money in cell A6 and add £220 to cell B6. Notice that the total amount of money coming in stays at £900. This is because a new formula is needed to add cells B5 and B6 together and put the result in cell B18. Enter the following formula into cell B18:

=B5+B6

How much does he now have left at the end of the month?

8 Luke can easily control some of the amounts in the spreadsheet, but others he can't. For example it is fairly easy for Luke to spend less on entertainment by staying in more often.

In small groups, discuss which of the amounts in the spreadsheet Luke can control and which ones he can't.

Those amounts that Luke can easily control can be altered in the spreadsheet to see what happens. These amounts are called variables.

KEY WORDS

variables – numbers in a spreadsheet that can be altered by the user to see what happens

9 Luke can use his model to help him make decisions. He travels to his day job by train and to his evening job by bus. Because the bar is open late, he walks home or if the weather is bad he will take a taxi.

Luke would like to run a car. He needs to answer the question 'can I afford to run a car?' using his model. Before doing this he investigates the cost of buying and running a car.

He intends to use all his savings to buy the car and the running costs of the car will be £200 per month. Add this, with a suitable label, to the spreadsheet.

Luke reckons he will be able to save some money elsewhere. Make the following changes.

- Food £120
- Delete the label 'Fares to work' and the amount
- Entertainment £160

After making these alterations, can Luke afford to run a car? Give reasons for your answer.

10 Save your spreadsheet under the file name 'Can Luke afford to run a car?'.

11 Print out a copy of this model. Remember to put your name and class somewhere on your spreadsheet before printing it out.

KEY WORDS

annotating – adding hand-written notes to computer printouts to add explanations

EXTENSION ACTIVITY

Luke likes to meet his mates and go out so he spends a lot on food, clothes and entertainment. Luke knows he could possibly reduce the amounts spent on all of these. He would like to go on holiday with friends and will need to save £100 per month to be able to do this. Use the spreadsheet model to experiment with the ways he could reduce certain amounts to do this.

Print out copies of each spreadsheet and mark on it (this is called annotating) what the alterations are.

Ways of presenting data from a spreadsheet

Data in a spreadsheet lacks impact. It is hard to take in the meaning of all the numbers. It is much better to use a graph or a chart to display numerical information. Sometimes these graphs and charts produced using spreadsheet software can be taken and put into a wordprocessed document. Taking a file from one piece of software and putting it into a different piece of software is called importing.

Background

A survey was conducted in a school to find out the types of crisps preferred by students in two different groups. Here are the results of the surveys for each group:

Group 7A	Number of students
Plain	10
Cheese and onion	9
Salt and vinegar	8
Barbecue beef	4

Group 9A	Number of students
Plain	10
Cheese and onion	10
Salt and vinegar	3
Barbecue beef	2

The class put each lot of data into spreadsheet software and produced the following pie charts:

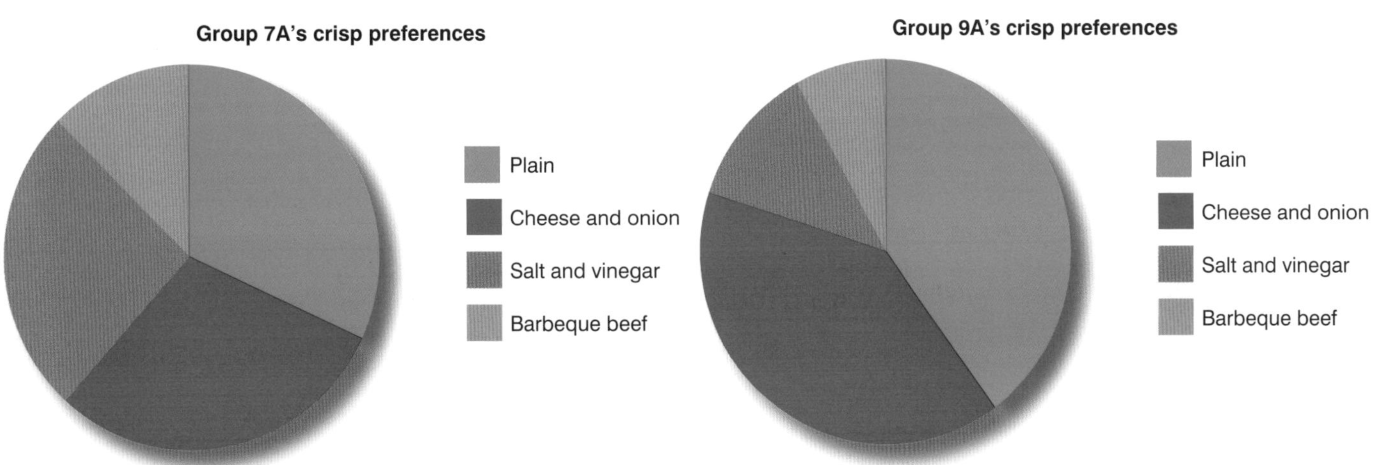

Presenting the data in the pie chart makes it easy to see the individual preferences of people in the class. Pie charts are good if you want to show the breakdown of a whole amount into parts. It is not a good idea to use a pie chart if there are too many parts (up to five or six parts is about right).

QUESTIONS

1 Do the charts by themselves tell us how many students like each type of crisp?

2 Can you tell from the charts by themselves how many students there are in each group?

3 Is it possible to compare the two pie charts with each other? For example, could you say that because the sector for plain crisps for group 9A is greater than the sector for plain crisps for group 7A that more people like plain crisps in group 9A?

4 Is the information on the pie chart easy to read?

5 Does the pie chart have a suitable title?

6 Is there anything that might be done to improve the presentation of the pie charts?

Make it happen

ACTIVITY 4: Producing the first pie chart

1 Key the following data into a spreadsheet:

	A	B	C	D	E
1	Results of a survey on crisp preferences for two groups in the school				
2					
3					
4					
5	Group 7A	Number of students		Group 9A	Number of students
6	Plain	10		Plain	10
7	Cheese and onion	9		Cheese and onion	10
8	Salt and vinegar	8		Salt and vinegar	3
9	Barbecue beef	4		Barbecue beef	2

2 Select all the cells from cell A6 to cell B9 (after selection they will be highlighted in blue).

3 Click on the 'Chart Wizard' button on the toolbar.

4 Here you choose **Pie** from the list of charts. There are some different ways the pie chart can be drawn and we will choose the first one.

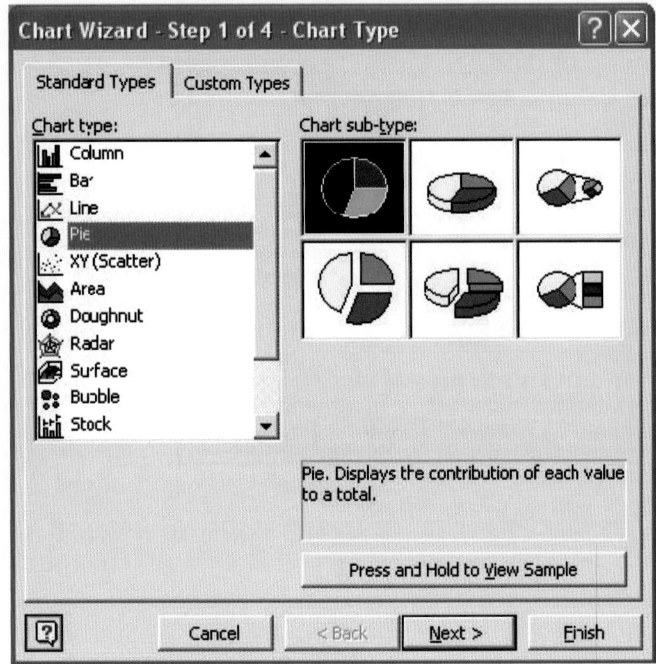

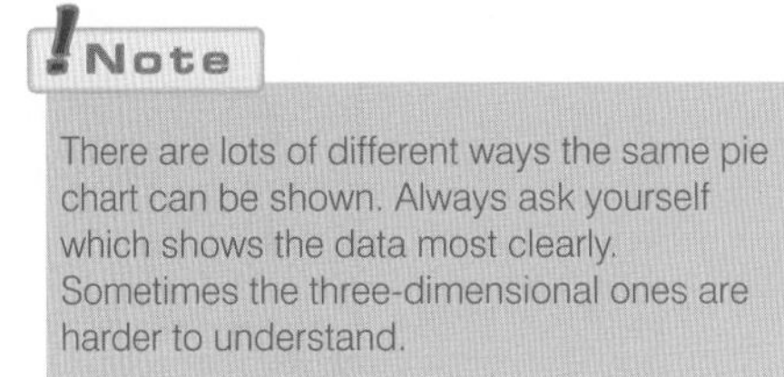

Note

There are lots of different ways the same pie chart can be shown. Always ask yourself which shows the data most clearly. Sometimes the three-dimensional ones are harder to understand.

Now click on **Next**.

5 You will see a dotted line drawn around the data that it is to be used for the pie chart. The following screen also appears:

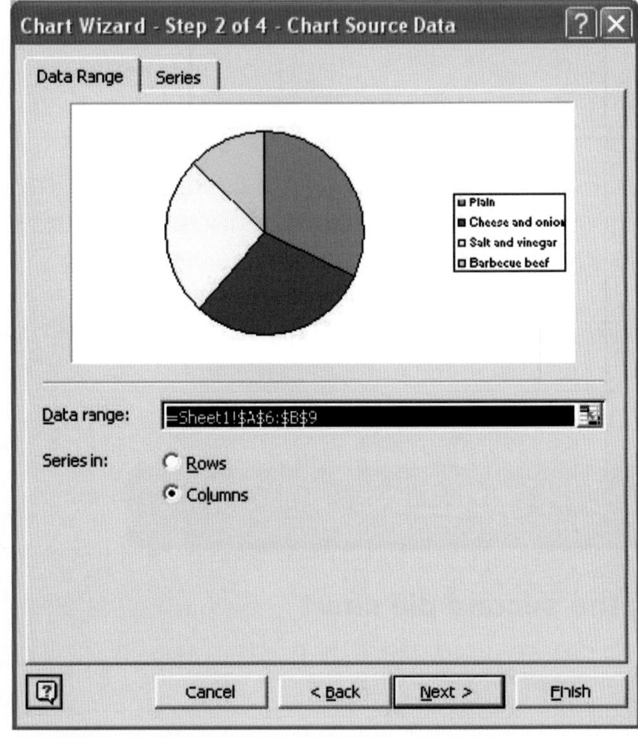

Click on **Next**.

6 The following screen appears, where you can add a title to the chart:

Chart Wizard - Step 3 of 4 - Chart Options

Titles | Legend | Data Labels

Chart title: Group 7A's crisp preferences

Category (X) axis:

Value (Y) axis:

Second category (X) axis:

Second value (Y) axis:

Group 7A's crisp preferences

Plain
Cheese and onion
Salt and vinegar
Barbecue beef

Cancel | < Back | Next > | Finish

Type in the title *Group 7A's crisp preferences*

Click on **Next**.

7 This screen appears, asking you where you would like to place the chart:

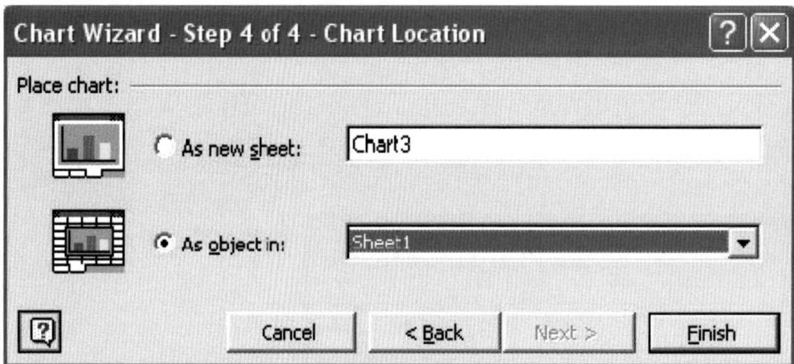

You can place the chart on a new sheet or you can place it in the same sheet as the data that was used to create it. We will choose the latter, which is already marked so just click on **Finish**.

8 You can position and size the chart by making use of the handles.

Make it happen

ACTIVITY 5: Producing the second pie chart

For this activity you have to create a pie chart by going through similar steps to those used to create the first pie chart.

Once you have produced the second pie chart, position it next to the first pie chart as shown in the following screenshot. You may need to resize the charts to do this.

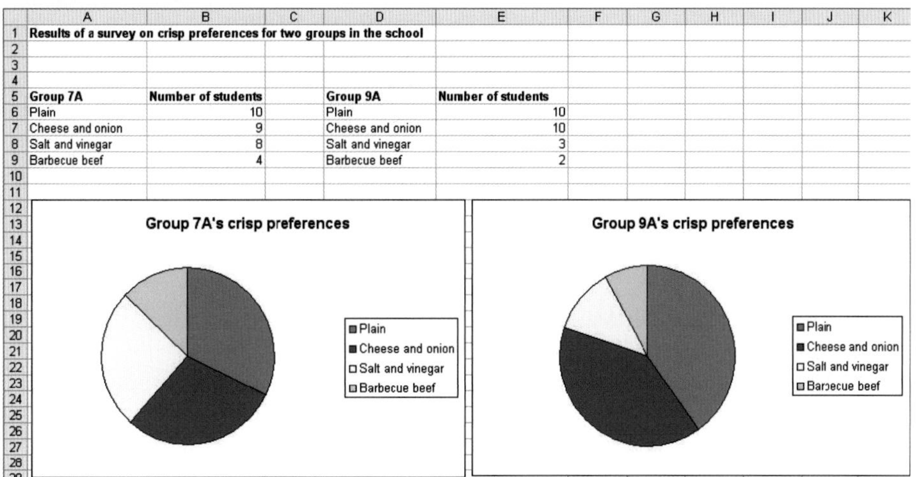

Results of a survey on crisp preferences for two groups in the school

Group 7A	Number of students	Group 9A	Number of students
Plain	10	Plain	10
Cheese and onion	9	Cheese and onion	10
Salt and vinegar	8	Salt and vinegar	3
Barbecue beef	4	Barbecue beef	2

Save your file using the file name 'Pie charts showing the results of the crisp survey'.

Make it happen

ACTIVITY 6: Importing the charts into a wordprocessed document

Importing means taking one file and incorporating it into another file. In this case a file (i.e. the chart) produced using spreadsheet software will be added to another file – a document produced using wordprocessing software.

1. Load the spreadsheet software and open the file (if it is not open already) called 'Pie charts showing the results of the crisp survey'.
2. Now click anywhere on the border (i.e. the line) around the first chart (i.e. the one for Group 7A). You will see small black squares appear around the border. These are the handles and they show that you have selected the chart.
3. Now click on the 'copy' button on the toolbar. A copy of your chart will be stored in a temporary area of memory, called the clipboard.
4. We now need to temporarily leave the spreadsheet, so minimise it by clicking on the 'minimise' button (situated at the top right of the

You can access this file via the 'Activity Files' link at www.oxfordsecondary.co.uk

screen) . Notice that it appears at the bottom of the screen and it is immediately available simply by clicking on it.

5 Load the wordprocessing software and open the file called 'Crisp preferences'.

6 Delete the text ('Pie charts to go here'). Position your cursor where this sentence started. Now click on the 'paste' button on the toolbar .

Your chart will now appear in the document.

You can resize and move the chart using the handles. Experiment with this until you are happy with the result.

7 Repeat these steps so that the other chart for Group 9A is imported into the document and is the same size as the other chart.

8 Save this wordprocesed file using the file name 'Report on the crisp survey'.

9 Print out a copy of your document, making sure that you put your name and class on the top.

Your document should look similar to this:

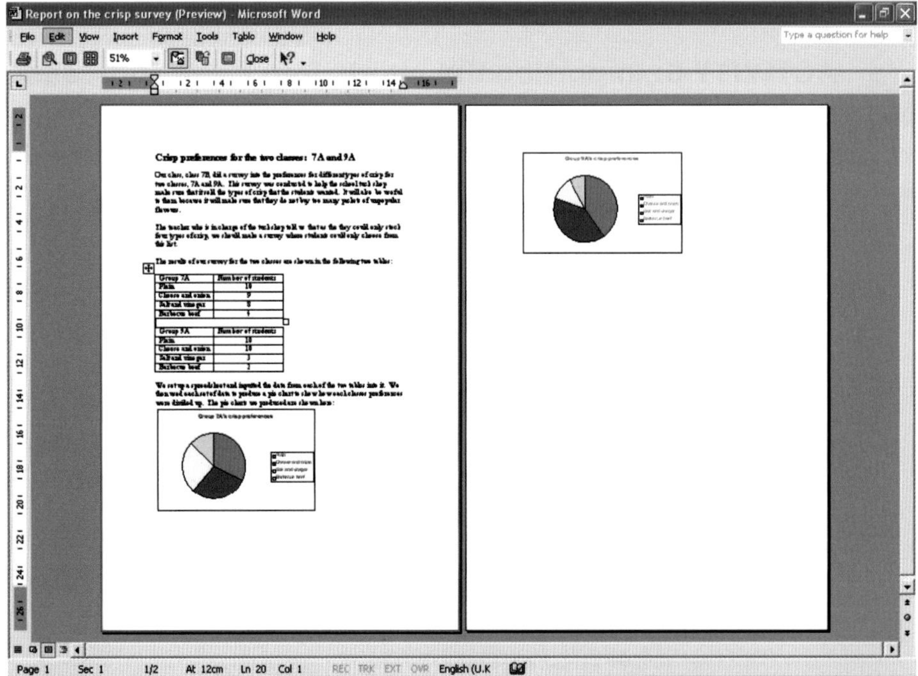

EXTENSION ACTIVITY

As you can see, the report produced in the last activity ended up on two pages. It is always better if all the material is on one page, especially when the figures refer to the diagram. You need to investigate if there is a way of getting everything on one page. In your alterations you need to make sure that you can read the text on the chart.

Here are a few hints of what you might do (there are others that are not mentioned here):

- close up any white space between the lines of text
- use a smaller font
- put the tables side by side
- put the charts side by side.

Produce some sample printouts of your alterations and annotate on them what alteration or alterations you have made. Which of your versions do you consider to be the best? Label it 'Best one'.

Phil got more attention when he used real pies for his pie charts – today it was apple – everyones favourite!

Lesson 4: USING SPREADSHEET SOFTWARE TO BUILD A MODEL

Background: Making a model to plan a school disco

Year 7 students Ashia and James propose to hold a disco for Year 7 in aid of a local charity. Their aim is for everyone to have a good time and raise as much money for charity as they can. Their headteacher has told them that the disco should run between 7pm and 11pm and that they must investigate the costs of holding the disco to make sure it does not lose money. Hopefully, all 220 of the Year 7 students will be able to attend the disco.

After making some telephone calls to local DJs they find that the cheapest disco and DJ is £60. This figure will not be altered in our model.

Hire of disco and DJ *£60*

Here are some items that could be varied:

Ticket price *£3.00*
Cost of printing tickets *£0.02 per ticket*

Note

Hint: When making a model you need to think about which items will be varied. If a number is unlikely to change, then it will not be a variable.

Because each of these numbers could easily be varied they are called variables. When the model is built, these variables can be changed to see what happens. For example, they may be able to get the tickets printed for less or they may charge more or less for the tickets. These are examples of 'what if...?' questions that the model is designed to answer.

We can use the model to answer 'what if...?' questions

The rules of the model (i.e. the formulae used in the spreadsheet)

In this model we are going to work out the money coming in and the money going out. The difference between these two amounts is the profit if we make money or the loss if we lose money. Our aim is to make as much profit as we can because this is the money that will be going to charity.

The rules of the model are the formulae that we put into each cell. Here are the formulae that we need:

- A formula to work out the money from ticket sales.
- A formula to work out the total income (i.e. the total money coming in).
- A formula to work out the cost of printing the tickets.
- A formula to work out the total costs.

All the above formulae depend on how many tickets are sold. We do not know for definite how many tickets we will sell so we will want to vary this to see what happens to the profit/loss figure.

The result from the spreadsheet is the profit that can be given to charity. If the result is a loss then we will need to do something about it. This is called the output from our model. It is the answer. So we also need:

- A formula to work out the profit/loss.

Planning the model

You should always think about your model design before using the spreadsheet software. Draw a quick sketch on paper before you start.

It is a good idea to plan your model on paper first

Here is the structure of the model:

	A	B	C
1	**Name:**	**Class:**	
2	**A Model to show the profit or loss for a disco**		
3			
4	Price for printing one ticket		
5	Number of tickets sold		
6	Ticket price		
7			
8	**Income**		
9	Money from ticket sales		
10	Total income		
11			
12	**Costs**		
13	Hire of disco and DJ		
14	Cost of printing all tickets		
15	Total costs		
16			
17	**Profit/Loss**		

Notice that:

- there is a space for your name and class to distinguish your work if it is printed out on a printer that is used by lots of other people doing the same work
- there is a title for the model

- the variables, income and costs are grouped together
- the output (i.e. the result) is shown separately.

When you design models of your own you should try to use a similar design.

WORKSHEETWORKSHEETWORKSHEETWORKSHEETWORKSHEET

WORKSHEET 7.4.3 Planning the model

Your teacher may give you a worksheet to complete or you may have to copy the grids and complete them in your book.

1. Look at the structure of the model. You have to decide by looking at the following cells if they should contain either a rule (i.e. a formula) or a variable (i.e. a number that we alter).

Cell	Write either 'rule' or 'variable'
B4	
B5	
B6	
B9	
B10	
B13	
B14	
B15	
B17	

2. Tick the cells that depend on the number of tickets being sold.

Cell	Tick if the number in the cell depends on how many tickets are sold
B4	
B5	
B6	
B9	
B10	
B13	
B14	
B15	
B17	

3. Using your answer to question 1, write down the formulae that each cell containing a rule should have in it. One cell has been done for you.

   NB: Not all cells have a formula in them.

Cell	Formula
B4	
B5	
B6	
B9	=B5*B6
B10	
B13	
B14	
B15	
B17	

Make it happen

ACTIVITY 7: Making the disco model

In this activity you will create a model using spreadsheet software.

1. Load the spreadsheet software and key in the information shown in the screenshot on page 155.

   You will need to widen column A and make some of the text bold.

   Your spreadsheet should look identical to the one on page 155.

2. The price for printing one ticket is *£0.02*. Put this amount in cell B4. Make sure that you enter the pound sign. Because of the pound sign the spreadsheet will know that you are dealing with currency.

You will need to format the cells to currency.

3. Enter the other variable data: *220* (for the number of tickets sold) into cell B5 and *£3.00* (for the ticket price) into cell B6.

4. The cost for the hire of the disco and DJ is *£60*. Enter this amount into cell B13.

(NB: This is the cheapest after shopping around so we have not thought of it as a variable.)

5 After checking with your teacher that your list of formulae in Worksheet 7.4.2 question 3 are correct you can now enter these formulae into the spreadsheet.

Your spreadsheet will now look like this, with your own name and class inserted:

	A	B	C
1	**Name: Stephen Doyle**	**Class: 7E**	
2	**A Model to show the profit or loss for a disco**		
3			
4	Price for printing one ticket	£0.02	
5	Number of tickets sold	220	
6	Ticket price	£3.00	
7			
8	**Income**		
9	Money from ticket sales	£660.00	
10	Total income	£660.00	
11			
12	**Costs**		
13	Hire of disco and DJ	£60.00	
14	Cost of printing all tickets	£4.40	
15	Total costs	£64.40	
16			
17	**Profit/Loss**	£595.60	
18			

6 Save your model using the file name 'Disco model 1'.

7 Print a copy of your model.

Make it happen

ACTIVITY 8: Using the model by asking 'what if...?'

By altering the numbers in the model we can see what happens to the profit. You must remember to return the other numbers back to their values in the spreadsheet above so that you are only varying one quantity at a time.

1. What if only 150 tickets were sold? Would we still make a profit and what would it be?

2. Ashia suggests that we should sell tickets to Year 8 as well. There are 200 students in Year 8 and added to the number in Year 7 this gives a total of 420 students.

   How much profit would be made if 420 tickets were sold?

3. James thinks that £3.00 a ticket is quite a lot to pay. What would be the profit if the price of a ticket was reduced to £2.50?

4. Ashia has volunteered to make the tickets herself using her computer at home. She will print the tickets as they are sold. The cost of the tickets will now be 1p per ticket. What will the profit be now?

5. How many tickets would need to be sold to break even? This would be the number of tickets that gives as near to zero pounds as the profit/loss. You will need to try lots of different numbers of tickets sold to arrive at this answer.

Make it happen

ACTIVITY 9: Developing the model

This model is quite simple. We often have to develop the model to include things we did not think of at first. Developing a model makes it more realistic.

Ashia decides that to make more profit they can sell soft drinks and crisps. She obtains the following costs from the cash and carry:

Cost of one can of soft drink: *£0.23*
Cost of one packet of crisps: *£0.14*

James and Ashia decide to sell the drinks and crisps for the following prices:

Selling price of one can of soft drink: *£0.40*
Selling price of one packet of crisps: *£0.30*

Note

You can access this file via the 'Activity Files' link at www.oxfordsecondary.co.uk

1. Load the file Disco Model 2. Check you have the correct model by comparing it with the following:

	A	B	C
1	**Name: Stephen Doyle**	**Class: 7E**	
2	**A Model to show the profit or loss for a disco**		
3			
4	Price for printing one ticket	£0.01	
5	Number of tickets sold	300	
6	Ticket price	£2.50	
7			
8	**Income**		
9	Money from ticket sales	£750.00	
10	Total income	£750.00	
11			
12	**Costs**		
13	Hire of disco and DJ	£60.00	
14	Cost of printing all tickets	£3.00	
15	Total costs	£63.00	
16			
17	**Profit/Loss**	£687.00	
18			

2 Each student will probably buy one can of soft drink and one packet of crisps during the evening.

The cost and selling price of each can of drink need to be added to the variable section of the model.

The cost and selling price of each packet of crisps need to be added to the variable section of the model.

Add this information (you will need to know how to insert a row to do this).

3 We now need some formulae to work out the income from the sale of drinks and crisps and also the costs of buying them.

We need:

- a formula to work out the cost of all the drinks from the cash and carry
- a formula to work out the cost of all the crisps from the cash and carry
- a new formula to work out the total costs.

We also need:

- a formula to work out the income from the sale of all the soft drinks
- a formula to work out the income from the sale of all the crisps
- a formula to work out the total income for the disco.

We also need suitable labels for the above.

Add all of this to your model.

EXTENSION ACTIVITY

Two teachers are needed to supervise the disco. The teachers offer their services free but they will need to cover the overtime for the caretaker who will need to be on the premises to clear away and to check the building and lock up. The cost of the caretaker is as follows:

Caretaking costs: *£12 per hour*

Add this to your model.

Make the changes to your spreadsheet to calculate the new profit/loss.

Save your work and then produce a printout.

Where do all the frogs go?

Background

Vicky says: 'In the spring my pond is full of frogspawn. If all the frogspawn changed into frogs my garden would be overrun with them. I hardly see any, so what happens to them?'

In the spring, Vicky took a small sample of frogspawn and put it into an aquarium to watch it grow. She noticed the following:

- Not all the frogspawn hatched – this might be because it was not fertilised
- Only about 70% of the spawn produced tadpoles
- Not all the tadpoles lived to turn into frogs. From Vicky's sample she estimated that of all the tadpoles that hatched only about 30% lived to become frogs.

REMEMBER!

Understanding the problem is essential for creating a good, realistic model.

Make it happen

ACTIVITY 10: Modelling frogspawn

For the following tasks you will need to work in a small group. Each task will need careful thought and it will be easier if you work on it together.

Task 1: Making the model

You have to produce a model where Vicky can input the number of eggs in a sample of frogspawn and the model will predict the number that will survive to produce frogs.

Task 2: Altering the model

Vicky kept her frogspawn in an aquarium. In the aquarium there were no predators, such as insects, fish and birds. Make your model more realistic by building this factor into it.

Are there any other factors that you could take into account? Add these to the model.

Save your model and produce a printout.

Produce a short piece of text using wordprocessing software to explain how you have constructed these extensions to your model.

Lesson 5: HOW MANY PIANO TUNERS ARE THERE IN LIVERPOOL?

Background

When you are asked a question in mathematics you are used to getting a right or a wrong answer. Real-life problems are very complicated and it is hard – almost impossible – to get a right answer. Instead we look for the best solution to the problem. The best solution to a problem will give the best answer.

Here is a problem to which it would be difficult to find a perfect answer. We want to know how many piano tuners there are in Liverpool. We could look in the Yellow Pages to see adverts for piano tuners. Maybe piano tuners belong to some trade organisation and we could ask them.

In this activity we will produce a model which hopefully will give us a good answer.

Make it happen

ACTIVITY 11: Planning and building a model

Task 1: Doing some research

Where can I find the population of Liverpool? The government collects facts and figures. It needs this information to make plans, such as how many schools to build (or close down), how many doctors need to be trained, and so on. There is a site on the Internet containing these facts and figures.

Access the following site using the Internet:

www.statistics.gov.uk/census2001/pop2001/united_kingdom.asp

Using this site select the area North West and then the city Liverpool.

You will now see an interesting table showing the population at various ages. Look for the total population on this page and write it down.

Age Range	Total	Males	Females
0 - 4	24869	12813	12056
5 - 9	26688	13801	12887
10 - 14	30789	15740	15049
15 - 19	33626	16826	16800
20 - 24	37115	17162	19953
25 - 29	29194	13556	15638
30 - 34	31175	15471	15704
35 - 39	32833	15417	17416
40 - 44	31188	14858	16330
45 - 49	26571	12810	13761
50 - 54	26987	13259	13728
55 - 59	20453	10053	10400
60 - 64	20895	10217	10678
65 - 69	19805	9477	10328
70 - 74	17889	8068	9821
75 - 79	13476	5320	8156
80 - 84	8736	3080	5656
85 - 89	4926	1387	3539
90 and over	2261	470	1791
Totals	439476	209785	229691

Print out a copy of this page.

Liverpool has a population of around 440,000.

Task 2: Thinking about the rules

The model will be created using the population of Liverpool. There are five questions we need to consider.

1. *How many pianos are in schools?*

   Most schools have a piano, but how do we find how many schools there are?

   We can use the table to look for the number of people in the age range 5–18. We will add up the totals for the age ranges 5–9, 10–14, and 15–19. The extra year here will not make much difference as we have not estimated for nurseries and playschools, etc. The total number of pupils in the population comes to about 91,000.

We now think about the average number of pupils per school. Junior and primary schools are much smaller than senior schools. Seven hundred pupils per school is about right.

If we divide the average number of pupils per school into the total number of schools, this will give the total number of schools. We will assume that each school has one piano.

2 *How many pianos are in homes?*

If we say that the average number of people in each household is three, then we can work out the number of households by dividing the population by 3.

We then consider what percentage might have a piano. This is quite hard, but we can say 3% (i.e. 3 in very 100).

The number of pianos in all the households can be found by finding 3% of the number of households.

3 *How many other pianos are there?*

We then need to consider the other places where pianos are used, such as theatres, dance schools and bars. One hundred seems a reasonable estimate.

4 *How is the total number of pianos found?*

The total number of pianos can now be found by adding up the numbers in schools, homes and theatres, etc.

5 *How do we find the number of piano tuners?*

We can estimate that a piano tuner would, on average, tune two pianos per day and would work about 200 days per year. By multiplying these two amounts we can work out the number of pianos tuned by each piano tuner each year.

However, pianos are not normally tuned every year. We can estimate that the average piano is tuned every four years. We can now divide the total number of pianos by the frequency (four in this case) to give the number of pianos tuned each year. This result is then divided by the number of pianos tuned per piano tuner to give the total number of piano tuners.

Task 3: Building the model

1 Load the spreadsheet software.

2 Type in the following headings and labels. Labels are used to describe the data that goes into a nearby cell.

	A	B	C	D	E
1	**Model to estimate the number of piano tuners in Liverpool**				
2					
3	**Finding out the number of pianos**				**Number of pianos**
4	Population				
5					
6	Number of population of school age				
7	Average number of pupils per school				
8	Number of schools				
9					
10	Average number of people in each household				
11	Number of households				
12	Percentage of households with a piano				
13	Total number of pianos in these households				
14					
15	Number of theatres, dance schools, bars etc. with pianos				
16				**Total pianos**	
17	Number of pianos tuned each day				
18	Number of days worked per year				
19	Number of pianos tuned in one year per tuner				
20					
21	Frequency with which average piano is tuned (every)		years		
22	Number of pianos tuned per year				
23					
24	**Number of piano tuners**				

3. Enter the number *440000* into cell B4, *91000* into cell B6, and *700* into cell B7.
4. Enter the formula *=B6/B7* into cell B8.
5. Enter the number *3* into cell B10.
6. Enter the formula *=B4/B10* into cell B11.
7. Enter *3%* into cell B12.
8. Enter the formula *=B12*B11* into cell B13.
9. Enter the number *100* into cell B15.
10. Enter the number *2* into cell B17 and *200* into cell B18.
11. Enter the formula *=B17*B18* into cell B19.
12. We now need to put the number of pianos into column E. Enter *=B8* into cell E8, *=B13* into cell E13 and *=B15* into cell E15.
13. Add up the total number of pianos by putting a formula in cell E16.
14. Put the formula *=E16/B21* into cell B22, to work out the number of pianos tuned per year.
15. To find the total number of pianos, enter *=SUM(E8:E15)* into cell E16.

Note

'3%' is still regarded as a number even though there is a percentage sign.

16 To find the number of pianos tuned per year, enter the formula *=E16/B21* into cell B22.

17 To work out the number of piano tuners in Liverpool, we divide the number of pianos tuned per year by the number of pianos tuned in one year per tuner. Enter the formula for this *=B22/B19* into cell B24.

18 Format cell B24 to integer, so that it shows the nearest whole number. To do this click on **Cells** in the 'Format' menu. Change the 'number' format to 0 decimal places.

19 Check that your spreadsheet is identical to this one:

	A	B	C	D	E
1	**Model to estimate the number of piano tuners in Liverpool**				
2					
3	**Finding out the number of pianos**				**Number of pianos**
4	Population	440000			
5					
6	Number of population of sc1ool age	91000			
7	Average number of pupils per school	700			
8	Number of schools	130			130
9					
10	Average number of people in each household	3			
11	Number of households	146666.7			
12	Percentage of households with a piano	3%			
13	Total number of pianos in these households	4400			4400
14					
15	Number of theatres, dance schools, bars etc. with pianos	100			100
16				**Total pianos**	**4630**
17	Number of pianos tuned each day	2			
18	Number of days worked pe' year	200			
19	Number of pianos tuned in one year per tuner	400			
20					
21	Frequency with which average piano is tuned (every)	4	years		
22	Number of pianos tuned per year	1157.5			
23					
24	**Number of piano tuners**	3			

20 Type in your name and class in a suitable place on the spreadsheet.

Save your model using the name 'How many piano tuners'.

Print out a copy of the model.

Task 4: Experimenting with the model

1 Load the model 'How many piano tuners'.

2 More thought has been given to some of the numbers used. Here are the alterations to the spreadsheet you need to make:

(a) More and more people are living on their own so reduce the 'Average number of people in each household' to 2.

(b) The number of theatres, dance schools, etc. needs to be changed from 100 to 200.

(c) The number of days worked per year needs increasing to 210.

Make these alterations.

3 Save this altered spreadsheet using the file name 'How many piano tuners version 2'.

4 Print out a copy of this spreadsheet, making sure that all the spreadsheet is on one page.

5 Using this model, write down the number of piano tuners in Liverpool.

EXTENSION ACTIVITY

You will now find out how many piano tuners there are in your nearest town/city.

Use the website to find the page containing the population and also the number of pupils of school age. Print out a copy of this page.

Alter the spreadsheet created in Task 3 (called 'How many piano tuners') so that the number of piano tuners in your town/city is worked out.

Now consider how some of the numbers in your town/city might differ (other than the population and the number at school). Make suitable alterations to the spreadsheet and save it using a suitable file name. Print out a copy of the spreadsheet.

Mark on your spreadsheet the figures you have altered and your reasons for altering them.

QUESTIONS

1 Explain one way that this type of model could be tested.

2 Some of the numbers have been an educated guess. Give two examples of numbers used in the spreadsheet where it might be possible to find out more accurate numbers.

3 This model can be re-used for any town or city. Explain what two main variables would change from one town/city to another.

Make it happen

ACTIVITY 12: Making your own models

Background

Up to now you have been guided through the things you have to do to create a computer model. It is important to be able to make up your own models from scratch. Here is a model for you to try.

How far is it worth travelling to get cheaper petrol?

Petrol varies from one petrol station to another. Some people will drive a few miles to the cheapest petrol station, but is it worth it? You could end up worse off because you will use petrol getting to the petrol station and back.

You need to produce a computer model using spreadsheet software to answer the following questions:

- Is it worth filling up from a distant petrol station or is it better to fill up at a near one even though it might be more expensive?
- How far is it worth travelling to save money on a tank of petrol?

EXTENSION ACTIVITY

Are there any other factors apart from the cost of the petrol? What about the time factor? Try to build this and other factors into your model.

5 Data handling

Lesson 1:
INTRODUCTION TO DATA HANDLING

Why and how do we collect data?

In this unit you will learn what a hypothesis is and how data can be collected to prove or disprove a hypothesis. You will learn how to collect data using questionnaires and how questions can be asked so that they cannot be misinterpreted. You will also look at how to ask questions in a way that makes processing of the data easier.

Data from questionnaires will be entered into a specially created database structure. This database structure will make use of validation checks to eliminate as many errors as possible. This unit will also look at how, once stored, the data can be processed to provide useful information in the form of statistics (mean, mode, etc.).

KEY WORDS

data – raw facts and figures entered into a computer

database – a series of tables/lists stored in a computer that can be accessed in a variety of ways

hypothesis – a statement that can be proved or disproved (i.e. proved right or wrong)

Why collect data?

By collecting data you can get answers to questions. These questions can be on just about anything. Here are some examples of questions:

- What percentage of Year 7 students in our school own their own computer?
- What is the most popular sport played in our school?
- What is the most popular sport watched by students in our school?
- What sport or leisure facility is needed most in the area where you live?
- Are boys taller than girls at all ages or just some?
- What is the average rainfall in Blackpool in July?
- According to the school tuck shop, which is the most popular flavour of crisp?

All of the above questions could be answered if data could be collected. The data you would need to collect to answer a question depends on the type of question.

Take, for example, the first question in the bulleted list on the previous page:

- What percentage of Year 7 students own their own computer?

This question could be answered by asking all the Year 7 students in the school if they had their own computer.

You can see that to answer questions, you need data. Sometimes the data you need is too difficult to collect yourself. For example, if you wanted to know the average weekly wage, this would be impossible to do yourself.

Luckily other people collect data, so you can sometimes use this to answer your question. The government collects data about everyone and this data can be used by anybody if needed. They conduct what is called a census, which asks lots of questions about everyone's household.

Questionnaires

KEY WORDS

questionnaire – a document containing questions, which is filled in to supply information

If you go on a package holiday abroad you will often be given a questionnaire to fill in at the end of the holiday. The holiday company uses your answers to their questions to find out how you enjoyed your holiday. They want to know about the things you liked as well as the things you disliked. They can then use the results of the questionnaires to improve the holidays and travel arrangements for next year.

Without these questionnaires the holiday companies would not know what people really thought about the holiday.

There are two main reasons for getting holidaymakers to fill in questionnaires:

1 *To provide feedback* – what people thought of the flight, the transfers, the accommodation, the food, trips, etc.

2 *To provide useful information about their customers* – how many holidays they take, what time of year they book, what papers they read, their ages, and so on.

Take a look at the following holiday questionnaire. There are lots of questions. Each one is asked for a purpose. With some questions, the purpose is easy to spot but with others it is harder.

See if you can identify the reason the holiday company is asking each of these questions.

On-line questionnaires provide a quick way of seeking lots of opinions. The advantage of these is that they do not cost much, as there is no need for postage, an envelope, etc. The disadvantage is that the people who reply are not representative of the population as a whole.

Global Holidays Questionnaire

Please [X] the appropriate box, or write in as requested

1. Your details

Title ______ **Initial** ______ **Other initials** ______
Surname ______
Partner's title ______ **Initial** ______ **Other initials** ______
Surname ______
Address ______

______ **Postcode** ______
Daytime tel. no ______
Mobile no ______
Preferred e-mail address* ______

Today's date ____/____/____

2. Your holiday details

A Which holiday company are you with?

Taylors ☐ Skyways Direct ☐
Worldtours ☐ Budget ☐
Lifestyle ☐
Other → (write in) ☐

B The name of your hotel/villa/apartments:
(name all accommodation stayed in)

☐

C Number of nights abroad:

6 or less ☐ 7 ☐ 8–13 ☐ 15–20 ☐ 21 or more ☐

D Board arrangements:

Bed and breakfast ☐ Self catering ☐
Half board ☐ Flexible dining (combining B/B & H/B) ☐
Full board ☐ All inclusive (all meals, drinks etc. included) ☐
Room only ☐

E If accommodation not included in your holiday price, was this an airfare/flight only to:

Own accommodation ☐ Independently booked accommodation ☐
Flydrive (flight & car rental only) ☐ Other ☐

F Did you use a brochure to select your holiday?

Yes ☐ No ☐

If yes, how accurate was the brochure description of your:

	Excellent	Good	Fair	Poor
a) Accommodation	☐	☐	☐	☐
b) Resort	☐	☐	☐	☐

G How did you book this holiday?

In a Travel Agency ☐ On the Internet ☐
Phoned Tour Operator/Travel Agency direct ☐ Other ☐

3. Flights

How would you rate:	Excellent	Good	Fair	Poor
A UK airport check-in	☐	☐	☐	☐
B Overseas airport check-in	☐	☐	☐	☐
C In-flight comfort	☐	☐	☐	☐
D Cabin interior appearance/cleanliness	☐	☐	☐	☐
E In-flight food	☐	☐	☐	☐
F Cabin crew: friendliness	☐	☐	☐	☐
G Cabin crew: service and assistance	☐	☐	☐	☐
H In-flight TV/radio	☐	☐	☐	☐
I Flights overall	☐	☐	☐	☐

4. Your accommodation

How would you rate:	Excellent	Good	Fair	Poor
A Rep's service	☐	☐	☐	☐
B Location	☐	☐	☐	☐
C Cleanliness	☐	☐	☐	☐
D Bedroom comfort	☐	☐	☐	☐
E Food quality	☐	☐	☐	☐
F Waiter service/buffet efficiency	☐	☐	☐	☐
G Accommodation overall	☐	☐	☐	☐
H Daytime activities and leisure facilities	☐	☐	☐	☐
I Evening entertainment	☐	☐	☐	☐
J Children's clubs	☐	☐	☐	☐
K Children's reps	☐	☐	☐	☐

5. In-resort service

How would you rate:	Excellent	Good	Fair	Poor
A Rep greeting on arrival at overseas airport	☐	☐	☐	☐
B Transfer journey to and from your accommodation	☐	☐	☐	☐
C On departure overseas: information given by Rep	☐	☐	☐	☐

Did you:	Yes	No
D Ask your Rep for any help or advice?	☐	☐
E Go to the welcome meeting?	☐	☐
F Go on any company excursions?	☐	☐
G Buy any excursions from another company?	☐	☐

6. Overall

Taking everything into account, how would you rate:

	Excellent	Good	Fair	Poor
A Resort	☐	☐	☐	☐
B Weather	☐	☐	☐	☐
C Reps	☐	☐	☐	☐
D Value for money	☐	☐	☐	☐
E Holiday company overall	☐	☐	☐	☐

F Holiday company service in resort compared to other package holiday companies travelled with:

Better ☐ Same ☐ Worse ☐

7. Holiday experience

A Have you been on a package holiday to this resort in the last two years? Yes ☐ No ☐

B Not counting this one, how many holidays abroad have you taken in the last 12 months?

	None	1	2	3+
a) With Taylors	☐	☐	☐	☐
b) With Worldtours	☐	☐	☐	☐
c) With other package holiday companies	☐	☐	☐	☐

C Where did you go for your last package holiday abroad?

Mainland Spain ☐ Greece (inc. islands) ☐ Majorca ☐
Canary Islands ☐ Florida ☐ Malta ☐
Portugal/Madeira ☐ Ibiza ☐ Cyprus ☐
Morocco/Tunisia/Egypt ☐ Caribbean ☐ Minorca ☐
Other (Europe) ☐ Other (Rest of the world) ☐

8. About you

A What is:

Your date of birth? ______ Your partner's? ______
Are you: (a) Male ☐ Female ☐
(b) Married ☐ Single ☐
Divorced/Separated ☐ Widowed ☐ Living with Partner ☐

B Are you:

In full/part time employment or self employed ☐
A full time housewife/househusband ☐ A student ☐
Retired ☐ Otherwise not employed ☐

8. About you cont.

C If you are in employment, which best describes the type of job you do, or if retired, the last job you did?

Skilled trade/craft ☐
Plant and machine operator/driver etc ☐
Foreman/supervisor ☐
Manual worker/factory worker ☐
Service worker (e.g. shop assistant/cleaner/catering/caretaker/goods delivery) ☐
Clerical/secretarial/other office work ☐
Technical (e.g. programmer/technician/nurse/representative) ☐
Junior management/junior professions/executive ☐
Senior and middle management/professions ☐
Other → (write in) ☐

D If unwell during your holiday, please specify:

Sunstroke/sunburn ☐ Infection ☐
Stomach upset (lasting more than 24 hours) ☐ Other ☐

E Does your home contents insurance cover items taken abroad? Yes ☐ No ☐

F In which month is your home contents insurance renewed? ______

G Whilst on holiday did you park your car at the airport? Yes ☐ No ☐

H In which month is your motor insurance renewed? ______

I Where do you live?

Own home (with mortgage) ☐ Own home (no mortgage) ☐
With parents ☐ Renting privately ☐ Renting from Council ☐

J When did you move to this address?

month ______ year ______

K How many times a year do you fly?

Never ☐ 1–4 ☐ 5–9 ☐ 10+ ☐

L Where do you fly?

Within the UK ☐ Europe ☐
Middle East ☐ Far East ☐ Latin America ☐
North America ☐ Australasia ☐ Other ☐

M Which newspapers do you read? (Please name)

a) Daily ______
b) Sunday ______

N In total, how much money do you estimate you and your party spent while on holiday? (Exclude flights & accommodation)

Up to £750 ☐ £751–£1000 ☐ £1001–£1250 ☐
£1251–£1500 ☐ £1501–£2000 ☐ Over £2000 ☐

O Which group in £000's best describes your COMBINED household income?

0–10 ☐ 11–15 ☐ 16–20 ☐ 21–25 ☐ 26–30 ☐
31–35 ☐ 36–40 ☐ 41–50 ☐ 51–60 ☐ 60+ ☐

P What are your interests and hobbies?

Golf ☐ Wild life/Environment ☐ Fashion/Clothes ☐
Dogs ☐ Gourmet Foods/Wines ☐ Health Foods ☐
CD's/Tapes ☐ Investments/Savings ☐ Books/Reading ☐
Cats ☐ Home Computing ☐ Excercise/Sport ☐
Gardening ☐ Hiking/Walking ☐ Theatre/Arts ☐

Q Did you place your unused change in the charity envelope provided?

Yes ☐ No ☐ No change left ☐

R What type of charity do you tend to support?

Health ☐ Third world ☐ Church ☐
Pets ☐ Youth ☐ Environment ☐
Wildlife ☐ Local Charities ☐ Childrens ☐

KEY WORDS

Internet Service Provider – a company that provides you with a connection to the Internet via their server

The Internet Service Provider AOL (America On Line) is seeking opinion on which is the most powerful celebrity couple

What is a hypothesis?

A hypothesis is a statement that can be proved or disproved. A hypothesis can therefore be proved right or wrong.

Here is a hypothesis:

Taller people, on average, have bigger feet.

How might you go about proving or disproving this statement? One way might be to collect your own data – you would need lots of pairs of measurements of shoe size and height. Once a large sample has been collected, you can set about seeing if the hypothesis is true or false.

Look at the small sample of data on the right showing height and shoe size. It is quite hard to tell from this data whether the hypothesis is true or false.

The data needs to be presented differently to help us decide. You often have to do something to the data (i.e. process it) to help you decide. Presenting the data graphically often aids our understanding of it.

On this scatter graph height is plotted against shoe size. A trend line (sometimes called the line of best fit) has been put in which is a line that shows the direction in which most points lie. This type of graph, called a scattergraph makes it easy to see that the hypothesis is true.

Height	Shoe size
183	11
167	6
169	6.5
172	8.5
175	8
174	7
180	10
178	9
181	10.5
173	7.5
168	7
175	7.5

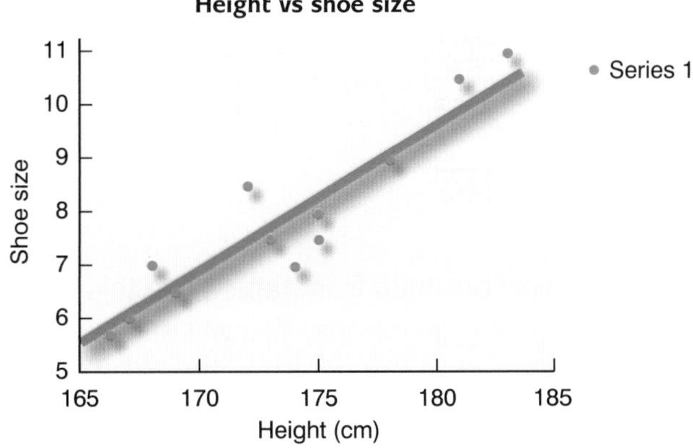

You can see that as a person's height increases then so does their shoe size. Data is often presented in different formats to test hypotheses. You should always choose the clearest way to present your data.

REMEMBER!

A line is drawn so that the distance to the points on either side of the line is the same. This is a called the trend line (or the line of the best fit).

WORKSHEETWORKSHEETWORKSHEETWORKSHEETWORKSHEET

WORKSHEET 7.5.1 Reading data from tables

Here is a table that shows the population distribution for Liverpool. This table was produced by the government after the census in 2001.

Age Range	Total	Males	Females	Difference
0 - 4	24840	12828	12012	-816
5 - 9	26670	13792	12878	-914
10 - 14	30771	15731	15040	-691
15 - 19	33626	16826	16800	-26
20 - 24	37112	17160	19952	2792
25 - 29	29194	13556	15638	2082
30 - 34	31175	15471	15704	233
35 - 39	32833	15417	17416	1999
40 - 44	31188	14858	16330	1472
45 - 49	26571	12810	13761	951
50 - 54	26987	13259	13728	469
55 - 59	20453	10053	10400	347
60 - 64	20895	10217	10678	461
65 - 69	19805	9477	10328	851
70 - 74	17889	8068	9821	1753
75 - 79	13541	5345	8196	2851
80 - 84	8736	3080	5656	2576
85 - 89	4925	1386	3539	2153
90 and over	2262	471	1791	1320
Totals	439473	209805	229668	

Note

The smallest sized number (positive or negative) shows the age range that has the least difference between the numbers of males and females.

You have to be able to understand how to find out data from tables like this one. Use the table above to answer the following questions. You will either be given a worksheet on which to write your answers or your teacher will ask you to write your answers in your book. When you have finished, your teacher will go through the answers.

1. What is the total population for Liverpool as shown in this table?
2. What is the total number of people between the ages of 10 and 14?
3. How many boys are there between the ages of 10 and 14?
4. How many girls are there between the ages of 10 and 14?
5. In the whole of Liverpool, and for all ages, are there more males or females?
6. Briefly explain a reason for your answer to question 5.
7. You would expect there to be equal numbers of males and females. In which age group is the number of males nearest to the number of females?
8. In which age group is there the greatest difference between the number of males and females?

What you should already know

You will need to know the basics of spreadsheets before starting this unit.

You will have used spreadsheets in your work for Key Stage 2. In this unit most of this Key Stage 2 knowledge will be assumed. Spreadsheets were also covered in Unit 4 'Modelling and presenting numeric data'. Your teacher has help sheets that he or she may supply or that you can ask for. Try to do the work on your own if you can and remember that you can always use the 'Help' supplied by the software.

You will also need to have an understanding of what databases are and how they are used.

In particular, you should already know:

- what a database is and what the terms 'record', 'field' and 'file' mean
- how to collect information using questionnaires
- how to produce pie charts to present information
- how to evaluate information and check for plausibility and accuracy.

What you will learn

In this unit you will:

- learn how to collect data to prove or disprove a hypothesis
- learn how to analyse data
- create a database structure to hold the collected data
- represent information (text, tables, graphs and charts) in the most suitable form
- prepare reports containing information suitable for the intended audience
- check data for accuracy.

WORKSHEETWORKSHEETWORKSHEETWORKSHEETWORKSHEET

WORKSHEET 7.5.2 How much do you already know about databases?

You should already know a bit about databases from your Key Stage 2 work. How much of it can you remember though? This topic introduces a lot of new terms.

Below are some basic questions to test your knowledge. You may be given a worksheet on which to write your answers or you may be asked to write your answers into your book. When you have finished, your teacher will either go through the answers or give you an answer sheet so that you can check

your answers yourself. You should have learnt most of this work when you did your Key Stage 2 work.

1. Some terms and their definitions have been mixed up. Sort them out and copy them into your book in the correct order.

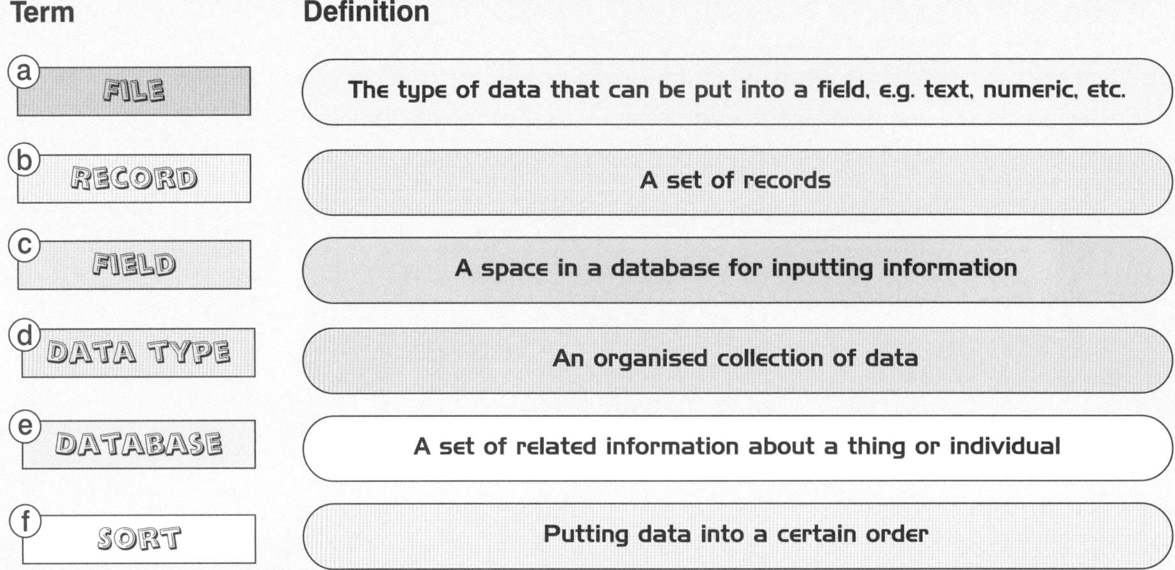

2. Here is a database set up using spreadsheet software:

	A	B	C	D	E	F	G
1	**Surname**	**Forename**	**Gender**	**Date of Birth**	**Year Group**	**Registration Group**	**Admission Number**
2	Hughes	Stephen	M	19/12/1984	11	L	121221
3	Chaudrey	Saleha	F	17/12/1987	8	F	110900
4	Robinson	Peter	M	18/09/1987	9	G	110899
5	Green	Amy	F	11/06/1986	9	H	150078
6	Roberts	Darren	M	18/11/1984	11	L	121897
7	Harman	Paul	M	11/05/1985	10	I	138988
8	King	Jason	M	11/07/1985	10	I	138971
9	Scott	Susan	F	04/06/1989	6	A	140087
10	Adams	Victoria	F	03/04/1989	6	B	140075
11	Wilson	Pamela	F	01/02/1988	7	C	149999
12	Mason	Veronica	F	03/08/1989	6	B	140090
13	Wiliams	Paul	M	01/02/1984	11	L	121223
14	Ferris	Jack	M	09/07/1989	6	B	140091
15	Corkhill	Kylie	F	01/02/1989	11	L	121223
16	Furlong	John	M	01/05/1989	11	K	121200

Using words from the following list, copy and complete sentences (a) to (d).

record
field
field name
item of data

(a) Surname is an example of a ....

(b) A row of data in the table is called a ....

(c) The first row in the table (i.e. the one in bold) represents the ....

(d) The admission number 121221 is an example of an ....

3. Explain the difference between the words 'data' and 'information'.

Lesson 2: COLLECTING DATA TO TEST A HYPOTHESIS

Background: asking questions

Once you have one or more hypotheses to test you then need to collect the relevant data. One way of collecting data is to use questionnaires.

What are questionnaires and why are they used?

Questionnaires enable people's views and opinions to be obtained by using a series of carefully constructed questions. Questionnaires provide data for further processing. The results from a questionnaire can be entered into a database structure to make further processing easy. This processing could be producing some further calculations, such as percentages, means, modes, etc. or it could be putting the data into a different order by sorting it or only selecting data with certain characteristics.

REMEMBER!

Questionaires are used to obtain data for processing.

Who do you give questionnaires to?

In Unit 2 you came across the words 'sample' and 'population'. Check that you understand these two words and if not take a look back.

If the population is small, such as your ICT group, or the group of Year 7 students, it may be possible to give the questionnaire to the entire population. If the population is large, you will need to give the questionnaire to a representative sample.

Types of questions

There are a number of different types of questions, namely:

- open questions
- closed questions
- ranking questions.

If you cannot remember what each type is, take a look back at Unit 2.

Testing a questionnaire

Sometimes the questions you ask will be confusing to the person answering them. They may misinterpret the question or they simply may not understand what answers are required. A good questionnaire can be answered without any further explanation of the questions. When making up questions always look at them carefully to see if they can be misinterpreted.

To test a questionnaire you can give it to a few people to answer. These people do not need to be part of the sample. You are just seeing if they understand the questions. Any questions that they do not understand can be changed. It is much better to spot these questions now than to get lots of questionnaires back with the questions unanswered or – even worse – with misinterpretations of the questions answered.

WORKSHEETWORKSHEETWORKSHEETWORKSHEETWORKSHEET

WORKSHEET 7.5.3 Good and bad questions

Below are some questions to be answered by Year 7 students. You have to spot and write down what is wrong with them.

1. What is your height?
2. What do you weigh?
3. How much time do you spend surfing the Internet?
4. How many cars do you own?

WORKSHEET 7.5.4 Rephrase the question

In the previous worksheet you saw that questions need to be precise so that they are not misinterpreted.

Rephrase the questions in Worksheet 7.5.3 to make them more precise.

WORKSHEETWORKSHEETWORKSHEETWORKSHEETWORKSHEET

WORKSHEET 7.5.5 **Making questions to give you data**

To test a hypothesis, you need to collect data. Write down what data you would need to test each of the following hypotheses:

1. The wettest month where you live is March.
2. The favourite meal in your class is pizza.
3. 80% of Year 7 students have their own mobile phone.
4. 90% of Year 7 students think that CDs are too expensive.
5. Three out of every ten students have admitted to copying CDs or software illegally.
6. The most popular holiday destination of Year 7 students is Spain.
7. The most popular boy's name in the school is Jack.

Using a questionnaire to try to find out what makes one person more popular than others

You may notice that some of your friends are very popular at school. You are interested to find out why and have decided to conduct a survey to find out.

You would like to find out the feature which most people rank the highest in a popular person. Here are the features you think are important and you would like to see how high they rank:

1 being good at school work

2 being good at sports

3 being attractive

4 having a good sense of humour

5 having lots of money.

Rather than simply ask 'Which is the most important quality?' you decide to ask your fellow students to put them in order of importance according to the following scale:

1 'most important' to 5 'least important'

This means they have to allocate all the numbers from one to five to the questions **1** to **5**. The advantage in doing this is that you can add up the scores people give for each feature. It makes processing of the data quite easy. You can also look at the number of 1s, 2s, 3s, 4s and 5s for each question.

Designing the questionnaire

Apart from asking the questions above, you need to think about if there are any other ways you might use the data. For example you might want to compare the response from girls and boys separately to see if there are any differences. If you intend to do this, you will need to ask whether they are male or female on the questionnaire.

Always think of hypotheses to prove or disprove as you are writing your questions. For example you may think that boys will think that looks are most popular. If you think that the way these questions are answered varies with age, then you would need to record the age of the person answering.

Do you need to record the name of the person answering the questions on the questionnaire?

You may get more honest answers to your questionaires if they are answered anonymously.

Sometimes you need to know who has answered the questions. In some cases, especially when the questions are a little personal, the person answering may prefer to remain anonymous. The questionnaire we are looking at here is quite personal, so it will be better to leave off the names or any other information that might identify the person filling it in.

If the data you collect is personal and it is about an identifiable person, to comply with the law you would need to register your use of the data with the Information Commissioner. There is a law called the Data Protection Act 1998, which covers the processing of personal information. The aim of this law is to protect personal data from being misused.

Producing the questionnaire

Once you have thought about any hypotheses you are testing, you can set about producing the questionnaire similar to the one opposite. Underneath is an example of the completed questionaire.

Using a database to test a hypothesis

Once the questionnaires have been completed and collected, the database structure needed to hold the answers is built. The fields to hold the answers are decided upon and the data is then entered into the database.

Questionnaire

Please answer the following questions to find out what makes some people more popular than others.

1 Are you

☐ Male? ☐ Female?

2 What is your age to the nearest whole year?

_________ years

3 Rank the following reasons why some people are more popular than others.
You need to place a number from one to five next to each reason.
1 = most important reason 5 = least important reason
(NB: all the numbers from one to five should be used.)

Being good at school work	________
Being good at sport	________
Being attractive	________
Having a good sense of humour	________
Having lots of money	________

Thank you for your time.

Questionnaire

Please answer the following questions to find out what makes some people more popular than others.

1 Are you

☐ Male? ☑ Female?

2 What is your age to the nearest whole year?

12 years

3 Rank the following reasons why some people are more popular than others.
You need to place a number from one to five next to each reason.
1 = most important reason 5 = least important reason
(NB: all the numbers from one to five should be used.)

Being good at school work	2
Being good at sport	3
Being attractive	1
Having a good sense of humour	5
Having lots of money	4

Thank you for your time.

Once all the data has been entered, the database can be used to test hypotheses such as 'do girls think having lots of money is the main reason for being popular?'.

Spotting a wrong item of data

KEY WORDS

dirty data – an obviously wrong item of data

When you look at data you can spot data that is obviously incorrect. If you use this data, your results or the conclusions you reach will be wrong. Wildly wrong data will distort your results, so you need to be able to spot it and remove it so that it is not processed by the computer.

Spotting obvious mistakes is easy. You can do this by looking through the answers to questionnaires or tables of the data.

When data is being entered into the computer it is possible to use the computer program to check the data being entered. Spreadsheet and database software can check the data as it is being entered to spot obvious errors. The problem is that you can only spot some errors. Data containing lots of obvious errors is called dirty data.

WORKSHEETWORKSHEETWORKSHEETWORKSHEETWORKSHEET

WORKSHEET 7.5.6 Spot the dirty data

Your teacher will give you a worksheet on which to work or a photocopy of the following table which has data containing errors (called dirty data).

Here is some of the data from the popularity questionnaires. Before data is processed to produce results, the dirty data should be identified and removed.

You have to spot the dirty items of data in the table and put a circle around them.

For each circle, you should say why the data it contains is dirty data.

A spreadsheet to hold the results of the popularity questionnaire

Sex	Age	Being good at school work	Being good at sport	Being attractive	Having a good sense of humour	Having lots of money
M	11	1	3	4	5	2
F		5	1	2	3	4
F	11	4	2	3	5	1
F	12	2	1	3	4	5
F	13	2	3	1	2	5
M	13	1	4	2	3	5
M	13	4	3	1	2	5
M	13	3	5	1	2	4
FM	13	5	2	1	3	4
F	13	4	3	1	2	5
M	111	4	1	2	4	3
F	12	3	1	2	4	5
M	11	5	3	1	2	5
F	13	2	3	1	5	4
F	12	3	4	2	5	1
F	13	3	1	2	4	5
M	11	2	3		5	4
F	12	4	3	2	1	5

What can you do about dirty data?

Dirty data contains obvious errors and if it is processed the results produced will be wrong. It is essential that these errors are spotted before the data is processed.

Here are some of the things you can do with dirty data:

- You can check the data and then correct it. Sometimes the questionnaires are numbered and these numbers are recorded on the spreadsheet. If there is an obvious mistake then it is possible to identify the questionnaire from which the data came in order to check it.
- You can delete the data. Rather than process records containing missing data or ridiculous data, it is better to simply delete the record.

Lesson 3: CREATING A STRUCTURE TO HOLD THE DATA

Databases

An organised store of data on a computer is called a database. The answers to the questionnaires need to be put into a structure on the computer so that further processing is made easy. A database can be created to hold these answers.

Choosing the software

There are two types of software you could use to process the results from a questionnaire:

- spreadsheet software
- database software.

You can build a simple database using spreadsheet software. In this database the columns represent each of the fields, and the rows are the records.

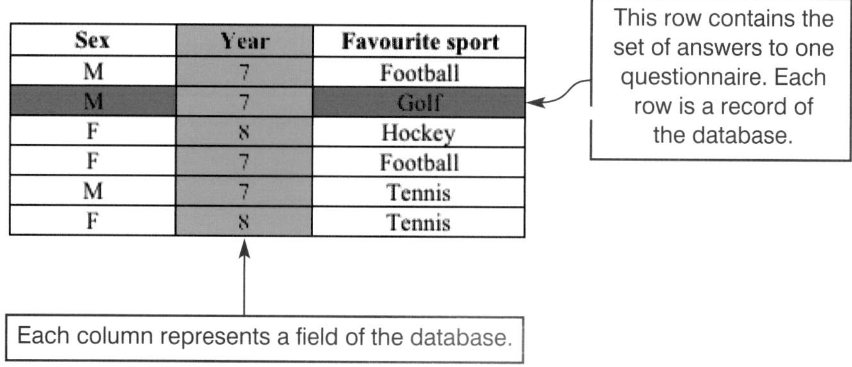

Sex	Year	Favourite sport
M	7	Football
M	7	Golf
F	8	Hockey
F	7	Football
M	7	Tennis
F	8	Tennis

Take a look at the above structure that is used to hold the answers to the following questions:

Sex? ....
Year at school? ....
Your favourite sport? ....

If you look at the diagram it is just like a list. When we are dealing with a database, we use the word 'table' rather than list.

Notice that the actual questions are used as the fields (i.e. Sex, Year, Favourite sport) and the results for each questionnaire given out are the rows in this table. These rows are the records, with each record holding the data for one questionnaire.

Why use spreadsheet software to produce a database?

It is very easy to use the spreadsheet as a database and then use the data to calculate means, modes, etc. and to produce graphs and charts.

Specialist database software is more difficult to use and for simple tasks such as analysing the results from questionnaires, the spreadsheet software is probably better.

Fields, records and files: What do they all mean?

There are some database terms you will need to familiarise yourself with. These are:

Data

These are facts about a specific person, place or thing.

Information

Information is data that has been processed into a form that is useful to the user.

Fields

A field is an item of data on the form. In other words it is a fact on the form. A surname would be an example of a field. A question in a questionnaire can be a field.

Records

A record is all the details relating to a particular thing or person. A record consists of fields. A record would be a row of data in a table.

Files

A collection of related records is called a file. The group of records for all the students in the school is called the student file. Often a simple file holding a single database is called a table.

Tables

In the databases we will be creating in this unit using spreadsheet software, only a single table is used. When only one table is used it is a very simple database and it is called a flat-file database.

For more complex databases created using specialist database software, lots of tables can be used. This is called a relational database. You will come across relational databases later on in your Key Stage 3 course.

Matching the fields to the questions in the questionnaire

Once the questionnaires have been filled in and returned you will then need to enter the answers into a database structure.

The database structure should be capable of holding all the answers to the questions in the questionnaire. For example if there is a question such as 'What is your sex?', there needs to be a field called 'Sex' as part of the database to hold the data (i.e. Male or Female).

Adding calculated fields

Sometimes in order to make data clearer you need to add an extra field that can be calculated from the other fields. An example of this would be percentages. In Activity 1, two extra fields will be added, and these can be used to present information in the table more clearly.

ACTIVITIES

Make it happen

ACTIVITY 1: Working out percentage figures

Sometimes it is better to present the data in a different form. For example, in the population distribution figures for Liverpool, it would be interesting to show how the percentages of males and females change for different age ranges.

For example, you might want to test a hypothesis such as 'I would expect the percentage of men to decrease with age, because I have heard that women outlive men'.

Note
You can access this file via the 'Activity Files' link at www.oxfordsecondary.co.uk

1. Load Excel and open the file 'Population distribution for Liverpool'.

Your teacher will tell you where this file is stored.

2. Check you have the correct file. Your spreadsheet should be the same as this one:

	A	B	C	D	E
1	**Age Range**	**Total**	**Males**	**Females**	**Difference**
2					
3	**0 - 4**	24840	12828	12012	-816
4	**5 - 9**	26670	13792	12878	-914
5	**10 - 14**	30771	15731	15040	-691
6	**15 - 19**	33626	16826	16800	-26
7	**20 - 24**	37112	17160	19952	2792
8	**25 - 29**	29194	13556	15638	2082
9	**30 - 34**	31175	15471	15704	233
10	**35 - 39**	32833	15417	17416	1999
11	**40 - 44**	31188	14858	16330	1472
12	**45 - 49**	26571	12810	13761	951
13	**50 - 54**	26987	13259	13728	469
14	**55 - 59**	20453	10053	10400	347
15	**60 - 64**	20895	10217	10678	461
16	**65 - 69**	19805	9477	10328	851
17	**70 - 74**	17889	8068	9821	1753
18	**75 - 79**	13541	5345	8196	2851
19	**80 - 84**	8736	3080	5656	2576
20	**85 - 89**	4925	1386	3539	2153
21	**90 and over**	2262	471	1791	1320
22	**Totals**	439473	209805	229668	

3. In cells F1 and G1 respectively, enter the headings *% Males* and *% Females*

4 In cell F3, add a formula to work out the percentage of males (no I'm not going to tell you!).

5 Check with your teacher that you have used the correct one and then copy this formula relatively down the column as far as cell F22.

6 In cell G3, add a formula to work out the percentage of females (again, you need to figure this out).

7 Check with your teacher that you have used the correct one and then copy this formula relatively down the column as far as cell G22.

8 Check that your results are the same as those shown here:

	A	B	C	D	E	F	G
1	**Age Range**	**Total**	**Males**	**Females**	**Difference**	**% Males**	**% Females**
2							
3	**0 - 4**	24840	12828	12012	-816	51.64251	48.35748792
4	**5 - 9**	26670	13792	12878	-914	51.71354	48.28646419
5	**10 - 14**	30771	15731	15040	-691	51.12281	48.87718956
6	**15 - 19**	33626	16826	16800	26	50.03866	49.96133944
7	**20 - 24**	37112	17160	19952	2792	46.23841	53.76158655
8	**25 - 29**	29194	13556	15638	2082	46.4342	53.56580119
9	**30 - 34**	31175	15471	15704	233	49.6263	50.37369687
10	**35 - 39**	32833	15417	17416	1999	46.95581	53.04419334
11	**40 - 44**	31188	14858	16330	1472	47.64012	52.35988201
12	**45 - 49**	26571	12810	13761	951	48.21046	51.78954499
13	**50 - 54**	26987	13259	13728	469	49.13106	50.8689369
14	**55 - 59**	20453	10053	10400	347	49.15171	50.84828631
15	**60 - 64**	20895	10217	10678	461	48.89687	51.10313472
16	**65 - 69**	19805	9477	10328	851	47.85155	52.14844736
17	**70 - 74**	17889	8068	9821	1753	45.10034	54.89965901
18	**75 - 79**	13541	5345	8196	2851	39.47271	60.5272875
19	**80 - 84**	8736	3080	5656	2576	35.25641	64.74358974
20	**85 - 89**	4925	1386	3539	2153	28.14213	71.85786802
21	**90 and over**	2262	471	1791	1320	20.82228	79.17771883
22	**Totals**	439473	209805	229668		47.74013	52.25986579

9 The large number of decimal places makes it harder to test our original hypothesis. We need to format the numbers in columns F and G to one decimal place.

To do this, select the cells from F3 to G22 by clicking on cell F3 and then, keeping the mouse button pressed down, drag it to cell G22. The selected cells will be highlighted in blue.

Click on Format in the toolbar and then on **Cells...**.

10 The 'Format Cells' window appears:

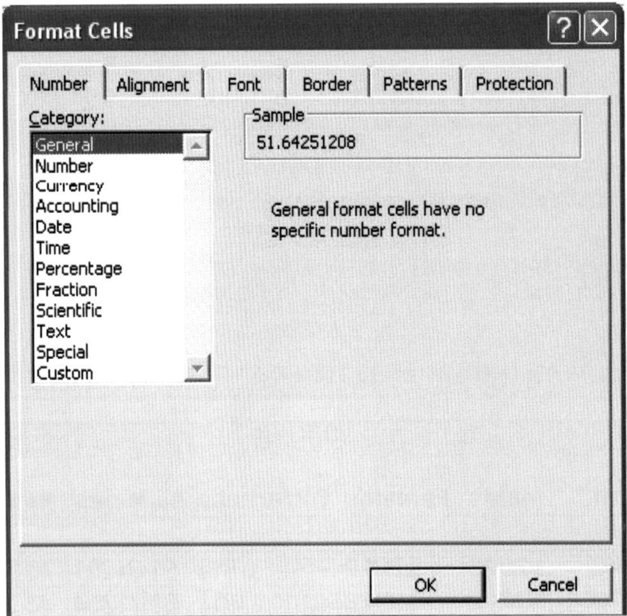

Click on the tab for **Number**.

11 In the 'Category' drop down list select **Number**.

This screen appears:

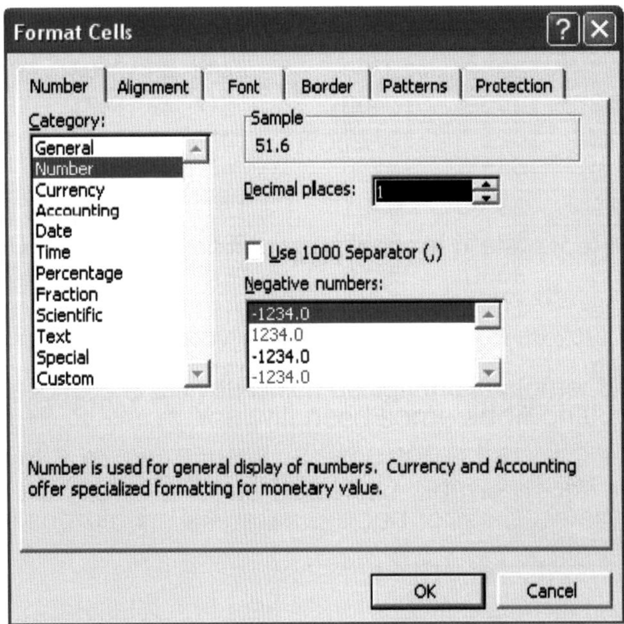

In the 'decimal places' section, decrease the number of decimal places to 1.

Now click on **OK**.

12 Check your figures are the same as this:

	A	B	C	D	E	F	G
1	**Age Range**	**Total**	**Males**	**Females**	**Difference**	**% Males**	**% Females**
2							
3	**0 - 4**	24840	12828	12012	-816	51.6	48.4
4	**5 - 9**	26670	13792	12878	-914	51.7	48.3
5	**10 - 14**	30771	15731	15040	-691	51.1	48.9
6	**15 - 19**	33626	16826	16800	-26	50.0	50.0
7	**20 - 24**	37112	17160	19952	2792	46.2	53.8
8	**25 - 29**	29194	13556	15638	2082	46.4	53.6
9	**30 - 34**	31175	15471	15704	233	49.6	50.4
10	**35 - 39**	32833	15417	17416	1999	47.0	53.0
11	**40 - 44**	31188	14858	16330	1472	47.6	52.4
12	**45 - 49**	26571	12810	13761	951	48.2	51.8
13	**50 - 54**	26987	13259	13728	469	49.1	50.9
14	**55 - 59**	20453	10053	10400	347	49.2	50.8
15	**60 - 64**	20895	10217	10678	461	48.9	51.1
16	**65 - 69**	19805	9477	10328	851	47.9	52.1
17	**70 - 74**	17889	8068	9821	1753	45.1	54.9
18	**75 - 79**	13541	5345	8196	2851	39.5	60.5
19	**80 - 84**	8736	3080	5656	2576	35.3	64.7
20	**85 - 89**	4925	1386	3539	2153	28.1	71.9
21	**90 and over**	2262	471	1791	1320	20.8	79.2
22	**Totals**	439473	209805	229668		47.7	52.3

13 Save your spreadsheet using the file name 'Percentage breakdown of males and females in Liverpool'.

Make it happen

ACTIVITY 2: Questions about the database

Use the data in the spreadsheet 'Percentage breakdown of males and females in Liverpool' to supply answers to the following:

1 Is the following hypothesis true or false: 'I would expect the percentage of men to decrease with age, because I have heard that women outlive men'?

2 For the age range 15–19 there are 16,826 males and 16,800 females, yet the percentages are both 50%. What is the reason for this?

3 Before you trust this data you must ask two important questions. Write down two questions you would like to ask about the data and explain your reasons for asking them.

Comparing local figures with national figures

The figures showing the population distribution for Liverpool may be the same as those for the whole of Britain or they may be different. You would expect them to be fairly close.

Here is a graph obtained from National Statistics On-line (**www.statistics.gov.uk**). It compares the population for Liverpool with that of the whole of the UK. You can see that there are slight variations. The data for Liverpool is shown as blue or pink bars (blue for male and pink for female) and the national data for the whole of the UK is shown by the blue lines.

Notice how easy it is to draw information from this graph rather than using the numbers in the tables.

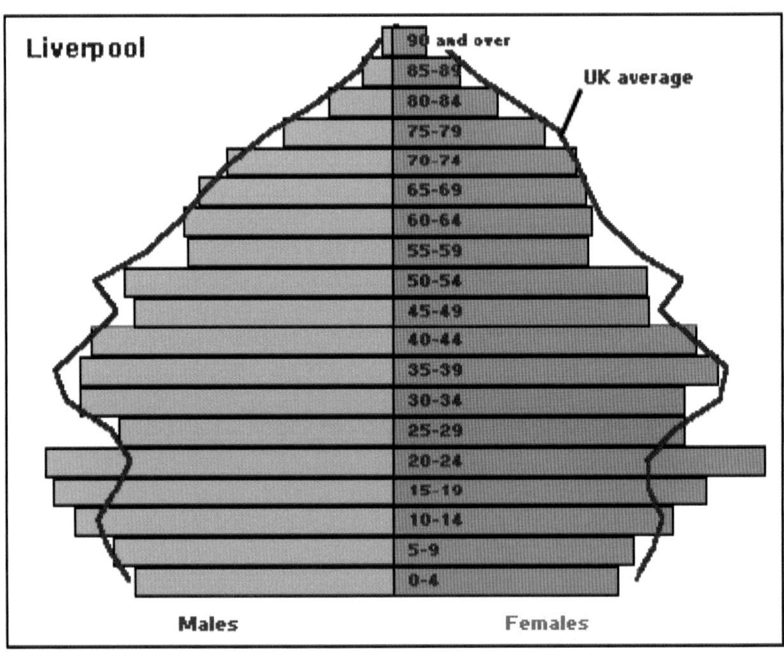

Comparing data you have collected with national data can also be done as a check. Usually your sample will only be small so it is a useful check to compare your results with a much larger sample. Do not expect to get the same answer, because your sample will reflect your local area and population.

KEY WORDS

validation – a check performed by the computer program to make sure that the data being entered is allowable

verification – checking the accuracy of data entry

How can the data I enter be checked?

Data can be checked by validation and verification.

Validation

Validation is a check that is performed by a computer program. When creating the structure of a database, you can include validation checks. These checks restrict the data that can be entered.

Verification

Verification involves simply checking that the data being typed in matches exactly the data on the document used to supply the information. In the case of a survey, this document would be a questionnaire. Verification checks to ensure that no errors are introduced during typing.

Verification normally means carefully proof-reading what has been typed in against what is on the document or questionnaire.

Make it happen

ACTIVITY 3: Validation checks in Excel

Using the spreadsheet software Excel, you can set a cell so that it can only accept certain data. You can therefore include validation checks.

Here are some of the things you can do:

1. Only allow numbers that are in a list to be entered (e.g. 1, 2, 3, 4 or 5)
2. Only allow numbers within limits (less than 10, greater than 20, etc.)
3. Only allow text of a certain length (e.g. only one character for either M or F)
4. Allow cells to be left blank
5. Not allow cells to be left blank.

If a user tries to input data into a cell that is restricted by the validation check, it will not be allowed. You can specify the message that appears when this happens. Usually it is best to explain what data is allowable in this message.

For each of the validation checks listed, use the on-line help or suitable books to find out how to restrict the data that can be entered into a cell.

EXTENSION ACTIVITY

Create a spreadsheet with cells that have each of the validation checks in the numbered list in Activity 3. Find out how and then make suitable messages to appear when the user tries to enter invalid data.

Lesson 4: SETTING UP THE DATABASE STRUCTURE

Background

It is very easy to create a database structure using Excel. You need to think about the fields you need to hold the answers to the questionnaires. Here are some very important points to consider when creating a database using Excel:

- Make sure you do not leave a blank row between the column titles (i.e. the field names of your database) and the first record. If you leave a blank row, Excel will not recognise that you are creating a database.
- Do not leave any blank lines in your list/table. A blank line indicates the end of the database above it.

Creating a database using spreadsheet software

The spreadsheet software Excel can be used to produce a simple database.

Using Excel, you can:

- enter data into a list
- search for data that matches certain conditions
- sort records into different orders
- produce totals
- calculate statistics such as means, modes, etc.
- produce graphs and charts of the data.

Setting up a database using Excel

The following series of activities shows you how to create a database using the spreadsheet software Excel.

Make it happen

ACTIVITY 4: Creating a database structure for the answers to the questions

1. Load the spreadsheet software Excel.
2. Type in the title of the spreadsheet in the first row like this:

	A	B	C	D	E	F	G
1	**A spreadsheet to hold the results of the popularity questionnaire**						
2							
3							
4							

Make the text bold.

3. In row 3, enter the following field names for the database, for example:

	A	B	C	D	E	F	G
1	**A spreadsheet to hold the results of the popularity questionnaire**						
2							
3	Sex	Age	Being good at school work				
4							
5							

Notice that the text entered into cell C3 starts to merge into the other cells. We need to keep all the text in cell C3.

4. One way to keep all the text in the same cell is to wrap it so that it looks like this:

Being good at school work

To do this:

Click on cell C3 to select it.

Now click on **Format** in the toolbar near the top of the screen.

Then select **Cells…**.

Now click on the **Alignment** tab:

The following window appears:

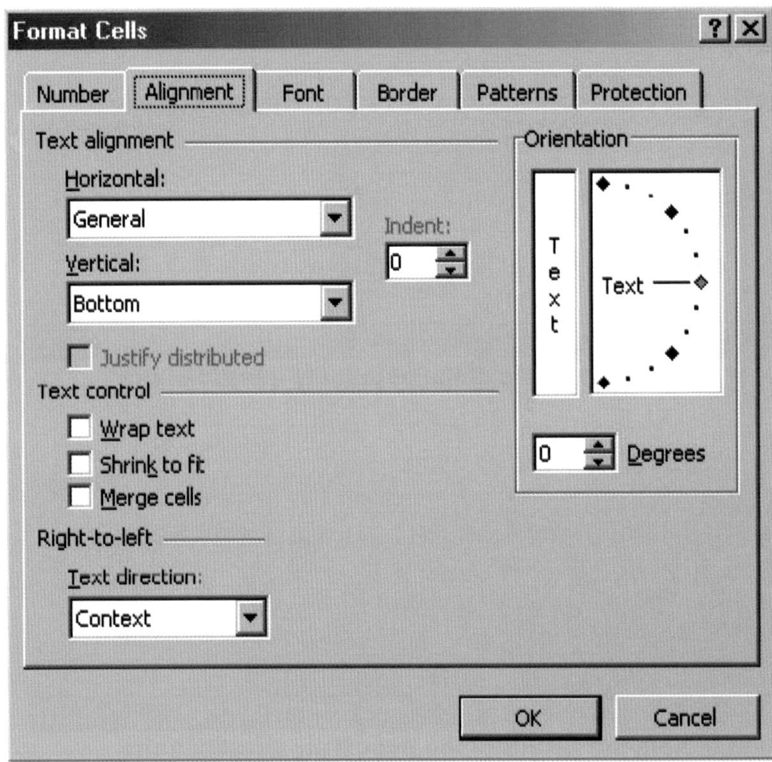

Take a while to look at all the things you can do using this window to format a cell. We want to control the text by wrapping it so that it fits in the cell.

Click on the box Text control ☑ Wrap text and then on OK.

Your spreadsheet will now look the same as this:

	A	B	C	D	E	F	G
1	**A spreadsheet to hold the results of the popularity questionnaire**						
2							
3	Sex	Age	Being good at school work				
4							
5							

5 We will now enter all the other field names into row 3.

Into cell D3 enter the text: *Being good at sport*

Now format the cell so that this text is wrapped.

Into cell E3 enter the text: *Being attractive*

Now format the cell so that this text is wrapped.

Into cell F3 enter the text: *Having a good sense of humour*

Now format the cell so that this text is wrapped.

Into cell G3 enter the text: *Having lots of money*

Now format the cell so that this text is wrapped.

When you have completed all these steps it will look like this:

	A	B	C	D	E	F	G
1	**A spreadsheet to hold the results of the popularity questionnaire**						
2							
3	Sex	Age	Being good at school work	Being good at sport	Being attractive	Having a good sense of humour	Having lots of money
4							

Note

Question: There is a quick way to format a series of cells before you put any text in them. Do you know how or can you find out?

6 The answers from the first questionnaire are entered in the row immediately below these field names. It is important not to leave a blank line between them, as this will make it impossible for Excel to recognise that you are creating a database structure.

7 Key in the first record. These are the answers from the first questionnaire.

	A	B	C	D	E	F	G
1	**A spreadsheet to hold the results of the popularity questionnaire**						
2							
3	Sex	Age	Being good at school work	Being good at sport	Being attractive	Having a good sense of humour	Having lots of money
4	M	11	1	3	4	5	2

8 The answers from the other questionnaires would now be keyed in carefully to make sure that no errors are introduced during typing.

To save time this has been done for you for the next activity.

You can now close this spreadsheet without saving it.

Make it happen

ACTIVITY 5: Adding data to the spreadsheet

1 To save you the job of entering the data, the spreadsheet containing the data has been set up for you.

Load the spreadsheet software Excel.

Open the spreadsheet file named 'A spreadsheet to hold the results of the popularity questionnaire'.

Your teacher will tell you where you can find this file. Check that your spreadsheet is the same as this:

> **Note**
> You can access this file via the 'Activity Files' link at www.oxfordsecondary.co.uk

	A	B	C	D	E	F	G
1	**A spreadsheet to hold the results of the popularity questionnaire**						
2							
3	Sex	Age	Being good at school work	Being good at sport	Being attractive	Having a good sense of humour	Having lots of money
4	M	11	1	3	4	5	2
5	F	11	5	1	2	3	4
6	F	11	4	2	3	5	1
7	F	12	2	1	3	4	5
8	F	13	4	3	1	2	5
9	M	13	1	4	2	3	5
10	M	13	5	3	1	4	2
11	M	13	4	3	1	2	5
12	M	13	3	5	1	2	4
13	F	13	5	2	1	3	4
14	F	13	4	3	1	2	5
15	M	11	5	1	2	4	3
16	F	12	3	1	2	4	5
17	M	11	5	3	1	2	4
18	F	13	2	3	1	5	4
19	F	12	3	4	2	5	1
20	F	13	3	1	2	4	5
21	M	11	2	3	1	5	4
22	F	12	4	3	2	1	5
23	M	13	5	3	1	2	4
24	F	13	3	2	4	5	1
25	M	12	3	2	1	4	5
26	F	11	2	1	3	5	4
27	M	13	3	2	1	4	5
28	M	11	1	2	3	5	4
29	F	13	4	5	2	3	1
30	M	12	5	3	2	4	1
31	F	13	5	4	3	1	2

2. Rather than enter the data into the spreadsheet grid, you can use a 'data form'.

   Move the cursor to any cell in the first row of data.

3. Click on Data on the toolbar and then select **Form...** from the list.

4. The data form now appears.

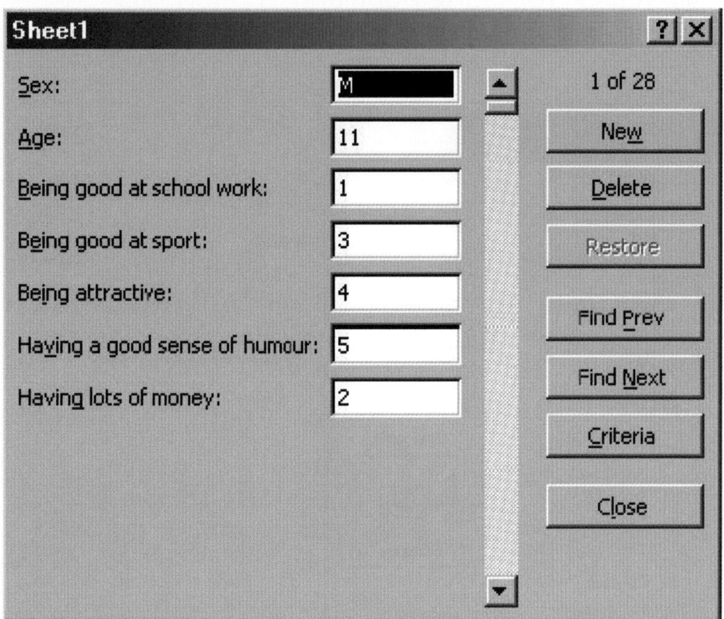

Notice the following buttons on this form:

This gives you a blank form into which you can type data for a new record.

Delete

This allows you to delete the current record (i.e. the one shown on the form).

Find Prev

This allows you to display a previous record.

Find Next

This allows you to display the next record.

Criteria

This allows you to find records that match certain conditions or criteria.

It is easier to use a form to type new data into the database because the data is shown one record at a time, so you don't get confused by looking at other rows of data.

6 A form can be used to search for certain records.

Click on Criteria.

7 A blank form appears. Here you can select values for each field to see if the data in the database has any matches.

Suppose we want to find any records for males aged 13 who think being attractive is the main reason for being popular.

Enter the data on the form as shown.

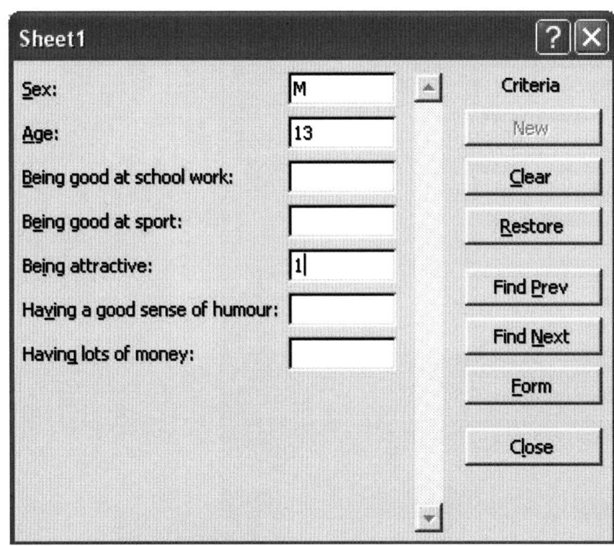

Click on Find Next

8 The first match appears on the form like this:

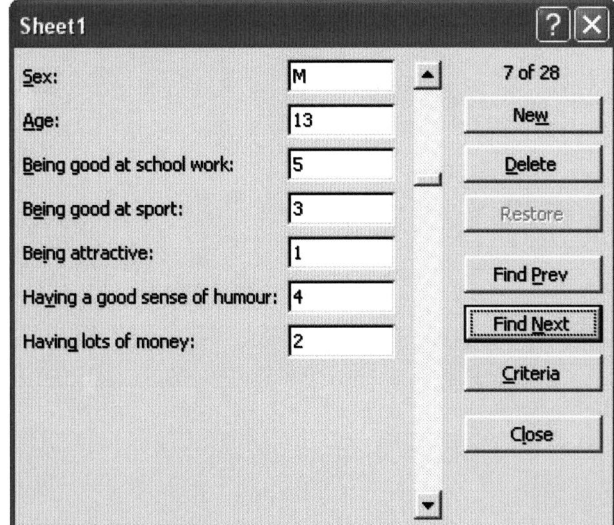

By clicking on **Find Next** repeatedly, you can see all the other matches (there are five in total).

9 Click on **Close** to leave the form.

10 Close the spreadsheet without saving it.

Make it happen

Note

You can access this file via the 'Activity Files' link at www.oxfordsecondary.co.uk

ACTIVITY 6: Working out totals

Since we have used ranking (i.e. 1 to 5), the totals of the ranks give us information for the whole group on those features of a person's personality that make them most popular. The smallest total will give us the feature people consider the most important and the largest number tells us which feature people consider to be the least important.

1 Load the spreadsheet software Excel.

2 Open the spreadsheet 'A spreadsheet to hold the results of the popularity questionnaire'.

3 In cell A32 enter the text *Total*. Make this text bold.

4 Move the cursor to cell C32. Here we need a formula to add up all the numbers in the cells from cell C4 to cell C31. An easy way to put the formula in is to use the 'AutoSum' button.

Now click on the AutoSum button Σ.

A dotted line is placed around the group of cells that the software thinks you want to add up and the formula is shown.

C	D
Being good at school work	Being good sport
1	
5	
4	
2	
4	
1	
5	
4	
3	
5	
4	
5	
3	
5	
2	
3	
3	
2	
4	
5	
3	
3	
2	
3	
1	
4	
5	
5	
=SUM(C4:C31)	

Check that this is correct and if so press **enter**.

6 Now produce totals for the cells D32 to G32. A quick way to do this would be to copy the formula in C32 relatively.

Check that your totals are the same as these:

32	Total		96	73	53	98	100

Remember that the lowest of these totals represents the most popular feature and the highest total (or totals in this case) represents the least popular feature.

You can see that by doing some further processing (e.g. calculating totals) we can make the information easier to see.

7. Save your spreadsheet using the file name 'Personality questionnaire results with totals'.

8. Exit the spreadsheet software.

Adding extra fields

When you create a database structure, you may forget a field and have to add it. Adding an extra field is easy, as you can insert a column between two existing columns. All you then need to add is the field name and the data for the field.

Adding extra fields usually means you will need to collect more data.

Problems in adding extra fields

Adding an extra field to a database is no problem. The problem is collecting the data to fill the field. If you have sent lots of questionnaires out and people have gone to the trouble to fill them in, then they might not be too happy about you troubling them again with a few extra questions. Also, there is the cost of obtaining the answers to these extra questions. If you sent out, say, 100 questionnaires by post enclosing a stamped addressed envelope for their reply you will need 200 stamps. If you decide you needed the answer to one extra question that you should have included, then you will need another 200 stamps.

This is why whenever you produce a questionnaire you need to plan it carefully and make sure that you have included all the questions.

Sometimes the extra field that is added to the database is simply calculated from the data in the other fields. An example of this would be a percentage field.

Merging data from two databases

Suppose you wanted to combine the replies you received with the replies other students received. You would need:

- to have exactly the same questions in the questionnaire
- to have exactly the same database set up.

Both of the above reasons mean that you would need to work as a team very early on in the project.

Lesson 5: QUERYING THE DATABASE AND EXTRACTING INFORMATION

What is a query?

A query is simply a question asked of a database. For example you might want to ask for the details of all the students in Year 7 or ask for only those girls in Year 7 who stay for school dinners.

KEY WORDS

query – a search for specific information contained in a database

Filtering data

Filtering is used with a list or table so that only rows of data matching certain criteria are shown. Basically, filtering hides those rows that do not fit your criteria. You will see this when you do the following activity.

Make it happen

ACTIVITY 7: Filtering out data

In this activity you will learn how to only show data matching certain criteria.

1. Load the spreadsheet software and open the file 'A spreadsheet to hold the results of the popularity questionnaire'.

Note

You can access this file via the 'Activity Files' link at www.oxfordsecondary.co.uk

2 Click on Data in the toolbar. Then select **Filter** and **AutoFilter**.

3	Sex	Age	Being good at school work	Being good at sport	Being attractiv	Having a good sense of humour	Having lots of money

Notice that the field names now have menus for each field. If you click on one of them, you will notice that all the different data for each field is shown.

3 Click on the drop down menu for Sex and you will see the choices M or F.

Click on M and you will see that all the records for males have been filtered out to give the following:

	A	B	C	D	E	F	G
3	Sex	Age	Being good at school work	Being good at sport	Being attractiv	Having a good sense of humour	Having lots of money
4	M	11	1	3	4	5	2
9	M	13	1	4	2	3	5
10	M	13	5	3	1	4	2
11	M	13	4	3	1	2	5
12	M	13	3	5	1	2	4
15	M	11	5	1	2	4	3
17	M	11	5	3	1	2	4
21	M	11	2	3	1	5	4
23	M	13	5	3	1	2	4
25	M	12	3	2	1	4	5
27	M	13	3	2	1	4	5
28	M	11	1	2	3	5	4
30	M	12	5	3	2	4	1

4 It would be more useful if the data for males could be sorted into age order so that data for the same ages are grouped together.

Move the cursor onto any of the cells containing data in the Age column.

Now click on the 'ascending' button in the toolbar

The data is now sorted in order of age from 11 to 13.

3	A Sex	B Age	C Being good at school work	D Being good at sport	E Being attractiv	F Having a good sense of humour	G Having lots of money
4	M	11	1	3	4	5	2
9	M	11	5	1	2	4	3
10	M	11	5	3	1	2	4
11	M	11	2	3	1	5	4
12	M	11	1	2	3	5	4
15	M	12	3	2	1	4	5
17	M	12	5	3	2	4	1
21	M	13	1	4	2	3	5
23	M	13	5	3	1	4	2
25	M	13	4	3	1	2	5
27	M	13	3	5	1	2	4
28	M	13	5	3	1	2	4
30	M	13	3	2	1	4	5

5 We would like to test the hypothesis that most boys think that being attractive makes you more popular.

Think about how you can use a filter to prove or disprove this hypothesis.

Using the power of Excel to help you extract information from your database

One of the reasons for using Excel to create a database is that it is so good at doing calculations. There are some very useful features in Excel that will help you when you process your data collected from questionnaires.

Make it happen

ACTIVITY 8: Using Excel to help analyse your answers to questionnaires

You have already seen how easy and useful it is to create a database structure to put your answers to the questionnaires into. In this activity you will see how easy it is to use some of the features of Excel to help supply some evidence to prove or disprove your hypotheses.

1 Load Excel and open the file called 'Part of a database of Year 7's use of technology at home'.

Your teacher will tell you where this file can be found.

Note

You can access this file via the 'Activity Files' link at www.oxfordsecondary.co.uk

2 Here is what you will see on the screen:

	A	B	C	D	E	F	G
1	**Part of a database of year 7's use of technology at home**						
2							
3	**Name**	**Do you have use of a computer at home?**		**Do you have Internet access at home?**		**Do you have your own mobile phone?**	
4	Amy	Yes		Yes		Yes	
5	Jack	No		No		Yes	
6	Joe	Yes		No		Yes	
7	Chloe	Yes		Yes		Yes	
8	Megan	Yes		Yes		No	
9	Danny	No		No		Yes	
10	Lesley	Yes		No		Yes	
11	John	Yes		Yes		Yes	
12	James	Yes		Yes		Yes	
13	Jackie	No		No		Yes	
14	Shakira	No		No		No	
15	Jennifer	Yes		Yes		Yes	
16	Stephen	Yes		Yes		Yes	
17	George	Yes		Yes		Yes	
18	John	Yes		Yes		Yes	
19	Marie	Yes		Yes		Yes	
20	Total with						
21	Total without						

Notice the names of the people questioned and the various questions with the 'Yes' and 'No' answers.

Also notice Cells A20 and A21. The idea is that the number of people with and without each device is to be recorded.

3 We could count all the 'Yes' and 'No' responses by adding them up ourselves. If there are lots of them, it could take a while and it would be easy to make a mistake. You can get the computer to do it for you.

Place the cursor on cell B20.

Type the following into this cell *=COUNTIF(B4:B19,"Yes")*

This counts all the Yes responses in the cells from B4 to B19 and puts the answer into cell B20.

Place the cursor on cell B21.

Type the following into this cell *=COUNTIF(B4:B19,"No")*

This counts all the No responses in the cells from B4 to B19 and puts the answer into cell B20.

4 In a similar way to that in step 3, find the totals for the other two columns, or alternatively you could copy the formulae. When you have completed this your spreadsheet will look like this:

	A	B	C	D	E	F	G
1	**Part of a database to hold details of year 7's use of technology at home**						
2							
3	**Name**	**Do you have use of a computer at home?**		**Do you have Internet access at home?**		**Do you have your own mobile phone?**	
4	Amy	Yes		Yes		Yes	
5	Jack	No		No		Yes	
6	Joe	Yes		No		Yes	
7	Chloe	Yes		Yes		Yes	
8	Megan	Yes		Yes		No	
9	Danny	No		No		Yes	
10	Les ey	Yes		No		Yes	
11	John	Yes		Yes		Yes	
12	Jarres	Yes		Yes		Yes	
13	Jackie	No		No		Yes	
14	Shakira	No		No		No	
15	Jonnifor	Yoo		Yoo		Yoo	
16	Stephen	Yes		Yes		Yes	
17	Gecrge	Yes		Yes		Yes	
18	John	Yes		Yes		Yes	
19	Marie	Yes		Yes		Yes	
20	Total with	12		10		14	
21	Total without	4		6		2	

Make it happen

ACTIVITY 9: Counting up the numbers of 1s, 2s and 3s in a questionnaire

For this activity we will use the popularity questionnaire database and the COUNTIF function again.

1 Load Excel and open the file 'A spreadsheet to hold the results of the popularity questionnaire'.

2 A blank column needs to be inserted in column A. All the data needs to be pushed one column to the right.

> **Note**
> You can access this file via the 'Activity Files' link at www.oxfordsecondary.co.uk

Place the cursor on any cell in column A.

Click on Insert in the toolbar and then on **Columns**.

You spreadsheet will look the same as this:

	A	B	C	D	E	F	G	H
3		Sex	Age	Being good at school work	Being good at sport	Being attractive	Having a good sense of humour	Having lots of money
4		M	11	1	3	4	5	2
5		F	11	5	1	2	3	4
6		F	11	4	2	3	5	1
7		F	12	2	1	3	4	5
8		F	13	4	3	1	2	5
9		M	13	1	4	2	3	5
10		M	13	5	3	1	4	2
11		M	13	4	3	1	2	5
12		M	13	3	5	1	2	4
13		F	13	5	2	1	3	4
14		F	13	4	3	1	2	5
15		M	11	5	1	2	4	3
16		F	12	3	1	2	4	5
17		M	11	5	3	1	2	4
18		F	13	2	3	1	5	4
19		F	12	3	4	2	5	1
20		F	13	3	1	2	4	5
21		M	11	2	3	1	5	4
22		F	12	4	3	2	1	5
23		M	13	5	3	1	2	4
24		F	13	3	2	4	5	1
25		M	12	3	2	1	4	5
26		F	11	2	1	3	5	4
27		M	13	3	2	1	4	5
28		M	11	1	2	3	5	4
29		F	13	4	5	2	3	1
30		M	12	5	3	2	4	1
31		F	13	5	4	3	1	2

3 Add the text *Total 1s* in cell A32, *Total 2s* in cell A33, *Total 3s* in cell A34, *Total 4s* in cell A35 and *Total 5s* in cell A36.

This section of the spreadsheet will look like this:

32	Total 1s		
33	Total 2s		
34	Total 3s		
35	Total 4s		
36	Total 5s		

4. We now need a function to count all the 1s in column D and put the answer in cell D32.

Click on cell D32 and enter the function *=COUNTIF(D4:D31,1)*

Notice how this function works. Inside the brackets there is the range of cells from D4 to D31 where the data is. After this is the number 1, which is what the function is looking for. It therefore counts all the 1s in cells from D4 to D31 and puts the answer where the formula is.

Check that your formula looks like this:

32	Total 1s			=COUNTIF(D4:D31,1)

Now press **enter** and you will see the result appear.

32	Total 1s			3

5. Now put similar functions in cells D33 to D36 to work out the totals for the other numbers. Do this manually rather than by copying the formula.

Make sure you check that this has been done correctly.

This part of the spreadsheet will look like this when you have entered all the functions correctly:

32	Total 1s			3	6	12	2	5
33	Total 2s			4	6	9	6	3
34	Total 3s			7	11	5	4	1
35	Total 4s			6	3	2	8	9
36	Total 5s			8	2	0	8	10

6. Save this spreadsheet using the file name 'Popularity'.

You will use this file later.

Using simple functions

Because the formulae are already set up, functions can save time and brainpower, so they are very useful.

A function must start with an equals sign (=) and it must have the range of cells to which it applies in brackets after it.

For example, to find the average of the numbers in a range of cells from A3 to A10 you would use:

=AVERAGE(A3:A10)

Here are some other functions:

Maximum

=MAX(D3:J3) displays the largest number in all the cells from D3 to J3 inclusive.

There are many more functions listed here. Use the on-line help to find more about the functions.

Minimum

=MIN(D3:J3) displays the smallest number in all the cells from D3 to J3 inclusive.

Mode

=MODE(A3:A15) displays the mode (i.e. the most frequent number) of the cells from A3 to A15 inclusive.

Median

=MEDIAN(B2:W2) displays the median of the cells from cells B2 to W2 inclusive.

Sum

=SUM(E3:P3) displays the total of all the cells from cells E3 to P3 inclusive.

Count

Suppose we want to count the number of numeric entries in the range C3 to C30.

We can use =COUNT(C3:C30).

Any blank lines or text entries in the range will not be counted.

Counta

To count a number of items or names of people we need to be able to count text entries. To do this we can use =COUNTA(C3:C30). You need to make sure that headings are not included in the range so that they are not counted as well. Again, blank lines are not counted.

There are lots of other functions you can use. For a list of them you can use the on-line help facility in Excel.

Presenting results as graphs and charts

Tables of figures can be hard to understand. It is much easier if we can show these figures as a picture using graphs and charts. Using graphs/charts makes it easy to:

- spot any inconsistencies in the data
- spot trends such as profits increasing or decreasing
- see the biggest or smallest reading.

There are lots of different graphs and charts to choose from so it is important to pick the one that is most suitable.

Pie charts

These are good for displaying categories as a proportion of the whole. For example, you could show a class's crisp preferences using a pie chart.

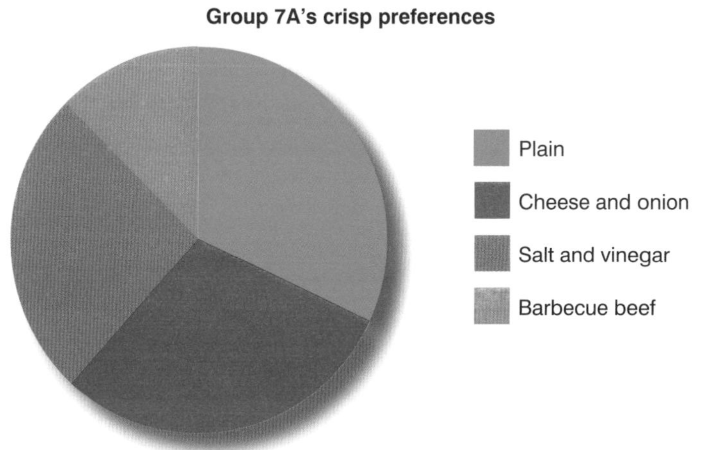

Bar charts

Bar charts are good for displaying the frequency of different categories. Here is a bar chart to investigate the types of vehicle using a certain road as a shortcut.

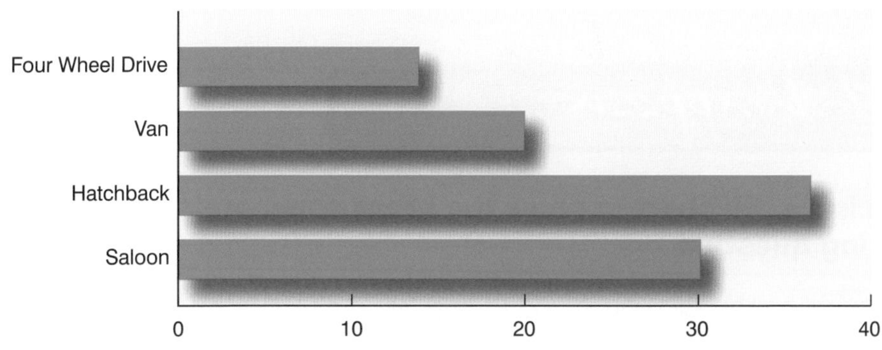

Scatter graphs

These are used to see how closely, if at all, one quantity depends on another. This is called correlation. For example, you might start with the hypothesis that someone who is tall will have bigger feet. You would collect height and shoe size data and then plot the pairs of values.

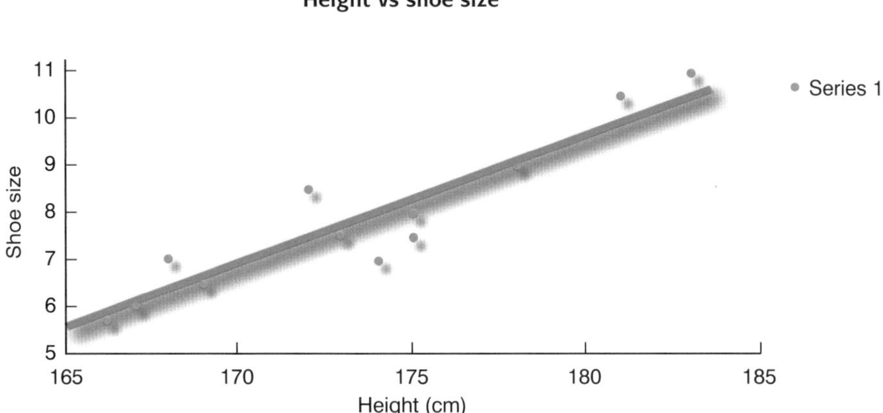

Line graphs

These can be used to show trends. The graph shows how the value of a car falls over the years. This is called depreciation.

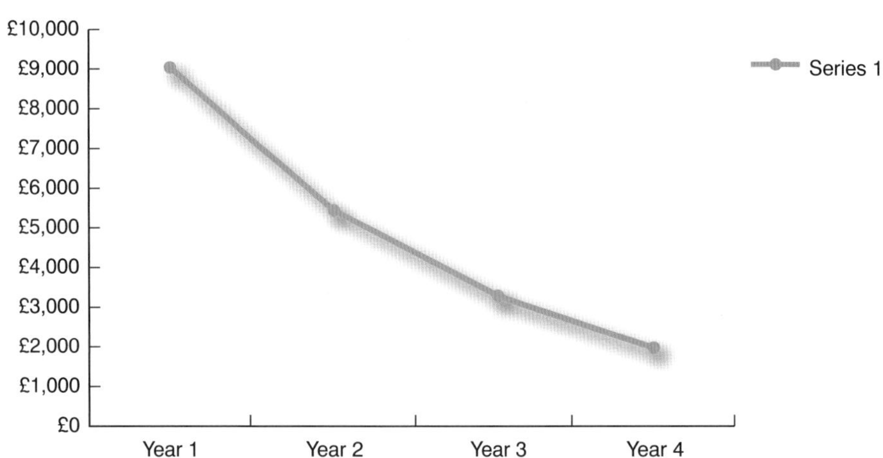

Make it happen

ACTIVITY 10: Producing a pie chart to show the breakdown of responses to a ranking question

1. Load Excel and then open the file you saved in Activity 9 called 'Popularity'.

2. You are going to produce a pie chart to show a breakdown of the rankings to 'Being good at schoolwork'.

To produce this pie chart you need to have the column containing the descriptions (i.e. column A, Total 1s, Total 2s, etc.) next to the column of data.

You could either move the descriptions next to the data (i.e. copy cells A32 to A36 and paste them into cells C32 to C36) or put them together on another part of the spreadsheet.

3. You now have to produce the pie chart to show the breakdown yourself. If you are stuck, look back at Activity 4 in Unit 4, where there is a description of how to produce a pie chart. You can also use the on-line help.

EXTENSION ACTIVITY

Produce pie charts for the other rankings and display them on a single page.

Make sure that you have suitable titles for each pie chart, as well as a suitable title for the whole page.

Making conclusions about the data

Once you have collected the data and have used it to prove or disprove your hypothesis you may spot other things about the data that you did not originally think of. Making conclusions about the data and writing about them is an important part of doing the research. Any conclusions reached must be supported by facts, such as figures from your data, calculated values such as means, modes, etc. or graphs and charts.

Checking to see if your answers were similar to ones collected by others

It is always interesting to see if your results and conclusions were the same as those of other people who collected similar data. Just because your results might not be the same does not mean they are wrong. Your data might simply reflect people's opinions locally rather than nationally or internationally. For example, the favourite sport in England might be football but in Wales it might be rugby.

Producing the final report

How can I check my results?

There are several ways you can check the results obtained from your questionnaire:

- you can compare your results with other students who are testing the same hypotheses
- you can check your results with web-based resources
- you can check with paper resources (books, newspapers, census results, etc.).

Considering the audience

Whenever you produce any material, you need to consider the audience. Anything you write needs to be explained in a way that is appropriate and accessible to your audience. As well as the text of your report, you will need to check that any charts or graphs have a clear title and that axes are suitably labelled.

Importing graphs, charts and spreadsheets into a document

As you will be using wordprocessing software to produce the report, any graphs or charts should be produced using the computer rather than hand drawn. The easiest way to import a graph or chart produced using spreadsheet software is to click on the graph/chart and then click on **Edit** and **Copy**. This places a copy of the graph/chart on the clipboard. You can then go to the wordprocessed document and click on **Edit** and **Paste**. This will paste the graph/chart starting from where the cursor was positioned.

Lesson 6: COLLECTING YOUR OWN DATA, ANALYSING IT AND PRODUCING A REPORT

In this lesson you will be given the opportunity to collect your own data, analyse it using a database and then produce a report using a wordprocessor.

Make it happen

ACTIVITY 11: Collecting, processing and representing data

Task 1: Collecting data

This activity involves creating a questionnaire to be answered by each member of your ICT group.

Here are some hypotheses to test:

People who most like fast food are the least likely to walk to school.
Are boys or girls more, less or equally likely to walk to school?

1. Produce another hypothesis, similar to those above, that you would like to test.
2. Produce a questionnaire containing only those questions needed to test your hypotheses.
3. Give a copy of your questionnaire to each group member to answer.
4. Collect the completed questionnaires.

Task 2: Creating the database structure

Think of suitable field names to hold your data and then create the database structure using Excel.

Task 3: Checking and inputting the data from the questionnaires

1. Check the data on the questionnaires and make a decision on what to do with any dirty data.
2. Type the answers from the questionnaires into your database structure.
3. Proof-read your table to verify that the data has been correctly entered.

Task 4: Analysing the data

1. Do any further processing of your data (e.g. percentages, counting different responses, working out mean, mode, median, etc.) that will help analyse the data.
2. Save and print a copy of your database.

Task 5: Producing graphs and charts

Produce any suitable graphs and charts so that you can explain your results and prove/disprove the hypotheses.

Task 6: Producing the final report

1. Produce a final report explaining what you did and whether each hypothesis is true or false. For each hypothesis you should support your answer using the data from the database or the graphs/charts you have created.
2. Try to incorporate copies of the data and graphs/charts into your wordprocessed report.
3. You should hand a printout of your work to your teacher.

6 Control and monitoring

Lesson 1:
INTRODUCTION TO CONTROL AND MONITORING

Issuing instructions and monitoring responses

You will have come across control in your Key Stage 2 work. You may have issued instructions to move a floor turtle around or used a control box to control a model in some way. In all of these examples, you had to issue instructions to the thing you were controlling. In this unit you will learn how to issue instructions. You will also learn about the importance of issuing instructions in the right order and structuring these instructions correctly.

The unit will also stress the importance of thinking about the problem carefully and structuring the program to make it easier to understand and change.

Background theory and key information

What is control?

Many systems are controlled in some way. For example, a central heating system is controlled to switch on and off at certain times of the day. During the times it is switched on it will still go on and off to keep the temperature of the rooms constant. The computer can detect and monitor devices such as temperature sensors and make decisions as to what to do on the basis of these measurements. Once the user has selected the times for the heating to operate the whole process is automatic. Such a heating system is very efficient because it is intelligent and knows when to turn itself on and off, so this saves fuel.

KEY WORDS

automatic – works on its own without needing further instructions from the user

control – getting the computer to operate devices automatically

efficient – making the best use of resources such as gas, electricity and water

monitor – continually take measurements of a quantity, such as temperature, so that action may be taken

system – a set of equipment arranged and organised together to perform a certain task

Proper control will keep a room at the same temperature when the heating is switched on

KEY WORDS

flowchart/flow diagram – a chart or diagram used to break down a task into smaller parts

input device – a device used to input data for processing by the computer

program – a set of instructions, written in a logical order that the computer obeys

The main features of control are:

- a sequence of instructions is obeyed (i.e. there is a program)
- there are instructions to turn things on and off.

In computer control the computer follows a set of instructions called a program. These programs instruct the computer on how to process the data it gets from sensors or other input devices. Programs can be planned using a diagram called a flowchart. You will learn how to draw your own flowcharts later on in this unit.

Common devices that use control

Most electronic devices use some sort of computer control to help them work. Below are some common household devices and what they use control for.

Washing machine – controls when to add water, what temperature to heat the water up to, when to add washing powder/liquid, how long to wash, when to empty water, when to spin, etc.

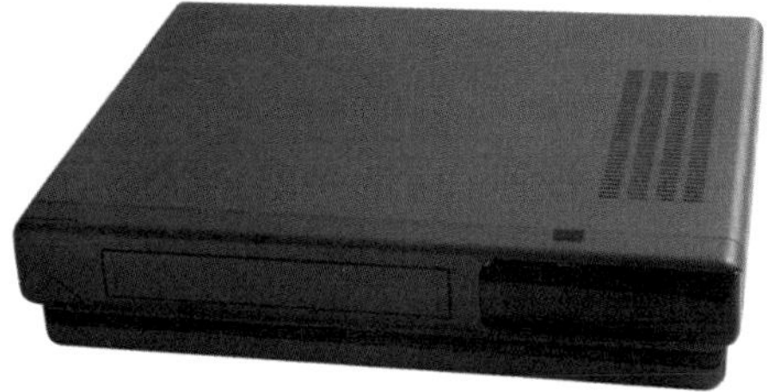

Video recorder – controls when to start recording, what channel to record, when to stop recording, etc.

Camera – controls the aperture (how much light to let in), the shutter speed, forwarding the film, etc.

Electric drill – controls the speed and the torque (turning power) of the drill.

The three steps in a control system: input, processing and output

Input and output devices used with computer control

The following diagram shows the three stages of control: input, process and output.

The three stages of control: input, process and output

Input data is gathered by an input device and sent to the processor for processing. The processor works with the data and a stored program to work out what it needs to output. Sensors are used to supply the data for control.

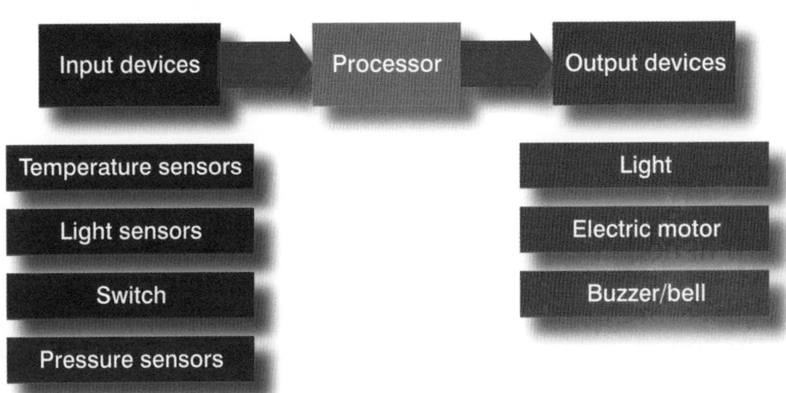

Input devices supply the input data that is processed and the data output is used to control output devices

Input

Inputs to a control system can come in different ways. They can be:

- given by the user as an instruction (e.g. press a button)
- sensed by sensors that send signals to the computer (e.g. a light sensor senses that a person has walked through a door).

Input devices

Input devices send the data to the processor. The processor uses its set of stored instructions (called a program) to decide what to do. On the basis of the input data, it may decide to switch the output device on or off, or it may decide to do nothing.

Switches

A simple switch that can be operated by the user is an input to a system. A use of this might be in a car park where the driver drives up to the barrier and presses a button to get a ticket.

There is a switch on a washing machine that stops the drum from revolving when the door is opened.

REMEMBER!

Sensors are input devices and they supply data for processing by the computer.

Light sensors

These detect light levels and can be used in street/security lights which come on when it gets dark.

A special type of light sensor can be used to detect whether a beam of light has been broken. This is used to sense a vehicle or a person passing by.

Pressure sensors

Pressure sensors detect something pushing down on them. This might be the weight of a liquid in a container or it might be the weight of a person or vehicle.

Infra-red sensors

Infra-red sensors can detect movement in a room or car and can be used as the input to an alarm system.

Sound sensors

Sound sensors detect the intensity of sound.

Proximity sensors

These sensors detect objects that pass over them or near them. You have probably seen these set into the road near traffic lights (they look like patterns of black lines set into the road). They detect vehicles approaching the lights.

There are many more sensors. If it can be measured, there will be a sensor to detect it.

Processing

Computers process input to produce output. Sensors can provide the input for processing. For example, if a door is opened, this can be sensed and data can be sent to the computer so that it can decide what to do. Making a decision about what to do is an example of processing. A signal can then be sent to an output device such as a buzzer to instruct it to sound for a certain period.

Delaying or waiting a certain amount of time before an output device is turned on or off is an example of processing.

Another type of processing performed by the computer is a calculation. Two counters would be needed in a multi-storey car park to count the number of cars entering and leaving the car park. This would enable the computer to work out how many cars were in the car park so that no more would be allowed in if it was full.

Examples of processing include:

- making decisions (i.e. asking questions based on the data so that one of two alternative actions can be taken)
- the use of counters
- obeying wait or delay instructions.

Outputs from the system

The outputs from the processor are the instructions on what the system has to do. For example, in a central heating control system, a sensor would measure the temperature in the house. The processing would involve comparing this temperature with the temperature setting the householder had chosen. If the temperature was lower than that required the system would send a signal that would turn the central heating on. If the temperature was higher or the same as that required the central heating would not come on, or if it was already on it would switch off.

The device that is controlled by the processor is called an output device.

Output devices

There are lots of different output devices that can be controlled by a computer. These output devices include the following:

Electric motors

Electric motors can be turned on and off. There are also special electric motors called stepper motors that you can instruct to turn through a certain angle. Stepper motors are ideal for raising barriers in car parks because the motor only needs to turn part of a revolution. Electric motors are also found in robots and robot arms.

You will find electric motors controlled by a computer in:

- lifts (to close the doors and also to move the lift up and down)
- car park and level crossing barriers
- children's toys (remote controlled cars, etc.)
- washing machines and dishwashers
- cameras (to move the film forward or to focus the lens).

Lights

Lights can be switched on or off or dimmed by a computer.

The following lights are controlled by a computer:

- traffic lights
- car park full signs
- green man and red man on pelican crossings
- motorway fog warning lights
- warning lights on a car dashboard
- the flashing lights of a burglar alarm or car alarm.

Buzzers or bells

Buzzers and bells are important because they can be recognised by people with impaired vision.

All of the following make use of a bell or buzzer:

- pelican crossing sounds
- burglar alarms
- warning sounds at railway crossings.

WORKSHEETWORKSHEETWORKSHEETWORKSHEETWORKSHEET

WORKSHEET 7.6.1 **Control in everyday life**

Most electrical/electronic devices use control.

Think about all the electronic devices other than those already mentioned and write their names down. For each device in your list you should say what the control does.

Your teacher may give you a worksheet on which to work or you may be asked to copy this table into your book. Fill in the table with your answers. The first one has been done for you.

Name of device	What the control does
Electric shower	Heats the cold water to a constant temperature according to the user's temperature setting. Switches off the shower if the water gets too hot.

WORKSHEET 7.6.2 **Is it control?**

Your teacher may give you a worksheet on which to work or you may be asked to copy the table overeleaf into your book. Fill in the table with your answers.

Here are some systems. You have to decide whether they are examples of control and give reasons for your choice.

Example	Is it control? Yes or No?	Reason for your choice
A shower		
A light dimmer switch		
A thermometer		
A speedometer in a car		
A burglar alarm		
A remote controlled garage door		
A light bulb		
A lift		
A set of traffic lights		

ACTIVITIES

ACTIVITY 1: Automatic washing machines

Washing clothes manually can take a long time. You need to be there for most of the time to add the correct amount of water at the right temperature, to add the soap powder and to actually move the clothes around. You then need to rinse them in clean water and then wring them out.

Automatic washing machines were invented to get rid of this drudgery. An automatic washing machine uses control to carry out a series of processes according to a series of instructions called a program. Washing machines have lots of different programs, one for each type of wash.

Think about what happens when clothes are washed and then answer the following questions:

1. Write down a list of the sensors a washing machine would have.

   For each of the sensors you write down you need to write a reason why it is needed.

2. 'Doing the washing' is an overall task. This task can be broken down into lots of smaller processes such as 'add soap powder'.

   Write a list of processes involved in 'doing the washing'.

3. In an automatic washing machine there is a processor. After processing the data input from the sensors, the processor sends signals to output devices to turn them on or off.

   Write a list of the output devices that a washing machine would have.

Make it happen

ACTIVITY 2: Sensors

Task 1

There are many input devices that supply the data for a control system.

Give two examples of each of the following used as inputs in a control system.

(a) Switches

(b) Temperature sensors

(c) Pressure sensors

Task 2

Modern cars contain lots of sensors.

Write down where you might find each of the following sensors in a car.

(a) Temperature sensor

(b) Pressure sensor

(c) Light sensor

Lesson 2: GIVING INSTRUCTIONS – MOVING A TURTLE AROUND A SCREEN

Logo is a programming language popular for teaching maths in schools.

Logo – What is it?

Logo is a set of instructions that can be used to control the movement of a turtle around the screen.

Why the name turtle?

When Logo was first developed, it was used to move a robot around on a piece of paper and it looked a bit like a turtle. The robot turtle contained a pen which left a track on the paper. It is easier to use Logo on the screen, and the turtle has been replaced by a triangle icon.

The original turtle drew a drawing on paper when it moved

Using MSW Logo

When you load the program you will see the following screen:

The opening screen. Notice it is divided into two. The MSWLogo Screen shows the turtle (the triangle) and is the area where the drawing appears

The 'Commander' half of the screen (the bottom part) is in two parts. The bottom part is called the 'input box'. The input box is the place where you type in the instructions.

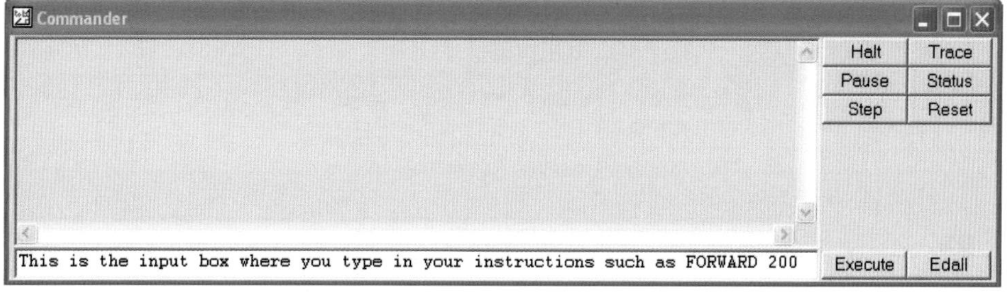

The input box, where instructions are entered

The top part is called the 'recall list box'.

A list of all the commands entered appears in the top part of the commander box. If you click on an instruction such as 'FD 100' in this part then it also appears in the input box. This saves time, as you will see later

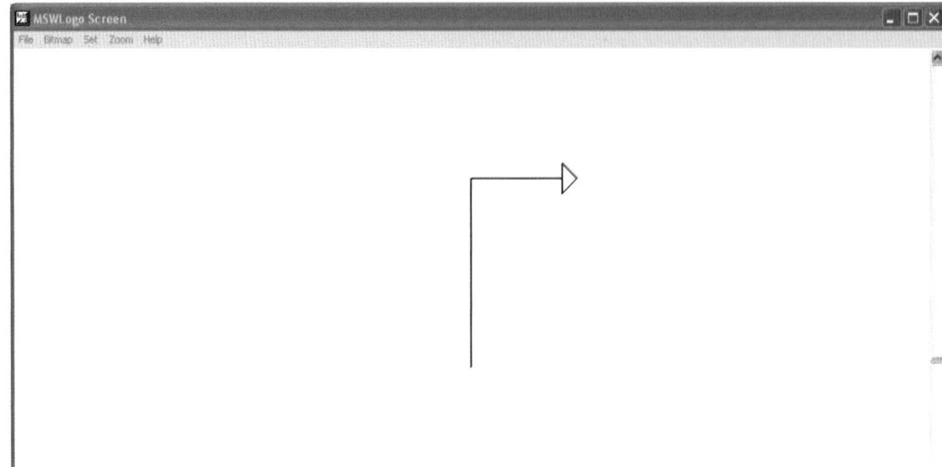

The top part of the screen is where the drawing appears

The basic instructions

Here are the basic instructions:

FORWARD 40	moves the turtle forward 40 units
BACK 50	moves the turtle back 50 units
RIGHT 90	turns the turtle 90 degrees to the right
LEFT 90	turns the turtle 90 degrees to the left
HOME	returns the turtle to its starting position (called the origin)
CLEARSCREEN	clears (i.e. erases) the screen

Shortcuts to save time

You can use abbreviations for most of the commands. For example:

FD 100	means forward 100
RT 90	means right turn 90 degrees
LT 45	means left turn 45 degrees
CS	means clear screen

Tips

You do not need to use capitals when giving instructions. Make sure there is a space between a word and a number (e.g. FORWARD 50).

Make it happen

ACTIVITY 3: A simple program

A set of instructions is called a program. Here is a simple program to draw a rectangle on the screen. Type these instructions exactly as they are here. Type each line into the input box and press **Enter**.

FORWARD 20
RIGHT 90
FORWARD 20
RIGHT 90
FORWARD 20
RIGHT 90
FORWARD 20

When you press **enter** after each instruction, Logo obeys the instruction.

This method is a bit tedious so there is a quicker way, like this:

To get rid of the previous drawing type in:

CS

Now type in the following program:

REPEAT 4 [FORWARD 20 RIGHT 90]

The above instruction tells Logo to repeat the steps in the square bracket four times. This is called a loop. Loops save you having to re-write lots of instructions if there is a part in your program that needs to be repeated a certain number of times. The instructions inside the square brackets are repeated four times.

To check that a series of steps works you should try obeying the instructions using a piece of paper. Make sure that at the end of each line, you know which way the turtle is pointing.

Look at this little program:

REPEAT 9 [FORWARD 100 RIGHT 80]

Can you work out what this program will do? Try drawing it out on a piece of paper using a pencil, ruler and protractor. Type in the program to see if you were right. Notice that the instructions in the square brackets are repeated nine times.

Make it happen

ACTIVITY 4: What will be drawn?

Here are some simple programs to give instructions to a turtle.

1. For each program, try to work out what shape will be drawn. Write this down.
2. Type each program into Logo. What shape does it draw? Were you right?

Program 1

```
FORWARD 10
RIGHT 90
FORWARD 10
RIGHT 90
FORWARD 10
RIGHT 90
FORWARD 10
```

Program 2

```
CS
RT 30
FD 60
RT 120
FD 60
RT 120
FD 60
```

Program 3

```
CS
RT 90
FD 80
LT 60
FD 80
LT 60
FD 80
LT 60
FD 80
LT 60
FD 80
LT 60
FD 80
```

Program 4

```
CS
REPEAT 4 [FD 100 LT 90]
```

Program 5

```
CS
FD 40
RT 90
FD 120
RT 90
FD 40
RT 90
FD 120
```

Program 6

```
CS
FD 60
RT 30
FD 60
RT 120
FD 60
RT 30
FD 60
RT 90
FD 60
```

Something for nothing!

If you are interested, you can get your own free copy of the Logo software at the following website:

www.softronix.com

Follow the instructions on how to download the program. If you have a computer at home you will then be able to experiment using the software at home.

More instructions

So far we have only looked at a very basic set of instructions. Here is a table showing some more:

Instruction	What it does
PU	Pen up – lifts the pen up so that the turtle stops drawing when it moves
PD	Pen down – puts the pen down so the that the turtle draws when it moves
SAVE "name of file	Saves the file using the name of the file entered
LOAD "name of file	Loads the saved file from disk
EDIT "subroutine	Allows a new subroutine to be started and edited or allows an existing subroutine to be edited
SETPC 1	Changes pen colour to blue
SETPC 2	Changes pen colour to green
SETPC 3	Changes pen colour to light blue
SETPC 4	Changes pen colour to red
SETPC 5	Changes pen colour to pink
SETPC 6	Changes pen colour to yellow
SETPC 7	Changes pen colour to white
SETPC 8	Changes pen colour to brown

Make it happen

ACTIVITY 5: Instructions that give colour to your drawings

The following two tasks will give you practice at using colour.

Task 1

Here are some instructions to set the pen colour. Try these instructions out by inputting each one in turn with an instruction to draw a line.

1. *setpencolor [0 0 0]*
2. *setpencolor [255 255 255]*
3. *setpencolor [128 128 128]*

Write down what colour each command gives.

Task 2

Try varying each of the numbers in the *setpencolour* instruction (each of the three numbers can have values from 0 to 255). Write down each instruction along with the colour that it produces in the form of a table.

Lesson 3: THE BUILDING BLOCKS OF PROGRAMS

Large programs are time consuming to type in and hard to understand. This is why it is much better to use subroutines. You may see the word 'procedure' sometimes being used in place of the word 'subroutine'. Subroutine and procedure mean the same thing.

Subroutines – what are they and why are they useful?

Programs are often built up of small sections called subroutines. Each subroutine performs a particular task and is given a name. For example, a subroutine to draw a square could be called SQUARE. Sometimes, the same subroutine is used more than once in the same program so you can simply type in the name of the subroutine rather than type in all the instructions again.

Make it happen

ACTIVITY 6: Creating a subroutine to draw a square

Load Logo and then follow these instructions:

1. In the input box type in:

   TO SQUARE

   Then press the **Enter** key.

   The word 'TO' tells the computer that a subroutine is being created and SQUARE is the name we are using for this subroutine.

2. The User Input Box appears.

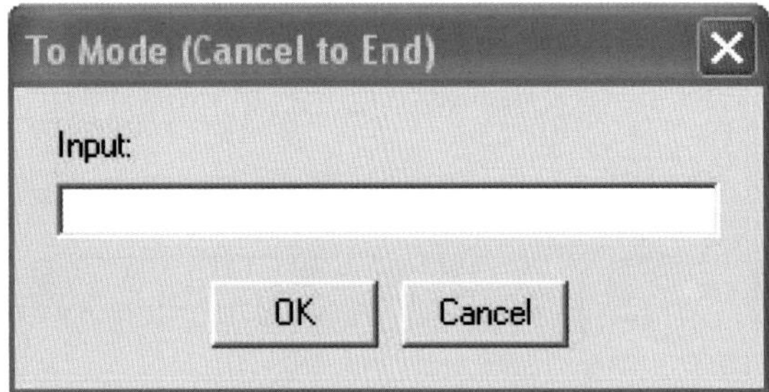

All the instructions that make up the subroutine to produce a square are typed in here.

Type in the first instruction:

FD 100

Press the **Enter** key.

3 You will now be presented with another blank User Input Box.

Enter the rest of the instructions to draw the square pressing the **Enter** key after each instruction.

Here are the instructions:

RT 90
FD 100
RT 90
FD 100
RT 90
FD 100

4 To end the instructions type in *END* and press the **Enter** key.

You will see that the subroutine to draw the square has been defined by looking at the Commander part of the screen.

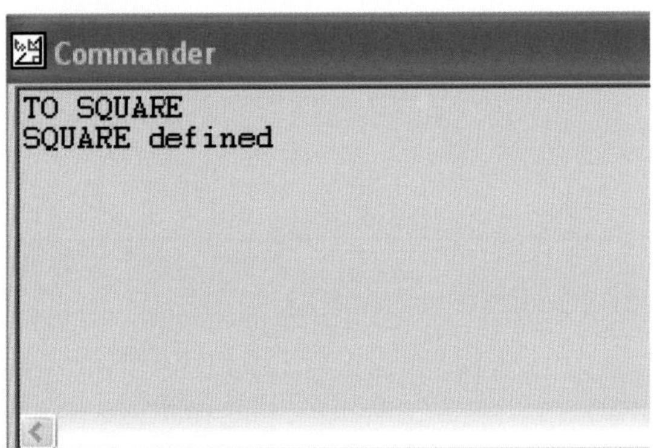

Note

Important: All subroutines must be given a name i.e. TO name of subroutine.

5 To run the subroutine type its name into the input box (at the bottom of the page) like this:

```
SQUARE
```

Now press the **Enter** key.

The square is now drawn.

All the instructions that are part of the subroutine must now be entered.

You must tell the computer that the subroutine has finished by issuing the instruction *END*.

It is possible to have one subroutine inside another subroutine, as you will see later.

Make it happen

ACTIVITY 7: Editing an instruction

Editing an instruction means changing it. It is easy to edit an instruction once the instruction has been put into the box on the screen called the edit box.

Follow these instructions to edit the program created in the last activity.

1. In the input box type in the instruction:

   EDIT "SQUARE

   A screen appears showing all the instructions in the subroutine called SQUARE.

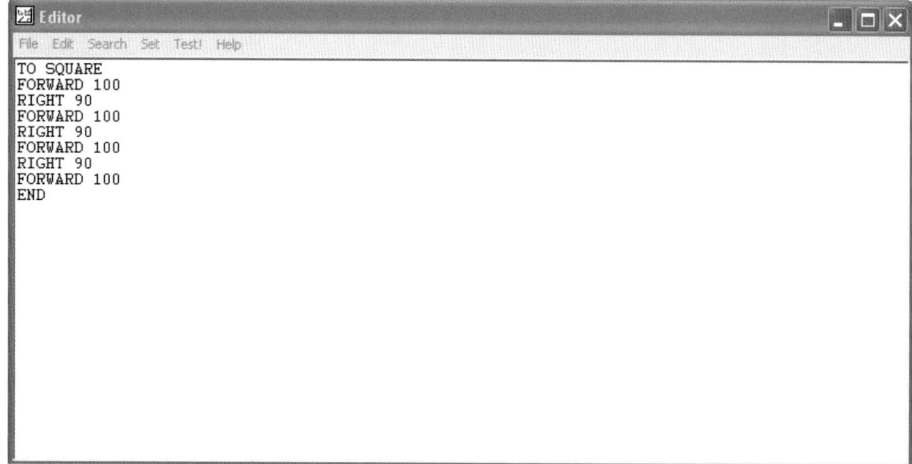

The editor window makes it easy for you to edit the instructions

2. We will now produce a larger square of side 200.

   Alter the relevant steps in the above program. To do this simply click and delete and alter the numbers. It is really just like editing a document using wordprocessing software.

3. Click on **File** and then on **Save** and **Exit**. This will save the subroutine called SQUARE.

4. Type in *CS* in the input box (at the bottom of the screen) to clear the screen.

5. Type in *Square* and press the **Enter** key.

   The larger square is now drawn.

6. Try practising using the editor screen to alter the program to different sized squares.

   See if you can work out what is the largest sized square that you can draw on the screen starting from the turtle's home position.

Make it happen

ACTIVITY 8: Drawing a house

In this activity you will be creating two subroutines together to form the cross-section of a house.

1. In the input box type in the instruction

   EDIT "

   This will open the Edit screen, where you can type in instructions.

   If you are typing in lots of instructions it is easier to do this using this screen.

2. Type in the following instructions

   ```
   TO SQUARE
   REPEAT 4 [FD 100 RT 90]
   FORWARD 100
   END
   TO TRIANGLE
   RT 30
   FD 100
   RT 120
   FD 100
   RT 120
   FD 100
   END
   TO HOUSE
   SQUARE
   TRIANGLE
   END
   ```

   If you look at this you will see the two subroutines called SQUARE and TRIANGLE. These are part of another subroutine called HOUSE.

   Your instructions should be the same as these.

3. To save this click on **File** and then click on **Save** and **Exit**.

4. Run the program by typing the following into the input box:

   ```
   CS
   HOUSE
   ```

   The house should appear on the screen like this:

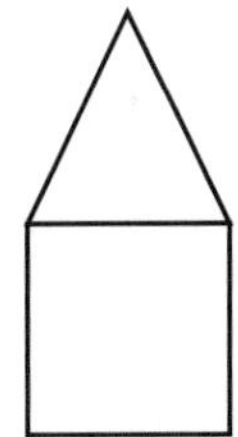

The outline of the house made up of the subroutines SQUARE and TRIANGLE

Make it happen

ACTIVITY 9: Tasks for you to try

Here are a number of tasks for you to try.

Task 1

By using a subroutine called RECTANGLE draw a rectangle on the screen of length 200 units and width 100 units. Save your subroutine.

Task 2

Here is a short program written in Logo.

REPEAT 5 [FORWARD 100 LEFT 72]

The above short program draws the pentagon shown here:

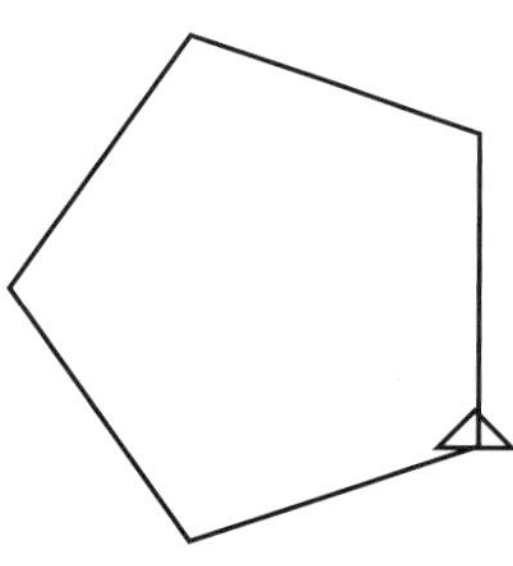

Here is another program that draws a hexagon. What should the missing
angle be?

REPEAT 6 [FORWARD 10 LEFT .....]

Task 3

Using a program similar to the ones for the pentagon and hexagon:

(a) Write a program to draw an octagon (8 sides). Check that your program works by typing it in and running it.

(b) Write a program to draw a decagon (10 sides). Check that your program works by typing it in and running it.

Task 4

A program written in Logo produced the following diagram. The size of the large square is 200 units.

Write a program to produce this shape.

You will need to use the PENUP (or PU) command to move the pen to the starting corner of the next square without drawing a line.

Make it happen

ACTIVITY 10: Loops inside loops – going loopy!

The following tasks will give you more practice at using loops and subroutines. You will even see how loops can be put inside other loops.

Task 1

Type in the following program:

REPEAT 9 [FORWARD 100 RIGHT 80]

Write down what you see on your screen.

Task 2

This program contains a loop inside a loop. The inner loop draws a square. The outer loop changes the starting angle by 10 degrees to the right each time a new square is drawn. This means that lots of different squares are drawn.

1. Open the edit screen by typing *EDIT "*.

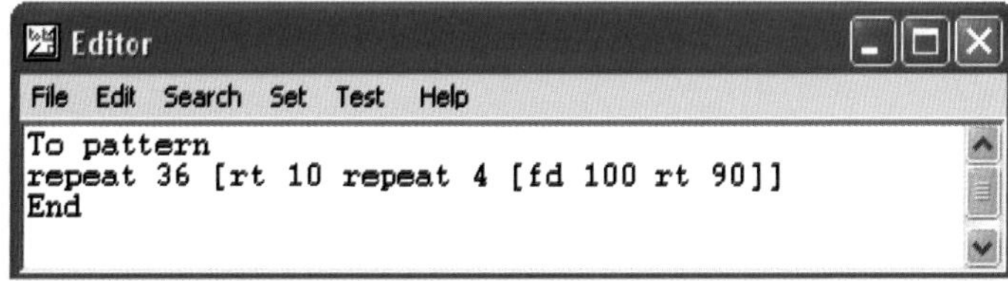

Enter the program instructions exactly as they appear here.

Run the program by typing the name of the subroutine *pattern*.

2. Try altering the instruction 'rt 10' to different numbers. You can make lots of interesting patterns like these:

Loops inside loops produce nice effects

If you find that the pattern is not complete, try changing the number in 'repeat 36' to a larger number.

3. Print any interesting patterns out by clicking on **Bitmap** and then **Print...**.

Subroutines in subroutines

Suppose we wanted to draw a diagram of a house. We would need lots of instructions. Trying to follow these instructions might be difficult if we came back to the program at a later date.

It is easier to break the whole task into smaller tasks. For example the instructions could be divided into the following subroutines:

- Walls
- Roof
- Windows
- Door
- Chimney.

Each of the above could be used as a name of a subroutine to draw part of the house. These subroutines would be structured like this, with the dots representing the program steps:

TO Walls
.
.
.
.
.
END

After the subroutines to draw all the other parts of the house have been created a main subroutine could then be written like this:

TO House
Walls
Roof
Windows
Door
Chimney
END

You will need some additional instructions to make sure that the turtle is in the correct position on the screen before each of the parts that make up the house are drawn.

Make it happen

ACTIVITY 11: Using subroutines to draw a house

Draw a picture of a house similar to the one shown below. You should use subroutines in your program.

Show your teacher your diagram on the screen when you have finished.

Write down the instructions that you have used.

See if you can produce this drawing by writing each part as a subroutine

EXTENSION ACTIVITY

1 Add instructions to change the lines in your drawings to suitable colours.

2 Add extra instructions and subroutines to include:

- a garage
- a tree
- a car.

Make it happen

ACTIVITY 12: Using variables in programs

This is a simple subroutine called SQUARE that contains a variable called size. We can make this program draw larger or smaller squares.

Type in the following subroutine.

TO SQUARE :size
REPEAT 4 [FD :size RT 90]
END

When you run this subroutine, as well as entering the name of the subroutine, you also have to enter a number which is the size you want for the sides.

Type in the following:

SQUARE 100

Try changing the numbers to draw different sized squares.

ACTIVITY 13: Changing sides

Here is a useful program that makes use of a subroutine and a variable called Sides. This program will draw a regular polygon having a number of sides that the user can specify.

1. Type in the program shown in this window, being very careful to include the spaces as shown.

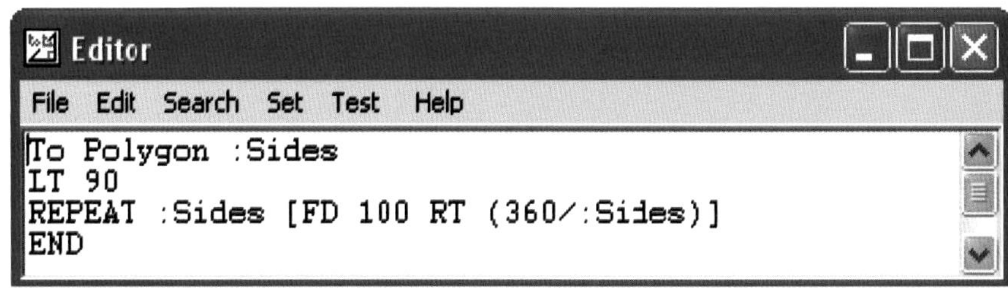

This program uses a variable called Sides

2. To run the program type in:

   Polygon 6

3. Clear the screen after each diagram by using the instruction *CS*

   Use the program to draw regular polygons with the following numbers of sides: 4, 5, 7, 9 and 10.

4. Look at the program carefully. Try to understand how it works. Here are a few questions to answer:

   (a) Why is the LT 90 instruction needed?

   (b) There is a loop in this program. How do we know?

   (c) Write down the calculation that works out the angle.

   (d) If you wanted to change the length of the side in this program, write down the step you would change.

(e) How does the program know how many times the instruction inside the loop should be obeyed?

(f) What instruction should always be placed at the end of a subroutine?

EXTENSION ACTIVITY

You can either:

(a) Put program instructions into the polygon program to draw the polygon using different colours;

OR

(b) Alter the program so that not only can the user select the number of sides, they can also select the length of the sides as well.

If you are really ambitious, you can try both!

Hint: You will need to add another variable to the subroutine.

Lesson 4: DRAWING FLOWCHARTS

Instructions for computers can be summarised in flowchart. Flowcharts are used to break down the overall task into lots of small steps arranged in a logical order.

The steps are written inside flowchart symbols.

KEY WORDS

flowchart – a chart or diagram used to break down a task into smaller parts. It can also show the order of the tasks and any decisions that need to be made

Flowchart symbols

Start or stop

Input or output

Process

Subroutine

Decision

Start or stop

These are placed at the start and end of the flowchart. They are also used at the start and end of a subroutine. A subroutine is a section of program that is written separately. We normally place the name of the box inside it like this:

Start, stop and subroutines share the same box shape

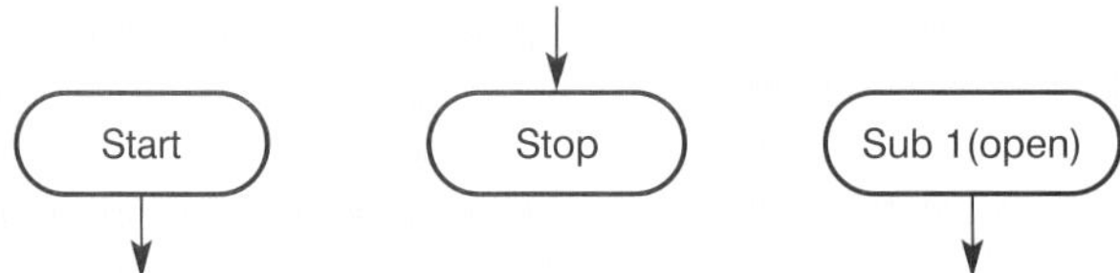

Input and output boxes

Input is what is required for the process to be done. Output is the result from the processing. An output might be to turn a motor on/off or turn a light on/off. The input and output are written inside the boxes. These diagrams show some examples:

Input boxes

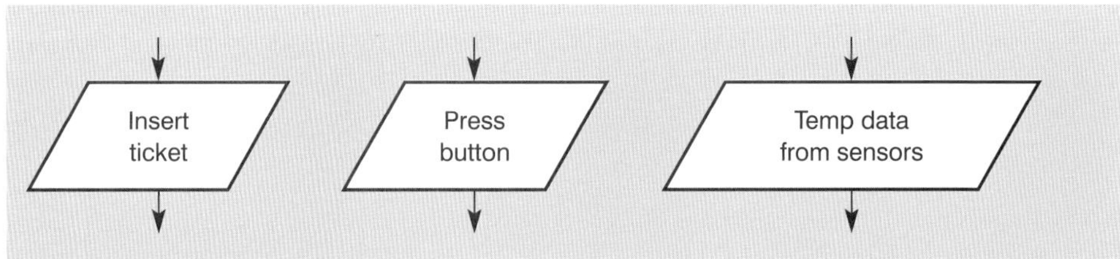

Output boxes

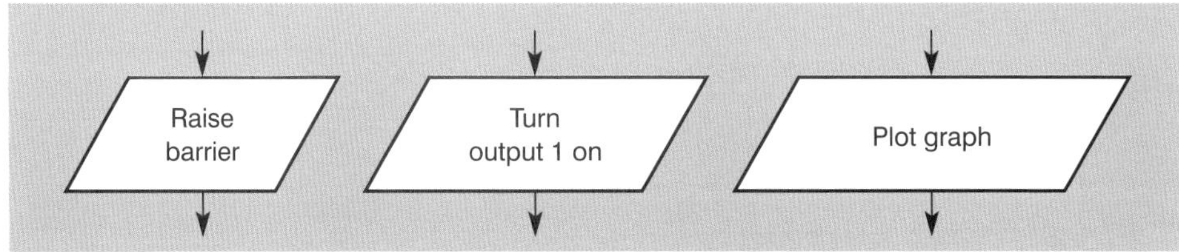

Notice the boxes don't need to be the same size.

Process boxes

Like input boxes, process boxes have one arrow going in and another coming out. They are also called activity boxes because something is done with the input.

Here are some typical processes:

Process boxes such as counters and delays.

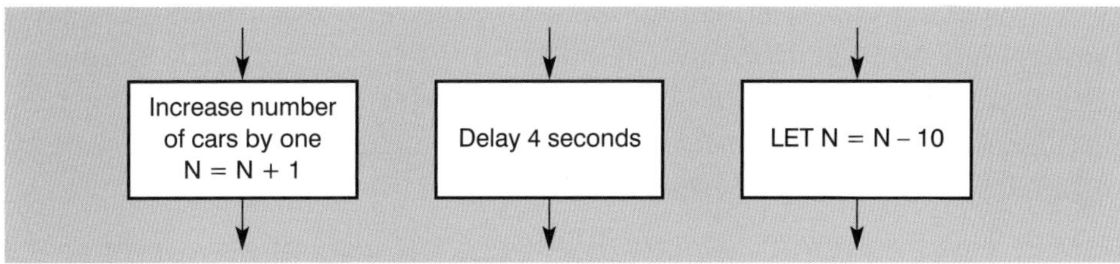

Subroutine boxes

Suppose you had a program that contained instructions that needed to be repeated several times. Rather than repeat each section, it is better to use a subroutine. A subroutine is a section of a program that can be called upon when needed. Sometimes you will hear subroutines referred to by the alternative name 'procedures'.

For example, you could have a series of steps to draw a window. If there were four identical windows on a diagram of a house, we could simply refer to the subroutine every time we needed to draw one of them.The subroutine box should be given a name. The flowchart for the subroutine is drawn separately.

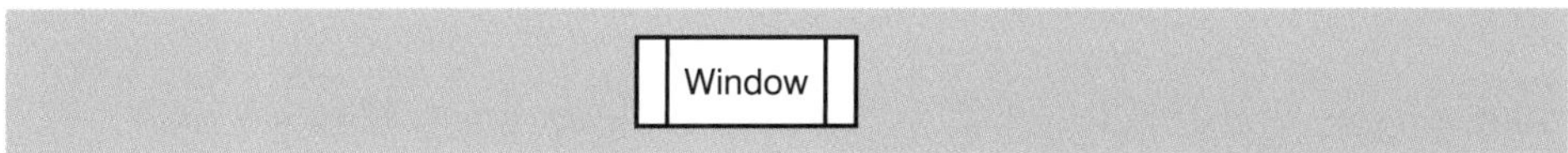

Another subroutine might be the beep at a pelican crossing or the flashing lights.

You came across subroutines when you used Logo.

Decision boxes

These boxes are used to ask questions to which there are two answers: yes and no. 'Yes' and 'no' must be written alongside the paths to show which path is being taken.

The flowchart will take one of two alternative paths, depending on the answer to the question in the decision box.

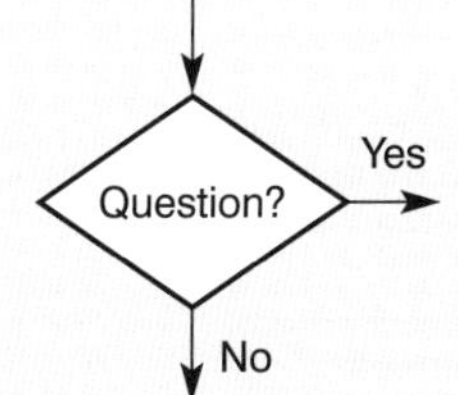

KEY WORDS

decision – a step that asks a question to which there is a yes or no answer. On the basis of the answer to the question one of two possible paths are then taken

They can be used to check for feedback from an input signal. For example, they could decide whether a temperature was more than, less than or equal to a certain value. Another use of a decision is to check whether a certain value has been reached. For example, a car park would need to check whether the number of cars in the car park has reached capacity so that a 'car park full' message can be displayed and the car park barrier will be instructed to remain closed until cars have left, thus freeing up spaces.

Here is a section of a flowchart that keeps the level of a swimming pool constant. The depth of the water in the pool could be measured using a pressure sensor. The pressure on the sensor varies with water depth. Deeper water means more pressure on the sensor.

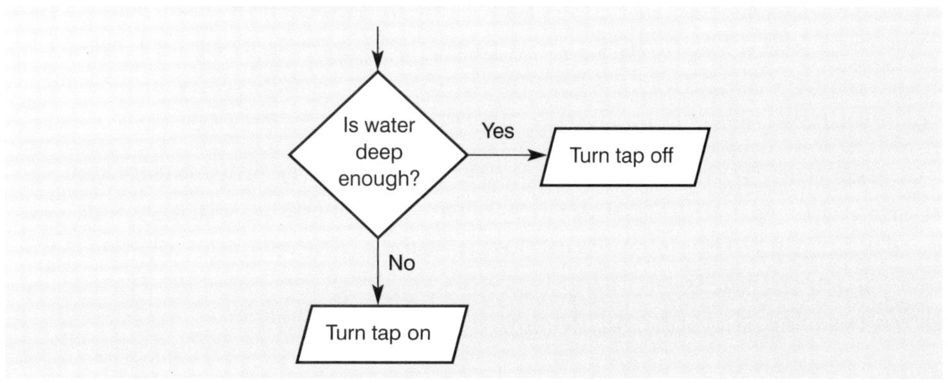

On the basis of the decision made, there are alternative outputs

Take a look at the following section of a flowchart. This section looks at the security light for a house. The sensor is continually checking for movement. If it detects movement the light comes on and it keeps checking for movement. This means if there is someone outside moving around, the light will stay on. If the movement stops, the answer to the question 'Has sensor detected movement?' will be no. The light stays on 2 minutes and is then turned off.

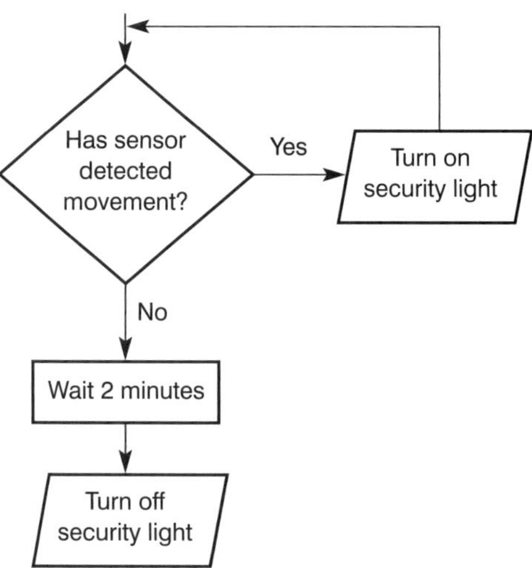

This security light system uses a decision box to decide whether to turn the light on or off

Notice that the lights are the outputs from this system.

WORKSHEETWORKSHEETWORKSHEETWORKSHEETWORKSHEET

WORKSHEET 7.6.3 Matching flowcharts to systems

Here are some simple systems and some flowcharts. You have to match the system to its correct flowchart. Put your answers into the table. Your teacher may give you a worksheet on which to work or you may be asked to copy the table into your book.

System 1: A beacon at a zebra crossing

The flashing beacons can be controlled by a computer

System 2: A buzzer that sounds when a shop door is opened

A system to alert the shopkeeper that a shopper has entered the shop

System 3: A system that fills a bath with water to a certain temperature and up to a certain level

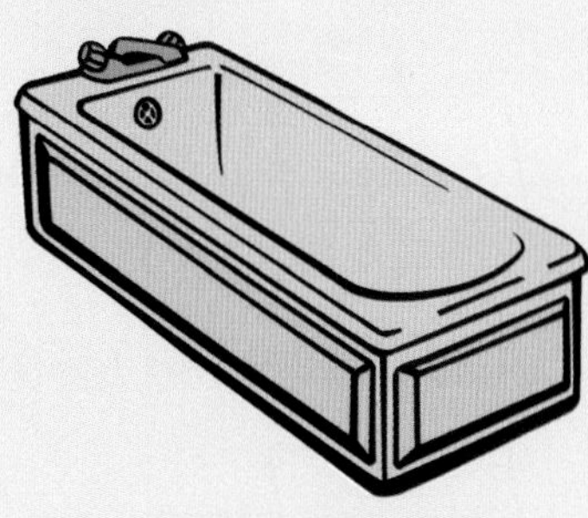

An automatic bath filling system

System 4: A traffic light system

A computer controls the sequencing of traffic lights

Here are some flowcharts. You have to decide which flowchart goes with each system. NB: You have not been told what each of the outputs are, as it would make the job too easy!

Flowchart 1

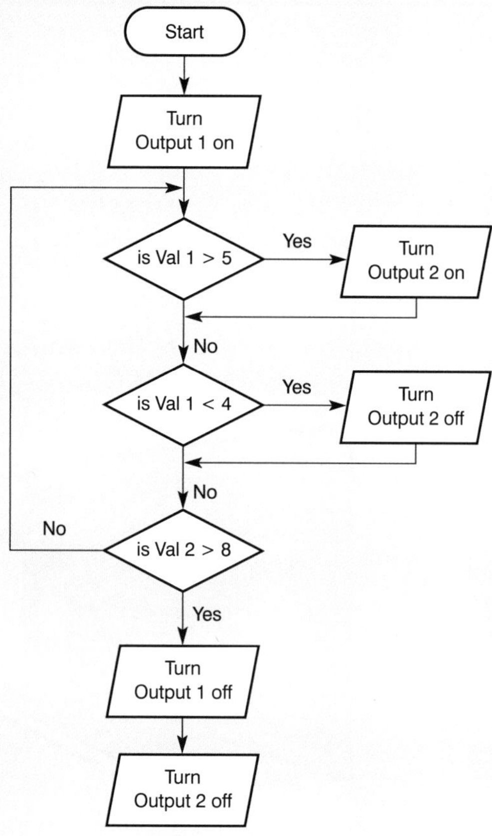

Flowchart 2

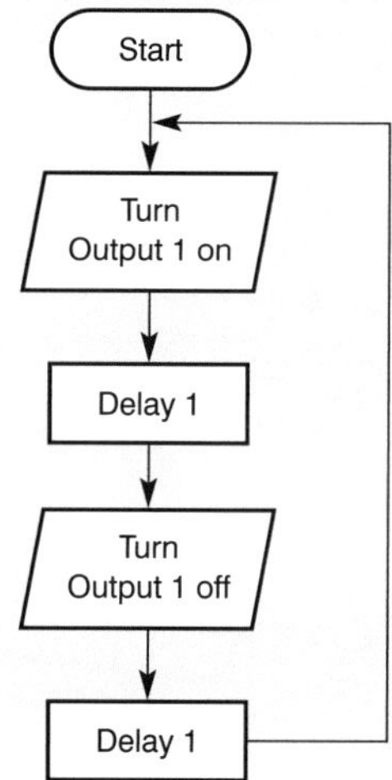

Flowchart 3

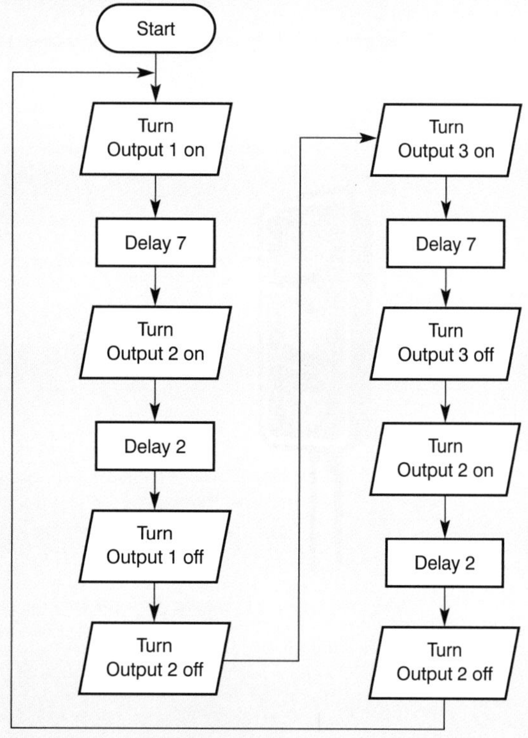

Flowchart 4

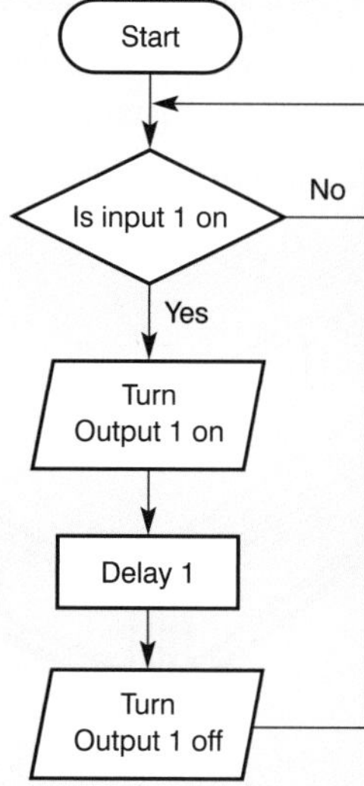

When you have worked out which flowchart matches each system, copy and complete this table:

Name of system	Matching flowchart number
System 1: A beacon at a zebra crossing	
System 2: A buzzer that sounds when a shop door is opened	
System 3: A system that fills a bath with water to a certain temperature and up to a certain level	
System 4: A traffic light system	

Lesson 5: CREATING AND TESTING CONTROL MODELS

In this lesson you will learn how to control a number of different models.

Traffic light control

Without traffic lights, the traffic in our towns and cities would probably grind to a halt during the rush hours. Traffic lights keep traffic moving. This reduces pollution, driver frustration, the cost of a journey and allows us all to stay in bed that little bit longer!

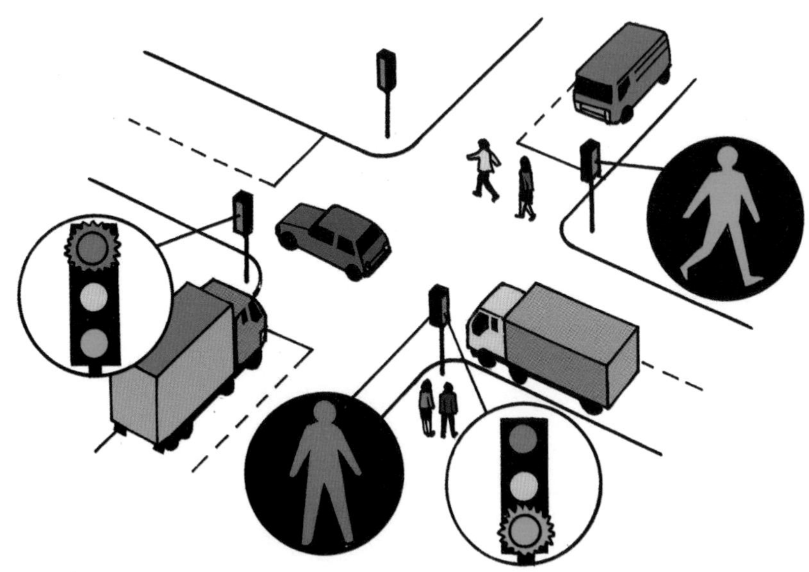

WORKSHEETWORKSHEETWORKSHEETWORKSHEETWORKSHEET

WORKSHEET 7.6.4 Traffic light sequences

Complete the worksheet, showing the sequence of traffic light signals for one complete cycle from red to green and back to red.

Your teacher may give you a worksheet to work on. If you do not get a worksheet, draw the blank diagrams and complete them.

Fill in the spaces on the worksheet to show which lights are on and off. You should also say what instructions each sequence tells the driver.

If you have coloured pencils you can shade in the appropriate lights, otherwise just write the name of the colour where the lights should go.

The first one has been done for you.

WORKSHEET 7.6.5 Putting the traffic light instructions into the correct order

Here is a set of instructions that can be given to control the traffic lights. They are not in the correct order. You have to write them down in the correct order. Use Worksheet 7.6.4 to help you.

Your teacher may give you a worksheet to write your answers on. If not, you will need to copy the answers into your book. Start the sequence from switching on the red light.

Switch on red
Delay 5
Switch on green
Switch on amber
Switch off green
Switch off amber

Delay 30
Switch on amber
Delay 5
Switch off red and amber
Delay 30

The numbers in the 'Delay' instructions represent a time in seconds and these instructions keep the lights on for a certain period.

This diagram shows a junction containing sets of traffic lights.

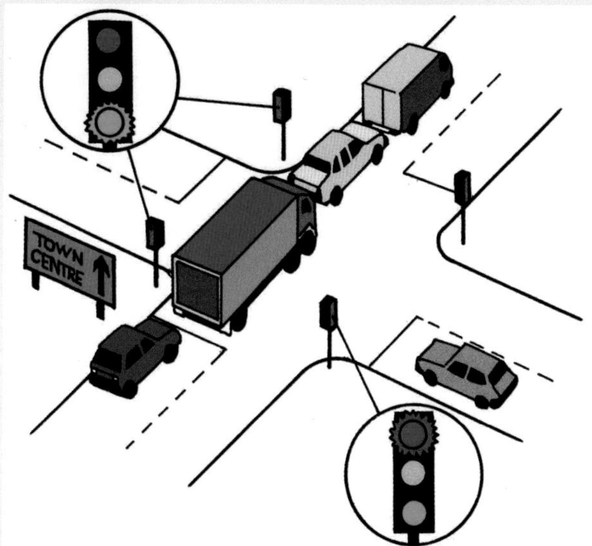

It is the morning rush hour and there is a lot more traffic travelling in the direction towards town. In the evening the main flow of traffic will be reversed as people travel home.

Explain why you think that some traffic lights should not have a set program for any time of the day.

WORKSHEET 7.6.6 Working out the outputs for a system

Your teacher may give you a worksheet to work on. If you do not get a worksheet, you will have to draw the following table before completing it.

An interface is needed when a device is connected to the computer. These are needed for several reasons, the main one being that the current required to operate a filament lamp or motor could damage the computer. The interface provides a connection between the device being controlled and the computer issuing the control instructions.

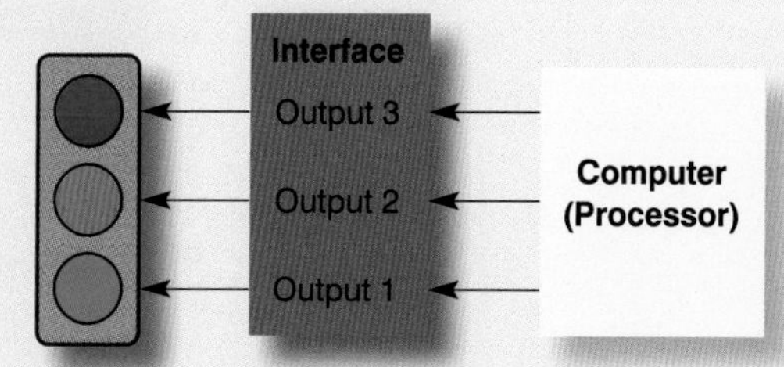

The interface sits between the output device (i.e. the traffic lights) and the processor

What it means	Instruction to control output (i.e. which outputs are on and off)
Stop	Turn output 3 on (Assume that outputs 1 and 2 are already off.)
Get ready to go	
Stop unless it is too dangerous to do so	
Go if it is clear	

Modelling traffic lights

Traffic lights can be modelled by using some equipment like that shown here:

A traffic light model that can be controlled by a computer

This equipment can be connected to the computer used to control the lights, and you can issue sets of instructions to create sequences.

If you do not have the equipment at school, an animation of the lights can be shown using a special piece of software called Flowol. Here is a picture of a set of lights at a pelican crossing. Using the software called Flowol you can issue instructions using a flowchart and then see what happens when they are obeyed. If you make a mistake, you can try to work out what happened and then alter the flowchart and try again.

A screen from Flowol. Using this software you can learn how to issue instructions to control a pelican crossing system

Make it happen

ACTIVITY 14: Understanding the problem

Here is a diagram of a junction. The side road is not as busy as the main road.

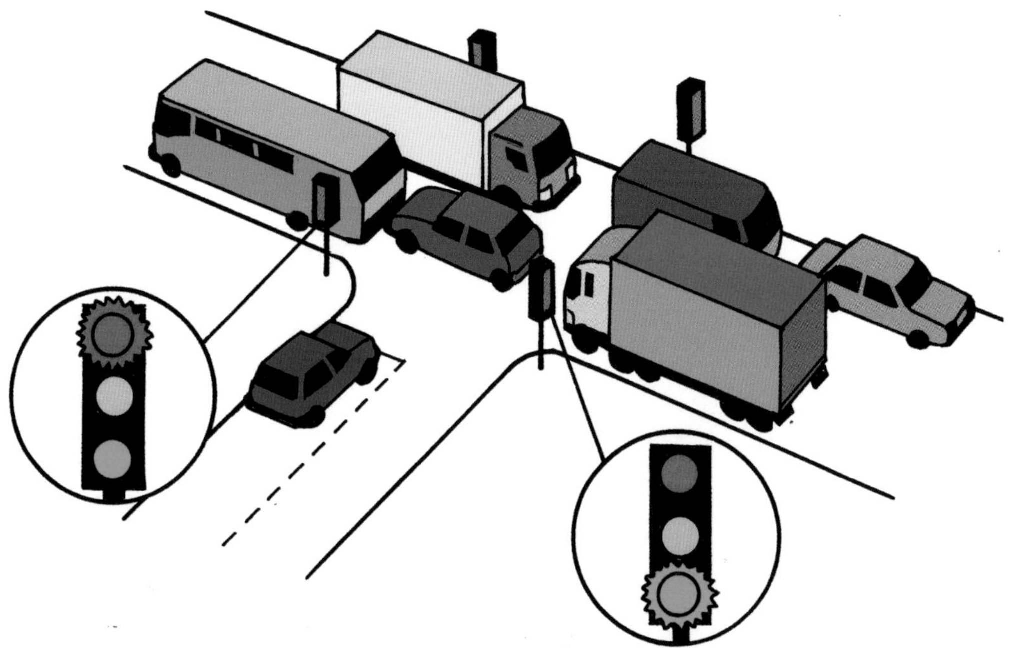

1. The green light stays on longer on the main road than on the side road. Why is this?
2. Traffic lights continually monitor themselves to check they are working properly. If they detect an error, all the lights are turned off. Why does the system do this?
3. The timing sequence of the lights might not be the same throughout the day. Why is this?
4. What may be added to a traffic light system to make it easier and safer for pedestrians to cross?
5. Cameras are sometimes seen at traffic lights. What are these cameras for and how do they make the junction safer?

Traffic lights: using sensors to make the system more intelligent

We have already seen that some traffic lights operate using a set sequence. Each traffic light has a set time for red and green to show.

If you arrived at these lights at 3.30 in the morning and they showed red, then even though there was no other traffic around, you would still wait the same length of time as you would have done during the peak period.

Some traffic lights are more intelligent than this and make use of sensors to detect the flow from all directions. If they detect that there are no other cars waiting or approaching, they will change the lights to let you through.

Make it happen

ACTIVITY 15: Traffic lights at road works

For this activity you have to design, build and then test a system for controlling a pair of traffic lights at road works. Before you start, read through the following description, which sets the scene for the activity.

Setting the scene

One lane of a two lane road has been closed for resurfacing works. Two sets of traffic lights have been set up to control the traffic. Only one line of traffic is allowed through at a time, so when one set of lights are on green, the other must be on red and vice versa.

There is a time delay to clear the line of traffic, so this means that as one light goes on red the other opposing light will not go on green immediately. The section of road to be closed is a quarter of a mile long.

A single lane being controlled by a pair of traffic lights

Look at the diagram carefully so that you understand the arrangement. There are two sets of traffic lights (Set A and Set B).

Here is a table showing the colours and the output numbers for each set of lights.

Set A lights	Outputs
RED	Output 3
AMBER	Output 2
GREEN	Output 1
Set B lights	**Outputs**
RED	Output 6
AMBER	Output 5
GREEN	Output 4

Task 1

Draw two flowcharts (one for each set of lights) to show how the system would operate. You should turn the outputs on and off by using commands such as

Turn output 3 on, Turn output 5 off etc.

If you have the Flowol software you can use it to draw the flowcharts rather than doing them manually.

You only need to complete this activity if you have the Flowol software.

Task 2

You are now required to use your flowchart to run the steps to check that the system works as expected.

EXTENSION ACTIVITY

How might the system be adjusted to make sure that the lane is completely clear of traffic before the opposing traffic is allowed through? Adjust your flowchart to take this into account and print out a copy of your flowchart.

Make it happen

ACTIVITY 16: A car park barrier

In this activity you will find out how to control a car park barrier.

Read the following story:

My mother drove up to the barrier but the barrier did not go up. Instead a message was displayed on a screen that the car park was full. We could not reverse because there was another car waiting to enter the car park behind us. Instead we waited. We noticed a car travelling in the opposite direction leaving the car park. As soon as the barrier went down after the car had passed through, the 'car park full' message went out and the car park barrier went up to allow us through.

Getting the computer to count for us

My mother and I thought it was clever that the car park knew that the car park was full and not to let any more cars in.

When we left the car park my mother approached the barrier, which went up automatically, and we drove out of the car park.

For this activity you will look at how this control system works and how it uses a counter to count the cars entering and leaving the car park.

There are two barriers and these are side by side: one at the entrance and the other at the exit. As cars are allowed in and out, the system will need to keep track of the number of cars so that it can tell when the car park is full. When the car park is full, a 'car park is full' notice is displayed and the barrier will not be raised until a car leaves to make space.

Using a counter

It is important to only allow cars into the car park if there are spaces left for them to park.

To make things simple we will assume that the car park is empty at the start of the day.

Two counters will be needed: one to increase the counter by one as the barrier is raised to allow a car into the car park and one to decrease the counter by one as the other barrier is raised to allow cars out of the car park.

Counters need to start off from a certain value. If the car park is completely empty this would be zero.

To understand counters you need to understand what a variable is. A variable is a letter that can be given a value. This value can be changed. It is just like a letter in a formula, where you use a letter to represent a number. Variables can have calculations done on them.

Take a look at this example of a counter.

Here is the subroutine that closes the 'In' barrier after a car has passed through.

This subroutine uses a counter to count the number of cars going through the barrier.

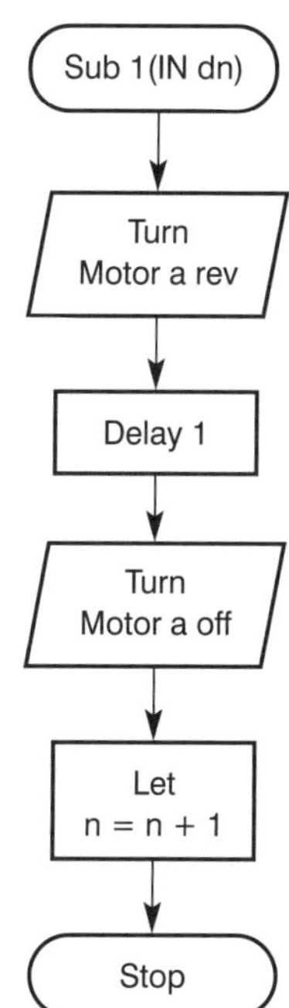

A flowchart to close the barrier from open and also add 1 to the number of vehicles in the car park

This subroutine is used to put the barrier down on the exit and to subtract one from the counter. This tells the system how many cars remain in the car park.

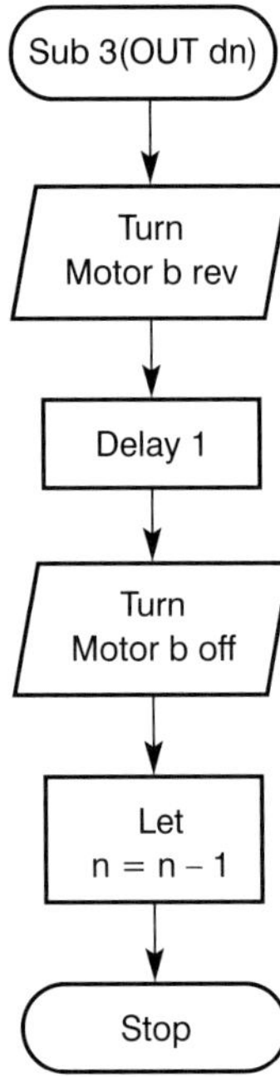

A flowchart to close the 'Out' barrier from open and to subtract 1 from the number of vehicles in the car park

Look at the flowchart below. It looks at the value of n, the counter. If n is greater than 3 (i.e. 4, 5, 6, etc.), then output 5 is turned on, which is the 'car park full' sign. If n is not greater than 3 (i.e. if it is 3 or less), then it loops around again to just after the start. This way it keeps checking to see if the car park is full.

Remember that n is changing all the time as some cars leave and some cars enter the car park.

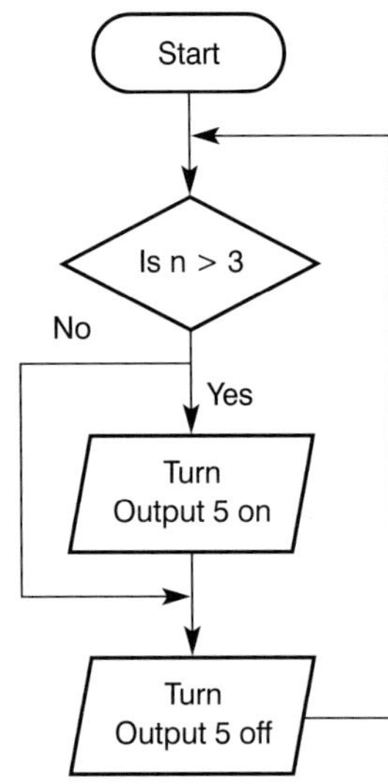

Notice that if the 'car park full' sign was on (because the car park was full – it only holds 4 cars) and then a car left the car park, the value of n would now be 3. If the answer to the decision 'is n > 3?' is NO, then output 5 (the 'car park full' sign) is switched off.

You can see that a control system that looks quite simple is in fact more complex. By using subroutines it makes it easier to break down an overall task into smaller, manageable tasks.

Part of the flowchart for the car park barrier system that turns on the 'car park full' sign

What you have to do:

1. This problem is best solved using subroutines, with each subroutine being used for part of the task.

   The operation of the barrier system can be divided up into the following steps.

   'In' barrier up

   'In' barrier down

   'Out' barrier up

   'Out' barrier down

   The flowcharts have already been drawn for 'In' barrier down and 'Out' barrier down.

   You are now required to produce flowcharts for 'In' barrier up and 'Out' barrier up.

   You can either use the software Flowol for this or you could draw them manually.

2. If you are using Flowol, you can test each subroutine separately, as it will be easier to sort out problems.

   Test each subroutine fully to check that it is working properly.

3. You are now required to produce the main program (or the main subroutine) which will join up all these subroutines. To do this you will need to draw a flowchart.

   Remember to use the subroutine boxes in this flowchart.

4. If you have Flowol you will be able to use the Car Park Mimic so that your flowchart can actually be used to run a simulation of an actual car park system. Do not worry if it does not work first time – they seldom do. Usually it is something you have forgotten.

5. You now have to test your system. Decide how you will do this. You will have to try all the combinations of the input to make sure that the outputs are what you expected.

6. Write an evaluation of your solution. How near was it to the real thing? Is there anything that can be added that will make it behave more realistically?

Feedback

Feedback is needed to make the car park barrier system more intelligent. Just because the computer has issued an instruction to turn the barrier motor on in order to raise the barrier, does not mean that the barrier is now fully up. There could be an obstacle in the way, such as a child swinging on it to hold it down. There needs to be two input sensors to know that the barrier is fully up or fully down.

What sensors would you suggest?

These input sensors feed back a signal to the computer to let it know that the barrier is fully up or down.

All control systems make use of feedback.

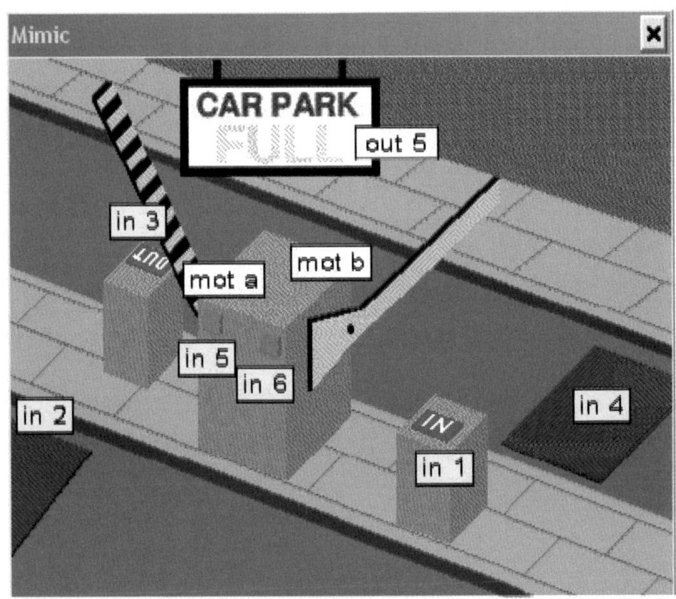

A car park barrier system. Notice there are two barriers: one for in and one for out

Look at the summary table of the inputs and outputs in this system on the opposite page. To understand this table you must look at the diagram above as well.

You may notice that there are some inputs that are included on the diagram that are not included in this table. Inputs 5 and 6 are feedback signals to check whether the barriers are fully raised or fully down. To keep things simple, we will not use these inputs.

Car park inputs	What it does
Input 1	Switch pressed by motorist to issue ticket and raise barrier
Input 2	Pressure mat to detect that car has passed the 'In' barrier
Input 3	Switch pressed by motorist to let them out of the car park
Input 4	Pressure mat to detect that car has passed the 'Out' barrier
Car park outputs	
Motor a	Raises 'In' barrier when motor goes forward and lowers barrier when motor goes backward
Motor b	Raises 'out' barrier when motor goes forward and lowers barrier when motor goes backward
Output 5	Lights up 'car park full' sign

Controlling the house of the future

You may think that controlling most things in your house using the Internet is something for the future. You would be wrong, because it is quite easy to do now.

What can be controlled?

- Lights can be switched on and off at different times when you are away to deter burglars
- Your alarm system could send you an e-mail if your burglar alarm has been triggered
- Switch the heating on from a computer at work so the house is warm when you arrive home. You can do this using timers, but you need to know what time you will arrive home.

More about feedback

KEY WORDS

feedback – where the output from a system directly affects the input

Feedback is used with most control systems. You saw in the last activity how feedback could be used to check the exact position of the barrier. Here is another example of how feedback can be used.

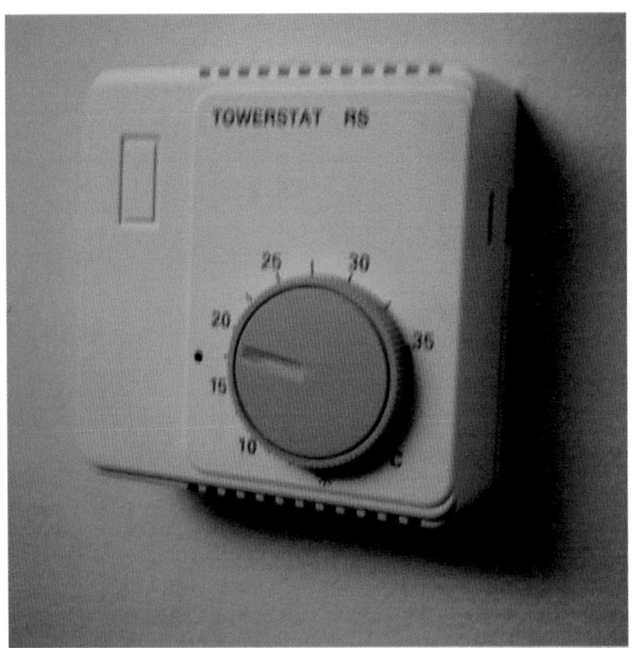

If a heater is switched on by a control system, the room will get warmer. A temperature sensor could be used to monitor the temperature in the room. The output from the system (i.e. the heat from the heater) is continually monitored and input into the computer to see if the temperature is high enough so that an instruction may be given to the output (i.e. the heater) to switch it off.

This is called feedback because the output (i.e. the temperature produced by the heater) is being used to alter the input (i.e. the temperature as measured by the temperature sensor). This, in turn, causes the computer to decide what to do with the output (i.e. whether to leave the heater on or to switch it off).

This is sometimes called a feedback loop because there is constant communication between the sensor and the processor so that the situation is continually being monitored.

If the room goes below the ideal temperature setting for the room, the processor will send a signal to turn the heater on again.

7 Measuring physical data

Lesson 1:
INTRODUCTION TO MEASURING PHYSICAL DATA

Using sensors and computers to measure change

You will have come across the use of sensors in the last unit as well as the work you did for Key Stage 2. In this unit you will learn about how sensors can be linked to computers and used to measure changes in the physical environment.

You will learn about how devices called data loggers are able to take readings and store them without the need to be permanently connected to the computer. You will get practice at using data loggers to perform your own experiments.

At the end of this unit you will be able to design and perform your own experiments using sensors and data loggers. You will also be able to interpret and present the results in the most appropriate way.

Background theory and key information

In the past, if you wanted to measure a physical quantity such as temperature, you would have used a thermometer to take the reading. The problem is that usually lots of readings are needed, and this involves being there at the exact place and time when the reading needs to be taken.

There are several problems with taking readings manually:

- You can forget to take a reading, so your data has a reading missing.
- You are late taking a reading.
- You take the reading incorrectly.

If readings are taken automatically using a sensor, all the readings are taken accurately and at the right time. This is why we now tend to take readings using sensors.

Measuring changes in the environment

The environment means the surrounding conditions. Our surroundings are important to us because we have to live in them.

Being able to measure changes in the environment is important to everyone. It is necessary to take regular readings to try to predict weather patterns or the effect that our lifestyle is having on the environment.

Why do we measure changes in the environment?

Environmental data is needed to:

- produce weather forecasts
- predict hurricanes, tornadoes and flooding
- assess the effect of global warming
- check for pollution in seas and rivers
- check that the conditions inside a room containing priceless paintings are suitable
- check that the working conditions inside a house or office are not damaging your health
- prosecute people who are making too much noise, creating lots of vibration, putting a neighbour's garden in the dark, etc.

Environmental data in the past would have been collected by humans. Now it would be rare to see humans taking these measurements, as it is much easier to take these readings automatically using sensors.

What is a sensor?

Sensors are used to detect and sometimes measure physical quantities such as temperature, sound and light. A sensor is an input device because it collects data.

Sensors can be used to take a single reading or they can be used to monitor changes over a period of time by taking lots of readings.

Taking lots of measurements over a period of time is called monitoring.

The data from the sensor is sent to the computer for processing. In some cases the data is simply stored, and when the rest of the readings are obtained a graph can be produced. In some cases a decision to do something can be made depending on the value measured by the sensor. For example, if the moisture level in the soil is low, the computer can decide whether it should turn on a sprinkler system.

KEY WORDS

data – information in a form that the computer can understand

monitoring – keeping a record of the measurements from sensors over a certain period of time

sensors – devices that measure physical quantities such as temperature, pressure, etc.

In Unit 6 sensors were used to input data into the computer so that the processor could decide which output devices to switch on or off.

What quantities can be measured?

There are sensors available to detect almost any physical quantity. Below, some of the main sensors are introduced.

Light sensors

Light sensors can detect brightness of light. They can be used to detect low light levels so that a light can be turned on. Light sensors are used to turn streetlights on when it gets dark. They can also be used to turn security lights on when it gets dark and to switch them off when it gets light.

Temperature sensors

Temperature sensors are used to detect and measure temperature. These can be used as part of a central heating system that switches a heater on when it gets cool. It can then be used to turn the heater off when the temperature has risen above a certain level.

Passive infra-red sensors (PIRs)

These are used to detect movement in a room. These are the sensors you see in corners of rooms as part of a burglar alarm system.

Sound sensors

Sound sensors detect the loudness or softness of a sound. They are used by councils to prosecute people who make too much noise.

Push switches

Push switches can be used to sense whether a door is open or closed. The interior light in a car has a push switch to turn on the light when the door is opened.

Humidity sensors

A humidity sensor determines how much moisture there is in the air or the soil. They are frequently found in greenhouses and art galleries.

KEY WORDS

humidity – the amount of moisture in the air

Pressure sensors

Pressure sensors can be found on roads to detect cars approaching a set of traffic lights. They can also be used to measure the depth of water in rivers (the deeper the water, the higher the pressure). You could put a pressure sensor under the carpet near the door in a burglar alarm system. When the intruder's weight pushes down on the pad, an alarm is set off.

ACTIVITIESACTIVITIESACTIVITIESACTIVITIESACTIVITIESACTIVITIES

ACTIVITY 1: Thinking about sensors

Here are some questions to get you thinking about the use of sensors:

1. Newer streetlights make use of light sensors. Older street lights had clocks in them. This meant that they could be set to come on and go off at a certain time.
   (a) Why might newer streetlights be more economical to run than the older ones?
   (b) Why do the streetlights making use of sensors provide greater road safety than those with a clock?
2. Write down a list of the sensors you might find in a home. For each sensor you should say the name of the appliance in which it is found and say why it is included in the appliance.
3. You have already come across many different types of uses for sensors in this unit. Copy and complete the following table. Make sure that you come up with some applications that are not mentioned in this unit.

The first one has been done for you.

Name of sensor	Application
Moisture sensor	To measure the percentage of water in brick or wood to indicate the presence of wet rot.

Applications of sensors to make our lives safer

There are lots of devices around that make use of sensors to make our lives safer.

Speed cameras

Some of these devices use radar to measure and detect the speed of passing motorists. If a car is over the speed limit, photographs are taken by the device to prove the offence. Some systems can recognise the number plates and look up the owner of the car on the computer and send him or her a warning letter or fine automatically.

Speed cameras reduce the number of serious accidents

Air pollution monitoring

Air quality is important to everyone, so councils monitor the quality of the air in their region. If the air is poor quality, they try to find out why so that the offenders can be prosecuted.

The quality of the air we breathe is continually monitored

Car exhaust monitoring

When a car is three years old it has to have an MOT every year. As part of the MOT, exhaust gases are tested with a sensor to make sure they are not too smoky.

Exhaust gases cause air pollution in cities. This is why cars have to pass an emissions test as part of their MOT

Sensors help to improve car safety

Sensors in cars

Sensors in a convertible car can detect whether the car is likely to roll over in an accident so that special protection pillars can be raised to protect the occupants. Sensors also sense when a car undergoes rapid deceleration when the car has hit something so that the air bags can be activated.

Red light cameras

Look at this photograph taken by a red light camera at a road junction. It shows a car jumping a red light. The light must have been red for some time because the traffic in the other two lanes has built up. And notice that a pedestrian has already started to cross.

Photograph of a car jumping a red light taken by a red light camera

This photograph shows how dangerous the situation was. The pedestrian could easily have been killed.

This pedestrian has had a lucky escape

Notice the readings displayed on the screen. These readings log the date and the time, and they work out the speed the car was travelling at. The registration number of the vehicle is photographed so that the driver can be prosecuted.

Why not take readings yourself?

There are several reasons why you might not want to take the readings yourself. In some cases it would be impossible to do this. Here are some reasons why you might not take the readings yourself:

The changes may happen so quickly that it would not be possible for you to take readings.

The readings may need to be taken in an inhospitable environment.

If you wanted to investigate the pressure and sound changes when a balloon burst you could not take the readings yourself because they happen so fast

Weather data from very cold or very hot places can be taken automatically

It may be too dangerous to take the readings yourself.

You may not have time, as the changes you want to measure happen so slowly.

It would be dangerous to take readings near sources of radiation

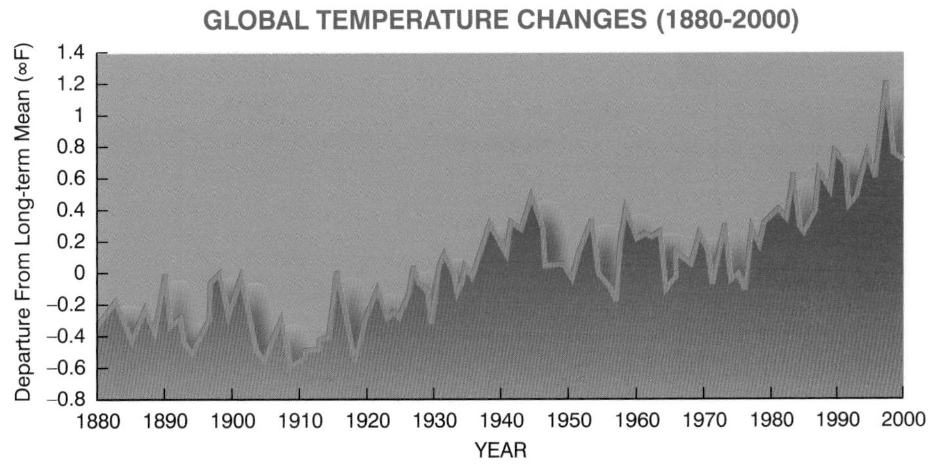

Some changes, such as global warming, take place so slowly you may not have time to take the readings

We have only mentioned a few of the sensors available. There are many more. Do some research to find out about these sensors.

Use the following website to help with your research:

www.data-harvest.co.uk/datalogging/ smartq.html

You need to write the following about each sensor:

- the name of the sensor
- what it measures
- one or more applications of how it can be used.

WORKSHEETWORKSHEETWORKSHEETWORKSHEETWORKSHEET

WORKSHEET 7.7.1 Which sensor is best?

Your teacher might give you a worksheet on which to work. If you are not given a worksheet, you should copy the answers into your book.

Here are some different sensors:

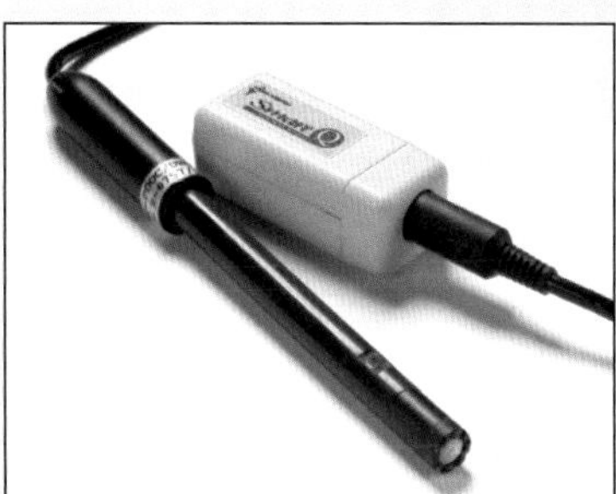

Oxygen sensor

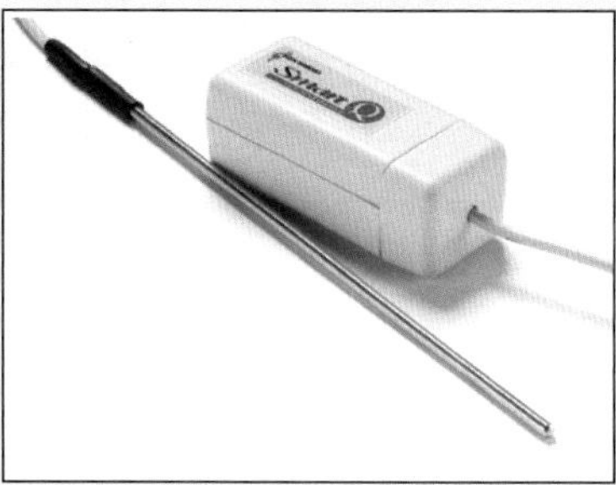

Temperature sensor

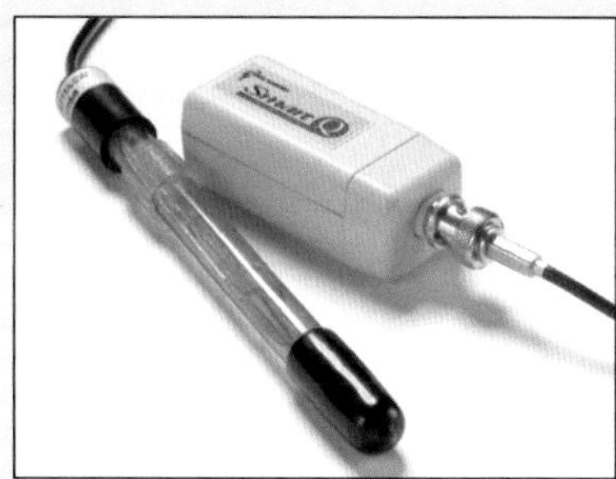

pH sensor (measures acidity and alkalinity)

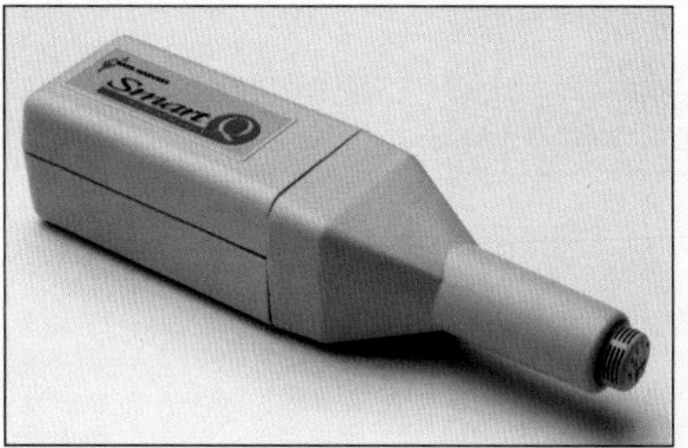

Humidity sensor

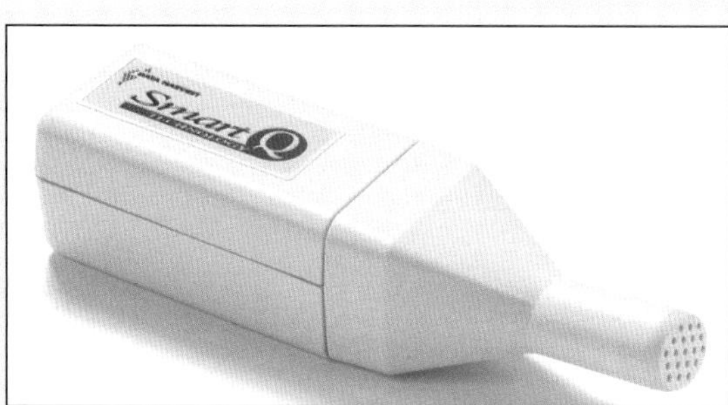

Sound sensor

Here are some things to measure. You have to decide which would be the best sensor for the job.

1. The noise made by a low-flying aircraft flying over your house
2. How dark it is in a garden surrounded by lots of trees
3. The acidity or alkalinity of the water in an aquarium tank
4. The loudness of the music from a bar
5. The temperature inside an oven
6. How hot or cold it is outside
7. The neutrality (i.e. neither acidic or alkaline) of a new soap for sensitive skin
8. How much moisture there is in the air of a room containing valuable paintings
9. The temperature of a car engine
10. The amount of oxygen in a polluted river

The advantages in using sensors and a computer

Take a look at the two temperature measurements on the right:

The computer display is much easier to read.

The computer display can show changes instantly.

The software can store and display data automatically in the most suitable format (e.g. line graph, bar graph, etc.). Look at the example below.

The graph (i.e. the red line) of how the current changes when a lamp is switched on is drawn from the data automatically. You can see that there is a current surge that dies down to a steady value. The blue line shows the light level.

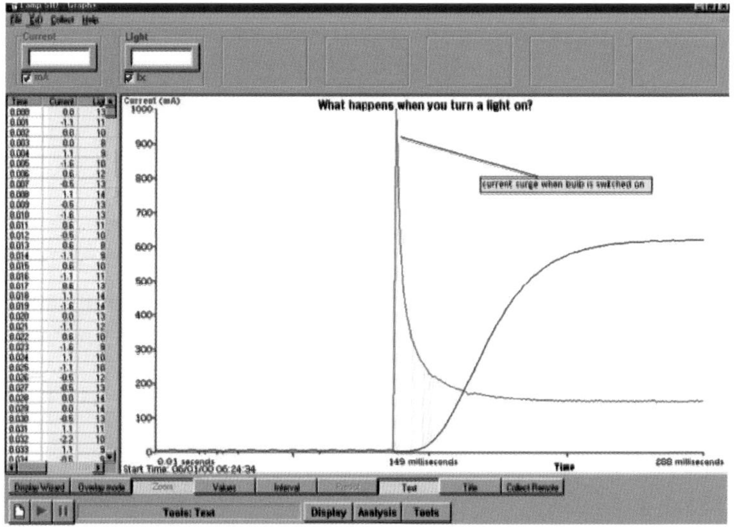

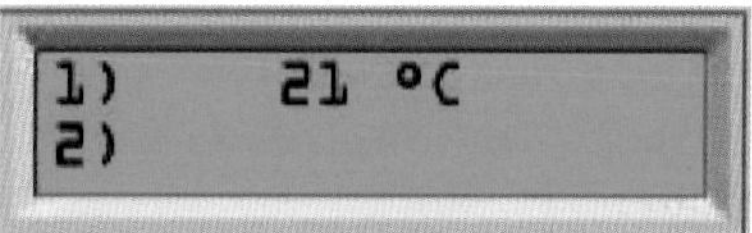

A temperature measured using a sensor

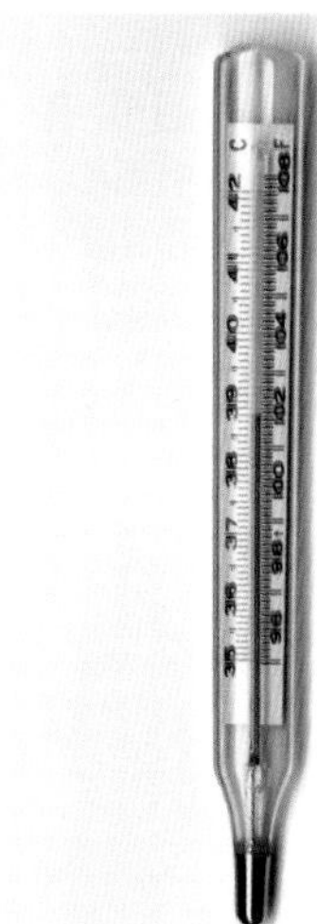

A temperature measured using a thermometer

Lesson 2: GETTING THE COMPUTER TO DO THE WORK

You cannot simply connect a sensor straight to a computer. A special device called an interface is needed, which makes sure that the computer and sensor are able to communicate with each other. Some sensors have their own interfaces built into them so that they may be connected directly to the computer. Most monitoring systems have separate interfaces.

Most interfaces are quite boring looking devices. They are simply boxes of electronics.

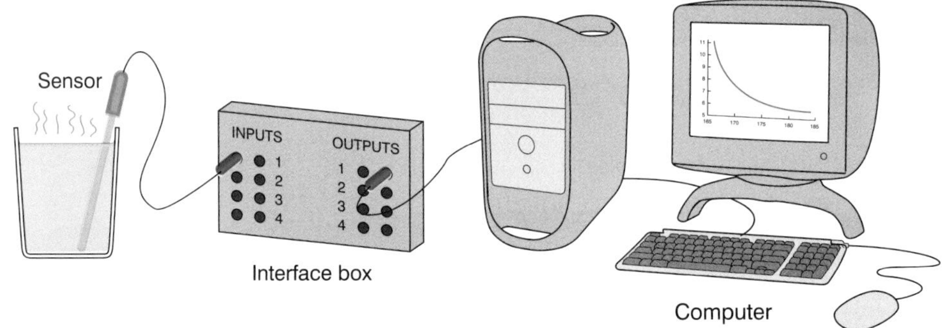

An interface box is connected between the sensor and the computer

KEY WORDS

data logging – a system that automatically collects data over a certain period of time. Remote weather stations use data logging

Data logging

What is data logging?

Data logging involves collecting readings over a certain period of time. These readings could be any physical quantity that varies with time, such as temperature, sunlight, oxygen levels and pollutants in the air.

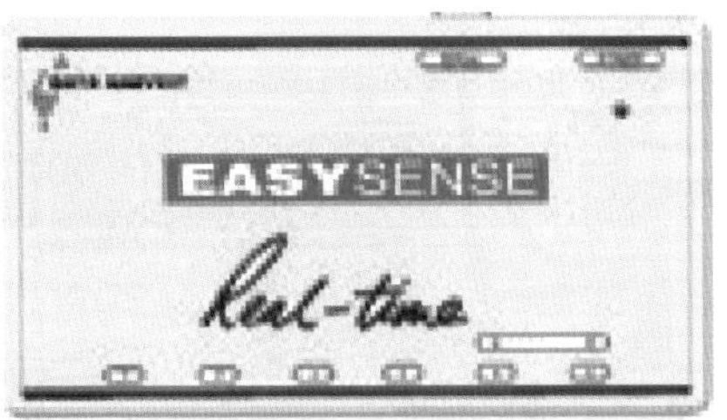

A real time data logger

This data logger operates in real time, which means that it needs to be connected to the computer when making its measurements. This is fine when the computer and experiment are in the same place. The readings are stored inside the computer.

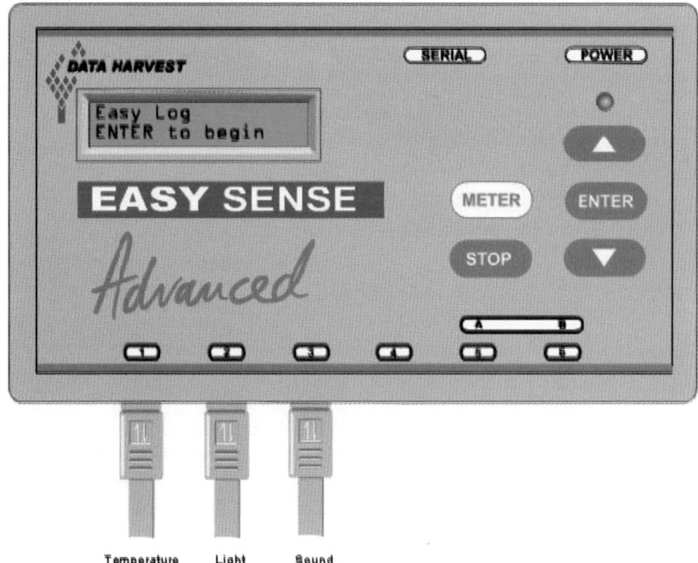

This data logger can be used remotely because it stores the data automatically over a period of time. It does not need to be connected to the computer when taking its readings

Data logging involves:

- collecting the readings automatically using sensors
- storing and processing the readings using a computer.

The advantages of using data logging

Data logging has several advantages over taking the readings manually. For example:

- You do not have to worry about forgetting to take a reading, as they are taken automatically
- There are no human errors in the reading so the readings are accurate
- You do not need to be present when the readings are taken
- Readings can be taken at exactly the same time (24 hours a day and 365 days a year)
- Data logging can be performed in areas where people would not want to live (e.g. the North Pole, up a mountain, in the middle of the ocean, etc.).

The disadvantages of data logging

There are a couple of disadvantages:

- Data logging equipment could malfunction and give false readings
- If they are used in very remote areas they may communicate back to the main computer using radio signals. This means the use of expensive communications equipment.

A remote weather station making use of data logging. The data is sent by radio signals to a main computer for processing

Logging period and logging frequency

The logging period is the time over which the readings are taken. For example, if you wanted to look at the cooling of hot coffee in different types of cup, a logging period might be one hour. If you wanted to investigate how the dissolved oxygen varies in a pond over a year, then the logging period would be a year.

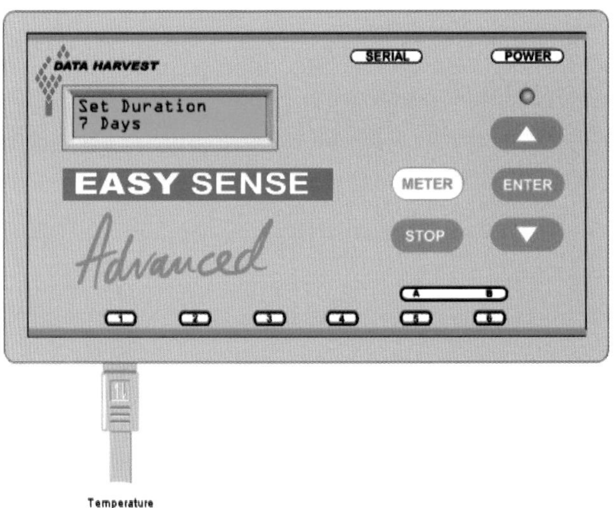

This data logger has a temperature sensor attached and the logging period has been set to 7 days

KEY WORDS

logging frequency – how often the readings are taken

logging period – the total amount of time over which the readings are taken

The logging frequency is how often a reading is taken (per minute, per hour, per day, etc.).

Data logging is ideal for monitoring those changes that take place very quickly or very slowly. In the case of very fast changes, the data logger can be set up to take lots of readings very close together. It would be impossible for a human to take the readings as quickly.

The stages of data logging

Here are the stages involved in data logging:

1 Set up the logging equipment (i.e. choose and connect the sensors to the computer). In some systems an interface is needed between the sensors and the computer, but in other systems the interface is included as part of the sensors.

2 Set the logging period (i.e. how long the data is to be logged for).

3 Set the logging frequency (i.e. how often a reading is to be taken (every second, every minute, etc.)).

4 Collect the data.

5 Transfer the data to the computer for processing. The data can be transferred as each reading is taken or stored inside the data logger for downloading into the computer later.

6 Process/analyse the data. This involves using software. Sometimes the data can be transferred to an applications package (e.g a spreadsheet) to calculate statistics such as mean, mode and median and to produce graphs and charts.

Make it happen

ACTIVITY 2: Using a data logger

Your teacher will show you a data logger and allow you to take readings using it.

As you will have to use the data logger later on, you will need to make sure that you understand how to connect all the parts together and how to set it to take readings using the sensors. Also make sure that you understand how to alter the period of logging as well as the logging frequency.

Make notes as your teacher explains the data logger so that you can refer to them when using the equipment yourself.

Lesson 3: GETTING THE COMPUTER TO TAKE THE MEASUREMENTS IN AN EXPERIMENT

There is more to data logging than simply getting the computer to take the readings at exactly the right time and over the right period.

Here are the steps you would normally take when conducting an experiment using sensors and a computer:

- Start with a hypothesis
- Plan the experiment
- Design a system to take the results (telling the computer/data logger the logging frequency and logging period)
- Obtain the data
- Analyse of the data
- Present the results
- Use the results to prove/disprove the hypothesis.

Testing a hypothesis using data logging

Have you ever heard anyone say that hot water freezes more quickly than cold water? You may think that this sounds a bit strange and wonder if it is really true.

An experiment can be designed to test the hypothesis: hot water freezes more quickly than cold water.

The next stage is to plan the experiment.

Planning the experiment

You need to think about how you will actually perform the experiment and how you will take the measurements. You will also need to ask yourself whether one experiment will be sufficient or whether the experiment will need to be repeated in a different way or under different conditions.

You can jot some notes down like this, which can be written up later when you produce your final report.

> **Two beakers (polystyrene cups) are filled with identical amounts of water. One is filled with hot water from a kettle and the other is filled with water straight from the tap.**
>
> **These beakers can be placed in a freezer.**
>
> **Two temperature sensors will used; one for each cup.**
>
> **These temperature sensors could be connected to a computer but this would mean having the computer and the freezer in the same place.**
>
> **A data logger is used. This could be put on top of the freezer with the wires going into the freezer to each sensor. Hopefully, the door will still make a good seal with the wires going in. You could consider placing the whole apparatus inside the freezer.**
>
> **The data logger will need to collect readings regularly over a period of time.**

Designing the system to take the results

Here are a few things to consider:

- Whether to use a real time data logger connected to a computer or a remote data logger
- As both cups of water must be allowed enough time to freeze, they must be in the freezer for a while. So what shall we set the logging period to?
- How often should the temperature readings be taken? This is the logging frequency.

Obtaining the data

This would involve setting up all the apparatus and computing equipment, loading the data logging software and actually carrying out the experiment.

Analysis of the data

You may wish to import the data into a spreadsheet package or use the analysis features of the data logging software.

You might want to print out the readings or work out statistics such as means, modes, medians, ranges, etc.

Presenting the results

Rather than working with a table of results, it is much easier to interpret the data if you draw graphs. In this diagram, two graphs of these readings have been produced automatically by the computer

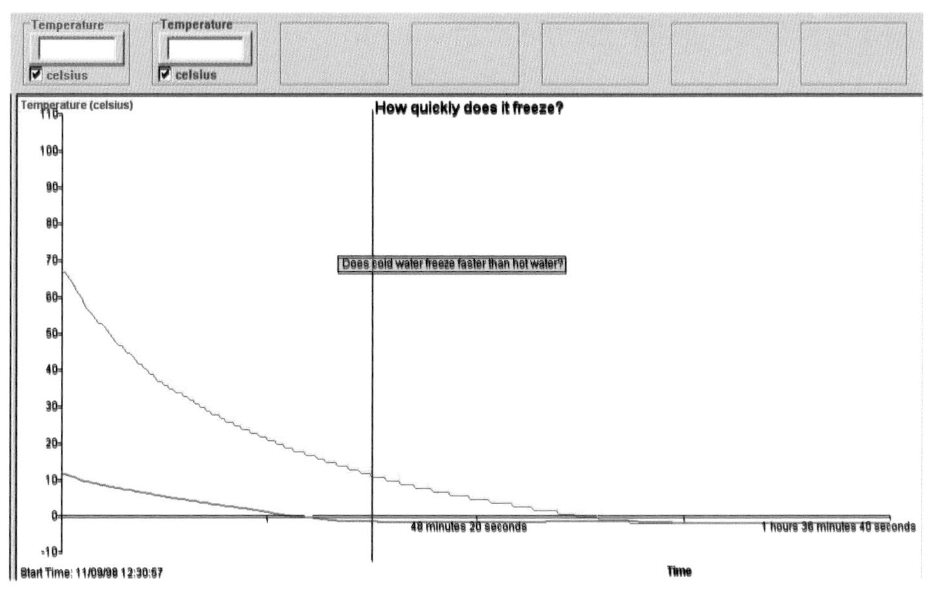

You can plot the cooling curve for the hot and cold water. Can you work out whether the original hypothesis is true or false?

with data logging software. One graph represents the cooling of the hot water and the other represents the cooling of the cold water.

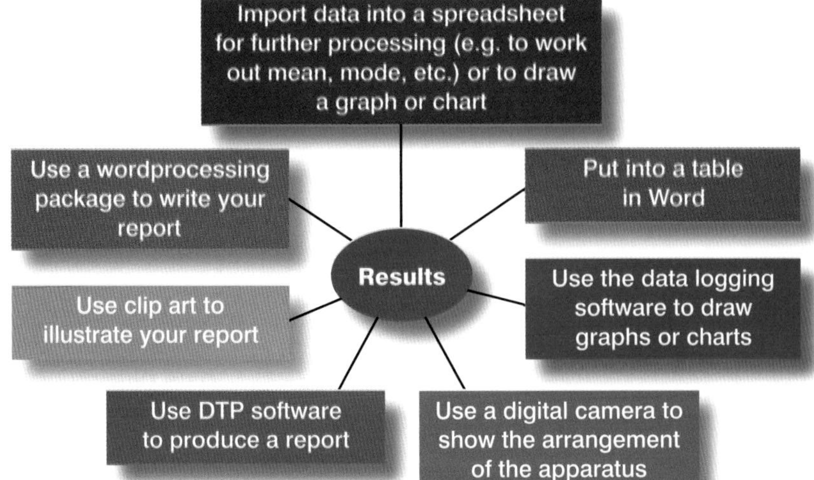

There are lots of ways that ICT can help present your results

Make it happen

ACTIVITY 3: Interpreting the graph

Look at the graph called 'How quickly does it freeze?' and then answer the following questions about it.

The graph shows a blue line and a red line.

1. (a) Which colour represents the graph for the hot water?

   (b) Explain how you knew this.

2. (a) Which colour represents the graph for the cold water?

   (b) Explain how you knew this.

3. (a) Is the hypothesis 'hot water freezes more quickly than cold water' true or false?

   (b) Explain how you arrived at this answer.

4. What can you tell from the gradient (or slope) of these two graphs?

Using spreadsheet software to help analyse results

Although a data logger takes all the hard work out of taking the readings, a human is still needed to interpret the results.

It is possible to save the data from a data logger and then import it into a spreadsheet package. This is useful if the data logging software does not have graphing and charting facilities. Once the graphs and charts have been produced using spreadsheet software, you can then import them into the wordprocessing or desktop publishing package that you are using to write up your report.

Make it happen

ACTIVITY 4: Drawing the cooling graph

Here is a section of the data produced at the start of the data logging experiment.

	A	B	C
3	Time (s)	Temp (°C)	Temp (°C)
4	0	67.0	11.7
5	20	66.9	11.6
6	0	66.1	11.4
7	60	64.9	11.2
8	80	63.8	10.9
9	100	62.0	10.6
10	120	61.1	10.3
11	140	69.7	10.0
12	160	58.3	9.8
13	180	57.1	9.6
14	200	56.2	9.5
15	220	54.9	9.3
16	240	53.9	9.1
17	260	53.0	8.9
18	280	52.7	8.7
19	300	51.7	8.6
20	320	51.0	8.4
21	340	50.0	8.2
22	360	49.2	8.1
23	380	48.0	8.0
24	400	47.4	7.8
25	420	47.0	7.7
26	440	46.0	7.5
27	460	45.5	7.4
28	480	45.0	7.3
29	500	44.1	7.1
30	520	43.8	7.0

Here is the end section of the data produced during the data logging experiment.

269	5300	-1.8	-1.9
270	5320	-1.8	-1.9
271	5340	-1.8	-1.9
272	5360	-1.8	-1.9
273	5380	-1.9	-1.9
274	5400	-1.9	-1.9
275	5420	-1.9	-1.9
276	5440	-1.9	-1.9
277	5460	-1.9	-1.9
278	5480	-1.9	-1.9
279	5500	-1.9	-1.9
280	5520	-1.9	-1.9
281	5540	-1.9	-1.9
282	5560	-1.9	-1.9
283	5580	-1.9	-1.9
284	5600	-1.9	-1.9
285	5620	-1.9	-1.9
286	5640	-1.9	-1.9
287	5660	-1.9	-2.0
288	5680	-1.9	-2.0
289	5700	-1.9	-2.0
290	5720	-2.0	-2.0
291	5740	-2.0	-2.0
292	5760	-2.0	-2.0
293	5780	-2.0	-2.0
294	5800	-2.0	-2.0

Task 1: Analysing the data

Carefully look at the data and then answer the following questions:

1. What temperature did the cold water start at?
2. What temperature did the hot water start at?
3. How often were temperature readings taken by the sensors?
4. Write down the logging frequency.
5. Over how many seconds were the readings taken?
6. Write down the logging period.
7. From the last section of data we can tell that the cooling process has ended. How do we know this?
8. What do you think the temperature in the freezer is and how do you know?

Task 2: Using the data to produce graphs

1. Load the spreadsheet package Excel and open the file called 'Data file for the freezing of hot and cold water'.

2. Check that you have the correct file by comparing the start and the end of the file with those shown at the start of this activity.
3. Both graphs need to be drawn on the same axes.

   Select all the data in the spreadsheet.
4. Click on the graph icon .
5. As there needs to be numbers plotted on both sets of axes we need to draw an XY (scatter graph). Make this selection.
6. Choose a chart sub-type that produces a curve.
7. Follow the steps to produce the graph as instructed by the Chart Wizard.
8. Choose a suitable title for each axis and also add an overall title for the whole chart.

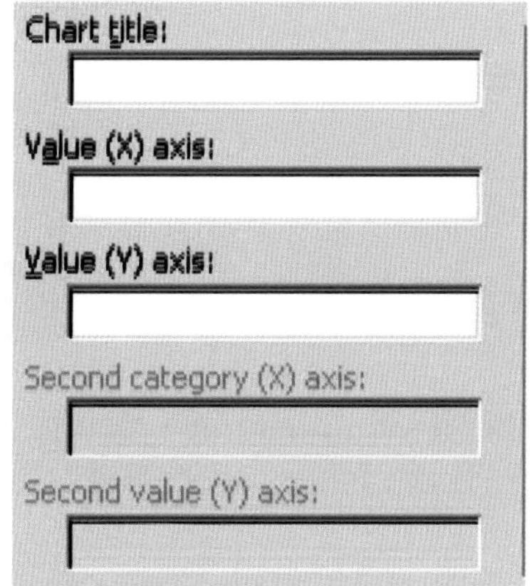

9. Check that your graph area looks like this:
10. Save your spreadsheet using a suitable file name.

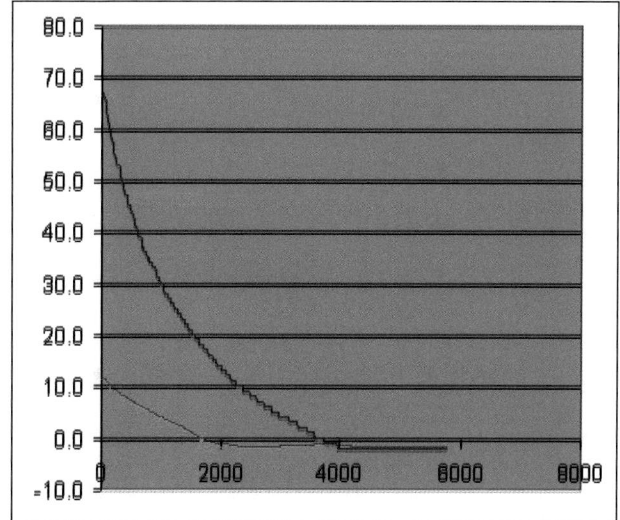

Make it happen

ACTIVITY 5: Writing the report

You now have to write a report that presents the results of this experiment. Your report should be wordprocessed. Make sure that you state the original hypothesis and say whether the results showed that it was true, false or inconclusive. You need to refer to the graph, and it would be best if you were to import the graph from the spreadsheet package into the wordprocessing package used to produce your report.

Make it happen

ACTIVITY 6: Monitoring the sound in a corridor at your school

You are going to carry out an experiment to test the noise level in a corridor at your school.

Task 1: Write down three hypotheses to test

To help with this, think about how you might expect the noise to vary during the day.

Think about the activities that make more sound and the times when they are likely to take place.

Task 2: Plan the experiment

Before you start you need to think carefully about what you are doing and how you are doing it. There are a number of decisions to make.

Things you will need to decide include:

- which type of sensor to use
- where the sensor should be placed
- the logging period (i.e. over what period you will log the data)
- the logging rate/frequency (i.e. how often a reading needs to be taken).

Task 3: Perform the experiment

You will need to be familiar with the way the data logging equipment works.

Task 4: Analyse the results

The data logger will collect the readings automatically over the period you have selected. The data logging software can then be used to load the readings into the computer so that they can be analysed. If you want to, you can see if you can load the readings into a spreadsheet package.

Tables of readings are hard to interpret so it is better to use graphs. You should produce a graph showing how the sound level varies with time. You can then look for the main features of the graph and try to interpret what they show. You need to make sure that you test the hypotheses that you wrote down at the start of the experiment.

Task 5: Produce a report on your findings

You should produce a wordprocessed report on your findings. Make sure that you refer back to your original hypotheses.

EXTENSION ACTIVITY

Can you think of ways you could do further experiments in your school to find out about sound levels?

Write down the hypotheses for these experiments and a brief description of how you would perform them.

Make it happen

ACTIVITY 7: Why do animals huddle together in the winter?

For this activity you are required to investigate why animals huddle together in the winter.

You have the following equipment to help you:

- a number of test tubes to be filled with hot water
- a number of elastic bands to bundle the tubes together
- several temperature sensors connected to a remote data logger
- a fridge or freezer to produce the low temperatures needed for the experiment
- a suitable computer to process the results.

1. Explain how you would carry out this experiment.
2. What logging frequency and logging period would you set your data logger to?
3. How would you process the results from the experiment?

EXTENSION ACTIVITY

Explain how you might extend this activity to investigate:

- how the temperature varies from an animal at the centre of the group to an animal at the edge of the group
- if it is more beneficial to the animals to have a much larger group.

Make it happen

ACTIVITY 8: The neighbours from hell

John and his dog Theo have 'neighbours from hell' living next door to them.

Here are some of the things they do:

Have smoky bonfires all the time

Play loud music into the early hours of the morning

Have loud rows

Do late-night DIY

Bang doors late at night

Refuse to cut down huge conifer trees that have put Theo's garden in darkness

John's parents contact the local environmental health officer, who asks the following questions: How often do they play loud music? ...have smoky bonfires? ...have rows? ...bang doors? ...do late night DIY?

1. Explain why the environmental health officer has asked them these questions.
2. What type of sensor would the environmental health office use to measure loudness?
3. The environmental health officer leaves them a data logger. The data logger records the noise and the time at which it occurred. Why does the time need to be recorded as well?
4. You can set a data logger so that it measures peak readings (i.e. the loudest sounds) or you can set it to average the readings out over a whole day or week.

Explain which setting you would use and why.

5 Give one reason why a data logger is used.

6 What sensor would be used to measure the darkness of the garden?

FIND IT OUT

Imagine you had the neighbours described in Activity 8 living next door to you.

Use the Internet to find out about laws to do with:

- noise pollution
- smoke pollution
- high conifer hedges taking light from your garden.

Explain what steps you might take (legal ones only!) to prevent the nuisance from occurring.

Lesson 4 DESIGNING AND CARRYING OUT YOUR OWN EXPERIMENT

In this lesson you will design and carry out your own experiment. The one in Activity 9 is a suggestion, but your teacher may ask you to perform a different one.

Make it happen

ACTIVITY 9: Battery life – do some makes last longer than others?

Duracell boasts that its batteries last longer than others. We need to design an experiment to test this. Your teacher will explain whether you have to actually do the experiment or simply describe how it might be done.

Task 1: What to test?

Write down a suitable hypothesis that you want to test.

Task 2: Planning the experiment

You are supplied with the following apparatus:

- wires
- bulb and bulb holder
- several brand new batteries (all the same size) including a Duracell one
- a current sensor
- an interface
- a computer with data logging software loaded.

Draw a diagram of how you would set up this apparatus.

Task 3: Collecting the readings

Describe how you would carry out the experiment.

In your description you should make sure that you use each term from the following list at least once:

- sensor
- interface
- data logging software
- period of logging
- frequency of readings.

Make sure you have described how the experiment is repeated.

Task 4: Interpretation and presentation of the results

Describe what you plan to do with the data that you collect from this experiment.

Glossary

absolute reference – in this type of reference, a particular cell is used in a formula, and when this formula is copied to a new address, the cell address does not change

animation – moving images

annotating – adding hand-written notes to computer printouts to add explanations

automatic – works on its own without needing further instructions from the user

bias – information that has been written to favour a particular viewpoint (e.g. an article on 'should fox hunting be banned?' written by a master of the hunt would be written in favour of fox hunting)

bitmap image – a file that represents a picture as pattern of 1s and 0s

bitmapped graphic – a file type where the image/graphic is stored as a map showing the position and colour of individual dots of light called pixels

browse – when you casually view something of interest whilst looking for something on the Internet

compression – storing data in a format that requires less space. Bitmapped graphics such as photographs are often compressed to a fraction of their normal size

content – material to be put into a document

contents list – a list of items on a website or a CD-ROM that enables you to jump straight to the section by clicking on the item in the contents list

control – getting the computer to operate devices automatically

data – the raw facts and figures entered into a computer

data logging – a system that automatically collects data over a certain period of time. Remote weather stations use data logging

database – a series of tables/lists stored in a computer that can be accessed in a variety of ways

decision – a step that asks a question to which there is a yes or no answer. On the basis of the answer to the question one of two possible paths are then taken

digital images – images that have been converted into a form that can be stored and manipulated on the computer

dirty data – an obviously wrong item of data

dpi (dots per inch) – a measure of the resolution of an image. The greater the dpi the better quality the image

DTP – this is short for desktop publishing

efficient – making the best use of resources such as gas, electricity and water

feedback – where the output from a system directly affects the input

fitness for purpose – making sure that a graphic is used in the correct context

flowchart – a chart or diagram used to break down a task into smaller parts. It can also show the order of the tasks and any decisions that need to be made

font – a set of letters and characters in a particular design

formulae – the plural of formula

frame capture – a moving image produced by a digital video camera is made up of lots of individual pictures (or 'frames'). It is possible to take one of these images and use it as a photograph

greyscale – black and white images consist of an unlimited number of greys. The computer can only use a limited number so a black and white image has to be converted to a greyscale so that it can be used by the computer

hits – the number of people who have accessed the website in a certain time

home page – the first page you reach on a website, which will usually contains links to other pages

humidity – the amount of moisture in the air

hypothesis – a statement that can be proved or disproved (i.e. proved right or wrong)

index – a list of words that you can click on, from which you are taken to the page where the word appears

input device – a device used to input data for processing by the computer

Internet – a worldwide network of computer networks that forms the largest connected set of computers in the world

Internet service provider – a company that provides you with a connection to the Internet via their server

legislation – laws

logging frequency – how often the readings are taken

logging period – the total amount of time over which the readings are taken

media – means of communication

models – systems that mimic a real situation or thing

monitor – continually take measurements of a quantity, such as temperature, so that action may be taken

monitoring – keeping a record of the measurements from sensors over a certain period of time

opinion – a person's own interpretation of some information

opinion poll – a survey to determine peop questionnaire – a carefully constructed set of questions to ask a person to find out information about a topic or their opinions

password – a string of characters chosen by the user. It is used to check the identity of the user. You are only allowed access to a network if you type in the correct password

pictures – photographs, clip art, paintings, graphs, charts and drawings

plagiarism – copying work and passing it off as your own

point – the unit of size for a letter, number or punctuation mark

program – a set of instructions, written in a logical order that the computer obeys

purpose – the use to which the information is to be put

query – a search for specific information contained in a database

questionnaire – a document containing questions, which is filled in to supply information

relative reference – when a cell is used in a formula and the formula is copied to a new address, the cell address changes to take account of the formula's new position

relevant – useful information that covers the topic you are looking for

reliable – trusted material

representative – a sample that reflects the whole population accurately

resolution – the sharpness or clarity (i.e. how clear it is) of an image

rule/formula – a mathematical equation that can be used to describe how the real thing behaves

sample – a smaller amount of data that reflects the whole set of data (or population)

sample composition – this is how the sample is made up so that it reflects the whole set of data.

For example, a sample in a mixed school would usually have equal numbers of boys and girls

sample size – the number of people asked their opinion

search – looking for specific information on a subject

search engine – a program that can be used to search for information on the Internet

sensors – devices that measure physical quantities such as temperature, pressure, etc.

shared area – part of the network that holds files that everyone on the network can access. Clip art would be stored in the shared area

sound – music, speech or sound effects

statistics – facts and figures on a subject, for example, the mean, mode, median, range, biggest, smallest, etc.

survey – collecting data by asking opinions or by observing

system – a set of equipment arranged and organised together to perform a certain task

test data – data which is entered into a model to test the way it behaves

text – letters of the alphabet, numbers and punctuation marks

URL – Uniform Resource Locator (formerly Universal Resource Locator) is the web address of the page where the information you want is located

user ID – a name or number that is used to identify the user of a network or system

validation – a check performed by the computer program to make sure that the data being entered is allowable

variables – numbers in a spreadsheet that can be altered by the user to see what happens

Vector image/graphic – image/graphic represented by a mathematical formula that can be enlarged or reduced without any loss in clarity

verification – checking the accuracy of data entry

Index